HOW TO MEASURE HUMAN RESOURCES MANAGEMENT

HOW TO MEASURE HUMAN RESOURCES MANAGEMENT

Third Edition

Jac Fitz-enz
Barbara Davison

McGraw-Hill

New York   Chicago   San Francisco   Lisbon   London   Madrid
Mexico City   Milan   New Delhi   San Juan   Seoul
Singapore   Sydney   Toronto

Library of Congress Cataloging-in-Publication Data

Fitz-enz, Jac.
    How to measure human resource management / Jac Fitz-enz.— 3rd ed.
        p. cm.
    Includes bibliographical references and index.
    ISBN 0-07-136998-8 (hc.)
        1. Personnel management.   2. Personnel departments.   I. Title.

HF5549 .F555 2001
658.3—dc21

2001056212

McGraw-Hill

A Division of The *McGraw·Hill* Companies

1 2 3 4 5 6 7 8 9 0   AGM/AGM   0 9 8 7 6 5 4 3 2 1

ISBN 0-07-136998-8

The sponsoring editor for this book was Richard Narramore, the production supervisor was Maureen Harper, and the editing supervisor was Scott Kurtz. The book was typeset by Pro-Image Corporation. The printer and binder was Quebecor Martinsburg.

How to Contact the Publisher
To order copies of this book in bulk, at a discount, call the McGraw-Hill Special Sales Department at 800-8842-3075 or 212-904-5427.

To ask a question about the book, to contact the author, or to report a mistake in the text, please write to Richard Narramore, Senior Editor, at richard_narramore@ mcgraw-hill.com

This book is printed on recycled, acid-free paper containing a minimum of 50% recycled, de-inked fiber.

Contents

Preface to the Third Edition

A great deal of change has taken place since the publication of the second edition of this book. Since the original edition, which was published in 1984, human resources has changed so much that in many companies it is no longer the same function.

When we entered the profession several decades ago, "personnel" was, in the words of the president of the company, "the place where they keep employee records." Today, at least in some companies, human resources (HR) is the place where they manage human capital. Unfortunately, in other companies it is still the place where they process things.

The important issue is not what has changed in the last several decades, but what is likely to change in the new millennium.

Technology

Clearly, the widespread introduction of technology is now the driving force in HR management. The human resources information system (HRIS) has evolved from mainframe-based, record-keeping systems in the 1970s to desktop, hands-on applications. With the arrival of the Worldwide Web, HR professionals have almost unlimited power at their fingertips. As a management tool nothing has ever been so powerful. As we go forward, the question will be how to make effective use of this tool, not only for management data and programs, but more importantly, for helping associates to expand their horizons.

As exciting and tantalizing as technology has become, technology today is nothing compared to what it will be like in another ten years. If this book requires another edition sometime in the future, it is difficult to imagine what the practice of human capital management will look like then. Nevertheless, within these three words—*human capital management*—lies the clue to what is likely to change.

Human Capital

Most top executives claim that the key to business success is largely a matter of the ability to attract and retain key talent. Some even believe what they say, while others believe privately that systems and technology can overcome the effects of talent. Clearly, that is not the case.

Given the criticality of people, how is HR going to strategically plan and act in the next several years? The traditional dichotomy between transaction administration and management consultation has to be resolved in order for HR to play an effective role. Transaction has to be attended to or the system will collapse. However, total attention to transactions at the detriment of strategy stunts growth. This decision is more important than which piece of technology to introduce next.

Return on Investment

Since HR is a business function, management has to ask what the value of the function is to the total enterprise. Traditionally, HR, like accounting, information technologies (IT), and other general and administrative units, has been treated as an overhead expense. The premise is that all overhead units should be managed as economically as possible. The value accruing from their operations has been viewed as a necessity or a nice thing to have. In the case of HR the alleged value is *keeping people happy*. This translates very loosely into retention and productivity. However, beyond turnover rates and meeting the budget, there has been little, if any, assessment of HR's performance.

For a growing number of firms this is no longer a viable position. In the pursuit of profitability and competitive advantage top management is looking at all functions for a return on investment. Operating within the budget is no longer sufficient. As more outsourcing firms prove their value, the question of keeping or outsourcing most of HR will rise on the agenda. There is no single right answer to the question of outsourcing. Its value has to be judged at the time for each situation. The point is this: What is the best way to spend money on HR services? That is the question that HR directors have to be prepared to answer, and the answer will have to come in terms of return on investment, not keeping people happy.

New Features

This edition offers significantly more than the previous editions did. First, there has been a great deal of change in the measures discussed and a substantial increase in the number of measures covered. Second, the issue of technology and information systems now accounts for a major section of the book. Third, a chapter on employee communications has been added because communication is at the heart of leading new employees. Fourth, there is a chapter on linking HR's activities to the business unit's objectives and ultimately to the organization's goals.

These changes bring the concept of how to measure HR management full circle. Starting by looking at the method for measuring individual activities, the book proceeds through each of the functions within HR from the perspective of human capital management. This is to say that the improvement in a single measure is not necessarily proof that HR has become more effective. Instead, one has to look holistically at the impact that HR programs and services have on the behavior and job performance of employees, who are now called associates. Finally, we roll it all up to the corporate level and try to determine the effects of HR activity on enterprisewide goals.

Acknowledgements

As always, we learn from each other. I am pleased to welcome Barbara Davison as coauthor of this edition. She has worked with me for more years than she will admit. Barbara knows as much as I do about the tactical application of measurement to HR activities.

Our patient editor, Richard Narramore, deserves mention for his tenacity. He has been after me for almost a year to produce this edition. His suggestions and offers of help have been invaluable.

Associates from among our customer base, those within the professional community, and others from the various boards in which I participate have broadened my outlook. They are, alphabetically: Nick Bontis, John Boudreau, Bob Coon, Marcela Echeverria, Mady Gorrell, Row Henson, Mark Hodges, Bob Hunter, Michael Kelly, Ann Lemmon, Mike Mitchell, Bob Stambaugh, and Dave Ulrich.

The staff members at Saratoga Institute have contributed through the evolution of their work and by making direct suggestions and contributions. In particular, the groundbreaking work on employee retention and commitment by Michael Kelly's group has helped us to formulate current measures in the areas of retention and employee communication. This has given me additional material for this edition as well as more up-to-date views of HR.

Jac Fitz-enz

Prologue: The Long Road to Today

Stage 1: A Slow Start

In the late 1800s the industrial revolution overwhelmed the United States. In just two decades giant manufacturing complexes replaced the small-business, cottage industry model that had been the focal point of commerce for hundreds of years. A hundred years later the arrival of electronic technology swung the pendulum back toward small business as a major source of production and employment. At the same time, as the giant corporations grew, they spawned the first staff departments, one of which was personnel. The personnel department was formed to meet the need to recruit thousands of people to work the machines of the new age. It was staffed by employees from line functions, and there was no formal education for personnel work. Since the value systems of nineteenth-century industrialists focused on new ways to engineer and manufacture, the people function and the worker in general were not highly valued. Employees were treated like production parts, and the personnel department like inventory clerks. Although most organizations are now more enlightened in their treatment of workers, this attitude has not completely disappeared.

Personnel departments often become the dumping ground for the organization's casualties. When well-liked employees began to have performance problems, a decision might be made to place them in personnel rather than fire them. After all, the feeling was, "They can't hurt anybody there." There were some individuals who willingly chose personnel as a career field, but this was more the exception than the rule in the early days.

Stage 2: The Service Model

Between the two world wars the personnel function began to develop. By the late 1940s it had become more than an offshoot of payroll. Besides being an employment service, it took the first step toward creating sophisticated compensation systems. Training blossomed during the postwar boom. The training technologies that had been developed in the armed forces began to find their way into industry. Labor relations had matured before most other functions had. When the unions again flexed the muscles they had voluntarily left unused during the war, labor negotiators became important.

Two traits characterized the changing personnel department. First, it was largely a reactive service; that is, there was not a great deal of forward planning. Some work was done to generate the gross numbers of employees needed to meet the business plan, but most companies did not begin to think of manning tables and succession planning with their implications for training until well into the second half of the century. Personnel was often not privy to the highest management councils. Hence, it had little choice but to be reactive.

The second characteristic of the postwar period was a continuation of the attitude that labor was an adversary, not a partner of management. This supported the view that employees were an element of cost not an asset. Not until the 1960s did this view begin to change, although very slowly. Given these attitudes and values, personnel work was directed toward a maintenance mode. The idea was that no news from personnel was good news.

Stage 3: Opportunity

The third stage owes its birth to government intervention in private business. As much as any other force, the federal government changed the way organizations related to and managed employees. It is a consistent phenomenon that when any individual, group, or institution achieves a power advantage, he, she, or it tends to guard that edge with great vigor. Change occurs when a greater power comes along. In this case the power was the federal courts and Congress.

The 1960s and 1970s saw the passage of the Civil Rights Act and the Employee Retirement Income Security Act (ERISA), along with the act that created the Occupational Safety and Health Administration (OSHA). This continued into the 1990s with the Americans with Disabilities Act (ADA). Each act found a different point of entry into the organization. In an effort to deal with these new realities, organizations placed the responsibility with the personnel group and staffed to meet the governmental intrusion. The new situation had created a need for new competencies. About this time the shift from personnel to human resources (HR) began. It looked like the opening of a new era. Young people saw an opportunity for interesting work and perhaps a satisfying career. As they entered the function and began to show results, management came to see possibilities it had never before imagined could exist.

Three other factors have played a role in the recent development of the HR profession. The first was the evolution of the workforce. A profound social change took place in the United States after World War II. The baby boom of the late 1940s and early 1950s threw a large number of young people into the labor market around 1970. Those workers were young and better educated than their parents. Their values were different. They were not content with just having a job; they demanded meaning and satisfaction from their labors. Compounding this trend, many oppressed people began to find a voice. Women and minority group members, with the support of federal agencies, pressed for a piece of the action and demanded that organizations provide a wide range of welfare benefits and social activities in addition to employment. By the 1990s the full impact was being felt, with support programs such as child and elder care and parental leave.

Another important factor was the rapid postwar growth of organizations. Both in the size and the scope of markets, the industrial concerns of the 1970s dwarfed those of the 1930s. Today international business is commonplace for most companies. This calls for specialists in areas such as expatriate compensation and intercultural training. Human issues arising from the restructuring of multinational corporations are being delegated to HR for study and implementation.

Finally, most recently, the slowdown in the growth of industrial productivity has become one of the nation's most pressing problems. Many HR departments are becoming involved in designing new pay systems, conducting more training, and getting involved in restructuring programs. It is here, within the productivity-quality dilemma, that HR has been handed its greatest opportunity. Some departments have taken advantage of this opportunity. In doing so, they have moved from the reactive and peripheral mode of stage 2 toward a more involved and strategic position.

It is clear that the HR function is moving into a fourth and perhaps final stage in its evolution, as will be discussed in Chapter 1.

Why Measure HR?

The New Human Resources

As a new century begins it is clear that the human resources (HR) function is moving into the fourth, perhaps final, stage of its evolution. In the last decade the authors have worked with a large number of HR professionals who bear no resemblance to their paper-shuffling predecessors. There is no complaining about lack of resources or appreciation. There is no acceptance of second-class citizenship or exclusion from strategic planning. Of course, not everyone loves them, and they have to face the normal percentage of difficult people in the organization, but these talented, insightful people have gone on the offensive. They are deeply involved in the operation of the company. Their work clearly affects the performance of the company. Best of all, their numbers are growing daily.

On the other side of the fence there is a force, growing in strength daily, that is saying, "Outsource!" One after another of the staff functions are being outsourced in the name of cost-effectiveness. Whether outsourcing really is cost-effective is not the point. There is an unquestionable groundswell in favor of outsourcing staff functions. One of the reasons for this is that it is an apparently simple solution. Management likes simple solutions such as layoffs, and outsourcing fits that criterion. All forms of transaction work are targets for outsourcing. Payroll and benefits administration are two currently popular candidates for outsourcing. What are the implications of this for your job? It depends on what type of HR practitioner you are.

There are three basic types:

1. *1950s style.* The familiar, traditional "HR as an expense" model continues, perhaps accounting for 30 to 50 percent of companies. It is found mostly in the lagging companies, which do not manage any function in an especially enlightened fashion. Very often these firms are family-owned or controlled by a small group of investors who milk the company and go to the country club every weekend. These are the types of companies that have very small pieces of the market. They pick up the leftovers. One venture capitalist described them as "the walking dead." A job in one of them is only slightly better than unemployment.

2. *Reactors.* The outsource-and-decentralize model with line managers taking back most of the responsibility they had in the early decades of the twentieth century accounts for perhaps 20 percent of companies. These people have never seen a fully functioning HR professional, and in desperation they have reverted to the old model. At least they have control, even though they wish they did not have to handle personnel matters. All in all, this type of department is not a bad place to work if one does not have too much ambition.

3. *Confidants.* The outsourced processes model with a few trusted, talented corporate HR people playing the role of internal adviser, consultant, and broker of outside services includes about 30 to 40 percent of companies. This is what enlightened managers wish they had. In this model HR truly is a lever that helps improve quality, productivity, and service, giving the company a competitive edge in the marketplace. If you have what it takes to operate in this highly accountable situation, go for it. It will be the best job you will ever have.

Thus, you have a choice of careers. It is up to you to pick the situation that best fits your ambition and aspirations. If you choose correctly, you can be contented. The questions are, How hard do you want to work? What do you want to spend your time doing?

and When you look back on your career, will you be able to say, "I made the world a better place in which to work and live"?

The Hope of the Future

Although many members of the early generation of personnel workers were good people, they were not business-focused, and that influenced what they did and how they did it. As management observed these administrative types, it came to believe that this was what personnel should be. As was mentioned above, some of these people are still working in HR. Last year I gave a talk at a national HR conference. At lunch I sat at a table with a number of ladies from a Fortune 500 company and asked them about the company's current activities. One lady volunteered that the company had just won a major government contract having to do with satellite communications. When asked for more detail, the lady said that she was not sure. Then she turned to one of her companions and asked what the contract was for. That woman replied, "I don't know. I try to stay out of the business."

During the decade of the 1990s a new breed of HR professional began to appear. Unlike most of their predecessors, these men and women are focused on participating in the business. Many have degrees in business; some even have MBAs with an emphasis on human resources administration (*administration* is a word that should be gotten rid of). They have been using computers since high school, and they know how to handle numbers. They view the work site as a place to learn, grow, make a contribution, and gain wealth. Gone are the days when most of the people in the personnel office were failed line personnel or social workers who lived to "work with people." Human resources has been energized by the new generation of business-oriented professionals. They are the ones who have dispatched the myth that said, "You can't measure what we do." After decades of arguing, it is now conceded by nearly everyone that it is possible to quantitatively measure the economic value of the HR function.[1]

---

[1] For the sake of brevity, I am going to use "HR" to mean the human resources department. I will use the terms *human capital, talent, employees,* and *associates* interchangeably to refer to the people who work in an enterprise.)

Technology to the Rescue

Computer technology arrived with a bang in the 1990s. Companies such as PeopleSoft and SAP designed massive HR information systems with analysis and reporting features. Personal computer (PC) capability was enhanced with new software, helping managers and associates in all functions to make quantum leaps in productivity as well as in understanding the business. Enlarged PC data storage allowed daily operations to reside on the desktop. This, along with word processing, spreadsheets, and desktop publishing tools gave everyone the power to collect, manipulate, display, and report data. The explosive growth of the Internet and the development of the browser in the middle of the decade connected everyone and enhanced the ability to communicate processes and results. Enlightened management has given employees access to their records on-line as well as a variety of other on-line self-services.

These technological advances removed the last barriers to financial accountability for HR. Now it is much easier for HR to be run like a business rather than an expense center. In fact, HR can show how its activities have contributed to revenue or expense reduction. That is the underlying theme of this and all the other books I have written. As you go through the various sections, you will find over 100 metrics that you can generate. They will help you understand how well you are doing and to report it to interested executives.

Support from the Top

For the first time in history senior managers have begun to pay attention to the HR function. This new attitude is due as much to economic expediency as it is to humanitarianism. With the well-known shortage of talent at all levels, management has begun to accept the fact that people are indispensable. Capable, motivated people are priceless and not interchangeable, as was long believed. As a result of this latent realization, HR is being both supported and challenged. Management is more likely to look favorably upon a request for funds or staff than it would have in the past, provided that HR makes a value proposition out of its presentation. Concurrently, management is beginning to press for a return on its investment above and beyond subjective testimony. Thus, the good news comes with a price, and fortunately, HR professionals are finding that price acceptable and within their reach.

THOUGHT I *Without data we have only opinions.*

Summary

As Bob Dylan said in the 1960s, "The times they are a changin'." Organizations can no longer afford to support people who are not clearly contributing to the strategic goals of the enterprise. Top management has only two choices today. One is to turn HR into a value-adding function; the other is to outsource it and pay for specific services as needed.

The good news is that all sides are coming together in a common quest for a more efficient and humane organization. Corporate culture, leadership, and human development are being blended into the concept of a good place to work and an employer of choice. The enterprise of the twenty-first century promises a better experience, with opportunity based on performance and rewards being distributed to those who make a measurable contribution to both financial and human goals.

Trends in Human Resources

From Feudalism to Collaboration

Typically, human resources work has been practiced in a fragmented fashion. Staffing groups focus on the job of providing qualified new hires. Compensation strives to maintain equity in pay and benefits for all employees. Training exposes people to new knowledge and skills. Each group seems oblivious to the others, working independently to achieve its individual objectives. This is inefficient in regard to optimum organizational performance. It is a sign of a unit that does not realize its higher purpose: the growth of human capital.

The most significant human capital management change we have seen in 40 years in business is the move toward collaboration. Executives have come to realize that there is a time and place for collaboration, even with competitors. Trying to go it alone in today's marketplace is an impossible challenge. The same applies to human resources (HR). It is the responsibility of the HR director to bring the concept of collaboration to the department. This means that the director has to show all the functions how they can enhance their growth through collaboration.

Fortunately, this is not difficult. Efficient and effective hiring depends at a minimum on knowledge of the compensation structure and the opportunities for an applicant's growth and advancement.

The staffing function also has to know the culture of the company and the company's economic viability. The development people can do a better job of designing a career pathing system if they understand what types of people are available in the labor pool and the organization's ability to compensate and promote high performers. Employee relations is often at the end of the line, inheriting the problems of the organization. The development people can help themselves as well as the organization at large and HR in particular by collecting and distributing data from their experience. Exit interview information should be pushed out to staffing, compensation, and development, where it can be employed to prevent future problems or solve current ones. By adopting with a broader view of its purpose, each HR function can expand its contribution to the department's objectives and the enterprise's goals.

Creating an HR Knowledge Exchange

A knowledge exchange (KX) can be created by setting up a file that is segregated by function. Everyone in HR has a duty to put in data from his or her experience. Everyone has access. Thus, the KX not only becomes an ever-growing source of knowledge, it also becomes a source of education for the whole staff. Everyone from the youngest, lowest-level HR person on up can learn from the experience of others. This is a high-tech mentoring system. It might even have a positive influence on the retention of junior staff. Where else could they learn so much so fast?

THOUGHT 2   *Success in the new market is built on collaboration.*

Reviewing HR's Vision

In the early part of the go-go 1980s it seemed that the secret to sustained prosperity had been discovered. America frolicked in what was up to that time one of the longest-running periods of economic growth. Then, all of a sudden, the facade began to wear thin and the first signs of new forces appeared. By the time 1990 arrived, the nation had entered what for a while seemed like an unending time of economic uncertainty. By the closing years of the decade we were again experiencing a period of unprecedented economic prosperity. Just as some people were thinking that we had overcome the laws of economics, the dot-com crash of April 2000 gave the country a dose of old-fashioned value-based reality. This cycle from expansion to contraction, stagnation, and wild speculation and back has driven executives to reassess what their organizations are about. People have returned to a more conservative view of how to run a business by creating lasting value. At this point new visions of organizational structure and the role of HR are emerging in which HR is moving up the corporate ladder of importance.

Vision statements were very popular at the time of the second edition of this book. Slogans such as Motorola's "Total Customer Satisfaction" and Chevron's "The Best in the Business" were meant to reaffirm management's dedication to employees and customers. HR departments were coming out with vision statements in an attempt to refocus their staffs in new directions. It was necessary to speak in terms more relevant to the new psychological contract between management and employees. Also, this was an attempt to regain employee confidence after the first great wave of downsizing. Visions are once again in vogue as a result of the upheaval brought on by the invasion and subsequent implosion of the dot-com phenomenon.

A vision is the essential foundation from which any function takes its direction. Today, as the new millennium begins, clarity of vision is essential. Management is finding it even more important and difficult to formulate and disseminate a vision. However, one of the major complaints we hear in the exit interviewing service at the Saratoga Institute is that the leadership of the enterprise has lost its way, leaving the employees floundering. As a result, employees have two choices. One is to search for and perhaps misperceive the organization's direction; the other is to leave for more stable ground. In the face of this HR needs to find its vision.

HR's vision for the new millennium must be drawn from the following ideas:

1. Human resources exists in an organization because it adds tangible value by providing necessary services at a competitive cost.

2. Human resources's charter is to enhance the productivity and effectiveness of the organization from the people side: the talent, the human capital.
3. Human resources should drive the organization's management in regard to people issues.
4. Human resources is a professional function staffed by professionals dedicated to the development of people in ways that are satisfying to the individual and beneficial to the organization.

Today's vision statements are shorter and focus more on the organization's goals. Typical examples follow:

• Strategic business partners
• Managers of human talent
• Change managers
• Supporters of the organizational goals

The exercise of establishing a departmental vision is very useful in unifying HR departments that were operating in a feudal mode. The defining characteristic of the best HR departments is the formal recognition of interdependence leading to the adoption of a collaborative culture. The best departments meet on a regular basis to share their plans and look for potential conflicts as well as synergy. If the process of creating vision and value is carried out in a participative manner, the staff feels a sense of ownership of and commitment to the product. Everyone is clear about what is appropriate.

Management Experts on Performance Measurement

There is ample support for performance measurement in the management literature. Practically every writer from Peter Drucker through Deming, Peters, O'Reilly and Pfeffer, Phillips, Huselid and Becker, Ulrich, Zenger, and Davenport has agreed that quantitative measurement is necessary. Chief executive officers (CEOs) also agree. Software companies have come out with HR-oriented analytic packages. Many consulting firms are scurrying to set up their versions of human capital performance measurement. There is no question that performance measurement is required of all people who choose to have an effect on their organizations. The only questions are how to do it, how to do it well, and what effect doing it well can have.

In the face of this overwhelming evidence, some people persist in the notion that they can survive without performance measurement. They consciously avoid connecting to business issues and bury their heads in their individual jobs. They blame the rest of the people in the organization—their customers—for not understanding that their function is somehow different from those of all the other organizational entities that depend on quantitative analysis. Deming died a frustrated and angry man because of people like this, who would not accept the need for a fundamental assessment of the need to change. Having spent over 20 years preaching the value of performance measurement to unreceptive HR practitioners, the authors of this book feel some of his frustration. The good news is that attitudes are changing and measurement is being accepted by more people every day.

The Bottom Line

Quantitative data are part of every organization's daily operations. Measurement plays a central role in our system; it does more than simply evaluate performance. A measurement system provides a frame of reference that helps management carry out several important responsibilities, including the following:

- *Communicate performance expectations.* Discussing work objectives in quantitative terms leaves less room for ambiguity. When objectives are set for cost, time, quality, quantity, and customer satisfaction, people understand what is expected of them.
- *See, feel, and understand outcomes.* Measurement systems involve, motivate, and foster creativity. Typically, the staff responds by meeting or exceeding objectives. Hard data make it clear what and how much happened.
- *Compare to standards and/or benchmarks.* The data indicate a company or department's relative position against internal objectives and external competitors. It is impossible to believe that

mediocre performance is acceptable when one can see where the markers are.

- *Identify performance gaps.* Now we know where we have to make improvements and how far we are behind or ahead of our goals. By trending, we can learn how fast we are moving compared to the market.

- *Support resource allocation decisions.* The data differentiate tasks for the staff according to higher and lower priorities. Scarce resources can be dedicated to the most important issues and to the areas that offer the best return on investment.

- *Recognize and reward performance.* Top performers often are de-motivated by qualitative goals. Quantitative evidence of performance gives the company a chance to show appreciation for excellent work.

One of the most consistent complaints of line management is that the HR staff does not seem to be interested in the important issues of the organization, such as return on investment (ROI). Studies have uncovered the belief that "HR doesn't understand the business." However, quantitative HR measurement systems include factors that relate to organizational quality, productivity, services, and profitability. Tracking and reporting hiring costs can be useful, but connecting a new hiring strategy with an improvement in operational quality, productivity, and service is much more compelling. It is this kind of attitude that links HR with its internal clients.

Summary

Human resources is a system within a system. Everything that happens within HR, to one extent or another, affects the larger system. HR has an effect on the organization because it is part of the organization.

To function at an optimal level, HR needs a vision of what it is about. That vision unifies the staff and provides a foundation on which to base future decisions. Knowing what you are about is one thing, but you still have to communicate it to your customers. That is called *positioning*. Every supplier or vendor occupies a position within the mind of its customers—whether or not either party realizes it. HR needs to position itself as a value-adding partner if it expects to gain the position it seeks.

We cannot just declare ourselves to be a partner. We earn partnership by acquiring the necessary skills and demonstrating to the customer-partner that we have something of value. When we operate in this way, we build visible links between our work and the bottom line of the company. How to show that is the subject of the rest of this book.

Designing a Measurement System That Works

The Global Standard

Until the mid-1980s there was no standard language that could be used to discuss performance across human resources (HR) programs. Only one book had been written suggesting the value of measurement. No seminars other than those offered by the Saratoga Institute were available, and no significant studies had been published. Even the simplest comparisons could not be made with any degree of confidence.

Since 1980 I had been advocating the development of professional standards along the line of generally accepted accounting principles. It was not until 1984 that the American Society for Personnel Administration (ASPA), now the Society for Human Resource Management (SHRM), endorsed that proposition. In July of that year, with ASPA's support, the Saratoga Institute assembled 15 HR professionals to develop the first set of formulas for measuring the work of HR functions.

Over the years there have been changes and additions to the initial set. By the turn of the century the methodology had been adopted in over a dozen countries in every continent except Antarctica. Most important, throughout this growth process and the subsequent modifications, the concept and methodolgy have remained consistent. This constancy is what gives the system its power.

This is the only human asset benchmark program that has endured the cyclonic changes in the global market. Virtually all major consultancies use and refer to the Saratoga Institute measures. More than 15 years after its inception, it is clearly the worldwide standard for measuring and evaluating human capital performance. What started as 30 metrics has grown to more than 75. With the permutations and combinations for location, level, growth rate, company size, and industry, over 250 metrics are currently available. The global database includes data from approximately 1,000 organizations. Figure 3-1 lists the Saratoga Institute Human Capital Benchmarks. It is important to note that the focus is not on the HR function but on total human capital investment.

This book will describe in detail over 60 ways to measure cost, time, quantity, quality, and human reactions. Important as these factors are, the most important measure is none of them. Every business depends on its customers for survival, and if one thinks of HR as a business, the most important measure is management's satisfaction with HR. Peter Drucker pointed out that the purpose of a business is determined not by the producer but by the customer, specifically by the needs the customer satisfies when purchasing the business's products or services.

That applies to staff functions such as HR as well. Staff departments are businesses within a market: the organization that the staff serves. When an internal department customer is dissatisfied with HR's service, there is a problem. There is a significant trend toward oursourcing staff services because management believes it can control costs and relieve itself of daily attention to a function that it believes does not add tangible value. If we want to keep our customers, we need to know not only what they want from us but how satisfied they are with our services and products and what we can do to increase their level of satisfaction.

Measuring Customer Satisfaction

There is no shortage of customer satisfaction surveys on the market. Most are adequate. The essential point is to use a consistent set of

ORGANIZATIONAL EFFECTIVENESS

Revenue factor
Expense factor
Income factor
Human capital value added
Human capital ROI
Human economic value-added
   outsourcing
Expense percent
Management ratio
Management investment factor
Average tenure*
Headcount percent—contingent
FTE percent by category
   Contingent on payroll
   Contingent off payroll
   Contingent total
   Management
Professionals
Sales
Office and clerical operatives

HUMAN RESOURCE STRUCTURE

HR expense percent
HR FTE ratio
HR exempt percent
HR FTE investment factor
HR headcount investment factor
HR outsourcing percent
HR consulting percent
HR compensation expense percent
HR employee cost factor
HR total employee cost factor
HR separation rate*
HR structure breakdown

Administration
Benefits
Compensation
Employee relatations
HRIS
HR management
Legal
Staffing

COMPENSATION

Compensation revenue percent
Total compensation revenue percent
Total labor cost revenue percent
Compensation expense percent
Total compensation expense percent
Total labor cost expense percent
Contingent cost revenue percent
Contingent cost expense
   percent—total compensation
   percent—by category
     Executives
     Managers
     Staff
     Variable
Contingent on payroll
Contingent off payroll
Contingent total employee cost
factor—by category
   Regular employees
   Workforce employees
   Executives
   Managers
   Staff
Total employee cost factor
Total labor cost factor
Contingent cost factor

*Shown by exempt, nonexempt, and total.

Figure 3-1 Saratoga Institute Human Capital Benchmarks

BENEFITS
Benefit revenue percent
Benefit expense percent
Benefit compensation percent
Benefit factor
Health care factor
Workers' compensation factor
Benefit cost breakdown
  Legally required payments
  Retirement and savings plans
  Life insurance and death
  Medical and medically related
    payments for time not worked
  Miscellaneous benefits

SEPARATIONS
Separation rate by category
  Exempt
  Nonexempt
  Management
  Professionals
  Sales
  Office and clerical
  Operatives
  Total
  Voluntary separation rate—by
    category* (same as above)
  Involuntary separation rate—by
    category* (same as above)

STAFFING
Accession rate*
Add rate*
Replacement rate*
Career path ratio*
Cost per hire*
Cost per hire breakdown
  Advertising
  Agency
  Referral bonuses
  Travel

Relocation
Recruiter cost
Time to fill*
Time to start*
Offer acceptance rate
Sign-on bonus percent
  Manager
  Executive
Sign-on bonus factor
  Manager
  Executive

TRAINING AND DEVELOPMENT
Employees trained percent
Training cost factor
Training cost percent—total
Training cost percent—external
Training cost percent—internal
Training cost HR expense percent
Training compensation
    percent—excluding trainee pay
    and benefits
Training compensation
    percent—including trainee pay and
    benefits
Training headcount investment factor
Training FTE investment
    factor—including trainee pay and
    benefits*
Training staff ratio
Headcount training factor
FTE training factor
Training cost per hour—excluding
    trainee pay and benefits
Training cost per hour—including
    trainee pay and benefits
Training hours percent—internal staff
Training hours percent—external
    staff

*Shown by exempt, nonexempt, and total.

Figure 3-1   (Continued)

questions so that HR can track trends and progress. At the Saratoga Institute we have designed a survey that we can use for our own staff and modify for external customers. Keep in mind that satisfaction is not a mysterious phenomenon. Ask yourself what causes you to be satisfied or dissatisfied as a customer. Chances are, the answer is the same for most people.

If you want to design your own survey, start informally. In the course of your daily contact with employees and managers, ask them the following questions:

- What are your expectations of HR?
- What do they do that you like?
- What do they do that you do not like?
- What do they do that you do not really care about?
- What really excites and pleases you?

By using the answers to these general questions you can build a formal survey. People often make things too complicated. The human desire for social and business interaction has not changed. It is based on the Golden Rule. Everyone wants integrity, responsiveness, reliability, competence, and empathy. I like to put it this way: Treat me like you really care, and I will be happy. This means that when a situation does not fit the rule, find a way around the rule. Don't tell me we can't do something because of the policy. Tell me how we are going to solve the problem, at least in a way where I get some of what I want. Do that and I will be a satisfied customer. Wouldn't you? Wouldn't your customer?

HR's Role in the Value Chain

Over the last two decades I have experimented with various ways to simplify the task of measuring the value of any HR process. I have found in countless trials that the simple process below yields a clear understanding of the value added, or not added, as the end product of any process.

These four points are the linked components of the value chain (Figure 3-2).

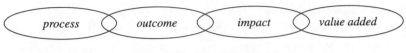

Figure 3-2   The Value Chain

All HR processes are supposed to add value. Any other purpose, by definition, would be wasteful. The objective is to develop ways to measure and evaluate HR processes, the resulting outcomes, and their ultimate value. Processes and outcomes in the various HR functions are shown in Figure 3-3.

For every process improvement in the HR function that is contemplated, the result should be a better outcome. The difference between this outcome and the outcomes before the process improvement is the impact. The dollar improvement represented by the impact is the value added. An example would be to change the sourcing method in hiring (process), which shortens the time to fill jobs (out-

Function	Processes	Outcomes
Staffing	Interviewing	Hires
	Job offers	Acceptances and rejections
Compensation	Job evaluation	Number of positions graded
Salary processing	Time to process	Record change
Benefits	Claims processing	Process cost
		Number processed
		Error rate
Employee relations	Employee counseling	Number counseled
		Time spent counseling
		Problems solved
Labor relations	Grievance processing	Number resolved
	Contracts negotiated	Wages rates in new contract
Training	Program design	Cost of training
	Program delivery	Hours of training provided
Organization	Problem solving	Time to solve
Development	Team building	Efficiency levels

Figure 3-3   Human Resource Processes and Outcomes

come). As jobs are filled faster, there is less of a need to use temporary or contract workers. The cost savings can be calculated. If, through HR's efforts, jobs are filled faster, not only does the company save the operating expense just described, the cost of the product or service is lowered and the product or service is gotten to market faster. Lower product cost and shorter delivery time create a competitive advantage in the marketplace, increasing the company's market share. That is an example of the tangible value added to the organization as a result of an improvement in an HR process.

Action Example

Figure 3-4 moves from the process of planning and hiring to an example of economic value added. Critics will argue that this is too simplistic. They claim that many things between the action and the result affect the outcome, and they are right. This is true in all cases of complex human interaction. It is impossible to account for all the variables and forces that affect a process–result chain. It cannot be done in production, sales, customer service, information technology, or any other function, yet people measure, evaluate, decide, and go forward, doing the best they can. HR activities are no different.

The Objective Is Results, Not Activity

A manager can be defined as a person who gets things done by directing other people. The focus is on working with people to get results. Many people in staff jobs fall in love with the process. A

Process	Change	Impact	Value
Recruiting Program	Time to fill shortened through new recruiting tactics	Production: Filling 14 days faster, meets shipment dates	Rev/day = $XXX and Market share increase
		Customer Service: phones answered	Customer retention increases = $XXX

Figure 3-4   Value-Added Example

description of their work might be something like this: "hires, pays, and trains people." More than one company has outsourced its HR function because there was a lot of movement but no visible value added. The focus was on activity, whereas we want to fix our attention on results.

As we proceed through the following sections, we will study many activities, tasks, and processes. We want to view them not for themselves but for their instrumental value, that is, how to improve them so that we will achieve positive results in terms of cost, time, quantity, quality, or human values. One way to keep focused on results is to do a functional analysis on each of the major HR department functions. Figure 3-5 provides a partial example of a functional analysis of staffing, one of the many HR activities.

There are many tasks and processes in acquiring a new hire. We will measure some of them to the degree that they can tell how efficient the staff is. However, the variable that ultimately makes or breaks the department is results or outcomes.

In the end we want to know the following:

Activities	General Recruitment	College Recruitment	Transfers
Tasks/Processes	Write and place ads	Contact placement offices	Post jobs
	Contact agencies	Schedule campus interviews	Screen
	Post on job boards	Interview on campus	Counsel
	Promote employee referrals	Invite to visit company	Interview
	Schedule interviews	Refer	Etc.
	Interview	Reject	
		Make offers	
	Impact on production and profits		
Results	Hires	Hires	Placements
			Counseling

Figure 3-5 Function Analysis: The Staffing Function

- What did the process cost?
- How much time did it take?
- How many hires did we obtain from each source?
- What was the quality of the process and the hires by source?
- How satisfied with the process and results were the applicants and the hiring manager?
- Eventually: How did the process and result affect organizational profitability?

All these questions should be answerable in terms of how they compare with previous periods. Just as corporate performance is monitored quarterly and from year to year, the same thing should be done with HR. These are the things we get paid to do well; they are the objectives of our jobs. When we can prove that we achieved positive results in key areas, we will have established ourselves as valued members of the management team.

The Importance of Reporting

We would like to conclude this section by making a few points about reports. The key issues in reporting are communication and persuasion. We can do a marvelous job, but if we can't communicate our worthwhile achievements, no one will know what we have done. If we want recognition for our results, it is almost as important to be an effective report writer as it is to be an effective manager. I'm not suggesting exaggeration; I'm calling for skills in communicating in one's native language.

Report generation often is approached as though reports were weak pieces of fiction or textbooks. In the first case there are a lot of unsubstantiated statements, loosely connected, leading to a conclusion that is all too apparent. In the second case there is a massive pile of information, seemingly with no form or direction, that challenges the reader to find something—anything—of value in it. The fact that computers can now store and spew forth mountains of data and desktop publishing can render it in a million colors makes the job of reporting more complicated than it was in the past, when collecting the data was a major problem. New extract tools are coming on the market that will make data collection easier.

Every report has a purpose and an audience. If both are not clearly defined before the data are assembled and the format is chosen, the chances for a meaningful document are lessened. Reports are not sterile descriptions of processes. Reports describe, or should describe, the results of the activity of large numbers of people who are expending resources to achieve predetermined objectives. As such, they deserve a spark of life and a hint of personality. They should be interesting as well as informative. Dull reports bore readers and, what's worse, do not get read.

A report cannot be a neutral, inert document. It must say something that causes the reader to make a decision. Even basic monthly reports of operations cause the reader to do something because a problem is evident or to do nothing because all seems well. Project and investigative reports usually evoke more action than conditional reports do. Whatever the type, the report writer should keep in mind that a report must have a specific value-adding purpose and should be readable at the sixth-grade level.

THOUGHT 3   *Reports are our opportunity to sell our point of view.*

The purpose of a business communication is to inform and persuade. If a report is primarily informational, it displays the following characteristics: clarity, conciseness, accuracy, and appropriateness. Whether the writer is using words or graphics, this is not meant to be a mystery story. Ask someone who is not involved in the process being reported to read the report for clarity. If that person, who knows nothing about the topic, can understand what you are trying to say, the chances are good that your reader also will understand it. If you use a chart or graph, remember that graphic formats have special attributes and certain limitations. Do not try to report too much on each graphic. Keep graphics simple and uncluttered.

Use charts for illustration.
Use words for explanation.

Here are some checkpoints to keep in mind when preparing reports:

- *Be concise.* Most businesspeople are busy. They want to get the information quickly and go on with their work. Get to the point, make it, and get out.
- *Be accurate.* Sloppy, careless, or wrong data destroy credibility. If you are not good with numbers, have someone who is check your work before it is published. Those who disagree with you will be looking for ways to discredit the report and the reporter. As consultants and survey producers, we run into this all the time. People's first reaction to bad news is to look for flaws in the data. If they find a flaw, they will let everyone know about it.
- *Be relevant.* Report what people want to know about, what you want them to know about, and what is important. Ideally these things will all be the same. It does more harm than good to report something that no one cares to know. All that does is to clog the report, make it harder to follow, and add to the fatigue of the reader.

The Fine Art of Persuasion

Persuasion makes up well over 75 percent of communications. Almost everything people say has a persuasive aspect. If you don't believe that, listen closely to informal conversations.

Reports are intended to do more than inform. They represent a chance to persuade. If we want to sell our ideas, we must understand the prospective buyers. Are they interested in the topic? How do they feel about it? Is it enough for them to merely agree with us, or do we want them to support us actively? Persuasive efforts always proceed from a central idea that the audience can comprehend. Points are made in a logical sequence that leads the reader in an orderly manner from the central idea to the desired conclusion. To show cause-and-effect relationships, it is usually necessary to have demonstrable supporting evidence. This is where the power of numbers is so strong. Graphics and pictures can add an emotional aspect to a presentation. Emotion plays a big role in all decisions, even those at the highest levels of executive deliberations. Don't be afraid to be passionate about your data and your point of view. If you don't feel strongly about it, your audience won't either.

The argument should proceed to the point at which the conclusion becomes self-evident. Two surrounding issues that help shape a persuasive outline are the situation and the audience. Ancient rhetoricians studied only the discourse between the speaker and the audience. However, modern system theories and holistic psychology have made people appreciate the impact of the environment on the persuasive event. We must consider how activities and events in the general area surrounding our point will influence it. If we are asking management to commit resources to a project, we must be sure that the financial condition of the organization will permit that expenditure. If we want the boss to do something, we must make sure that it is something top management does not oppose. Putting one's immediate supervisor in a delicate situation is not a path to success.

Audiences (buyers of ideas) are diverse. Organizations make the mistake of viewing their employees as a monolith. That is, they tend to communicate with their people as though there were only one personality for the whole group, yet every individual has a different combination of interests, values, attitudes, and needs. We can communicate effectively if we take this into consideration. Engineers, salespeople, accountants, customer service personnel, and information scientists all have their own set's of values and aptitudes. What makes a strong argument for one is ineffective for another. Keep in mind the personalities and positions of your audiences.

The questions are simple and straightforward. Think of them in terms of Interest, Value, Attitude, and Need (IVAN). This is a time-proven sales technique, and we are all sellers whether we want to admit it or not.

1. How *interested* are the readers in the subject?
2. How much *value* do they place on it?
3. What are their individual *attitudes* toward it?
4. Do they feel a *need* for it?

Assuming that the readers are interested enough to read the report, what format do they relate to best? Some people like a lot of detail. They want to see tables of numbers, sometimes out to two decimal places. Other readers prefer the big picture. They will accept bar charts or trend lines, which are not as specific but give a quick impression of the situation. There is no way to persuade a big-picture person to plow through tables of numbers. Likewise, an accountant type feels insecure with only a line slashing across a graph. If you want people to read, comprehend, and react favorably to your recommendations, you must do them the courtesy of providing them with data in the form they prefer.

Summary

Measurement starts with the conviction that we can and should evaluate our work in both qualitative and quantitative terms. Without some type of objective review, it is very difficult to improve performance. For the past 15 years a series of international reports have been published in a dozen countries by the Saratoga Institute's global network. Collectively, they represent the standard measures for the HR profession. Beyond that, the most important measure is what the customer says about our work. For us to be successful, our customers must be satisfied.

Management wants to know how we are performing. To impress the top executives, we have to use terms they understand and appreciate. This means numbers describing costs per unit of service, cycle times of various processes, the quantity or volume of work completed with a given level of resources, the quality of the result, and the level of satisfaction of the customers. For management to know that we are doing something valuable, we have to show value added. After all, that is what management pays for. By following the logic of the value chain, we can find the potential and actual value of nearly everything we do.

The last factor in the success formula is communication. You can do great work, but if no one knows it, you will be devalued within the organization. You can overcome this potential problem by applying recent advances in computer and software technology to structure reports so that the audience will understand and appreciate what you have contributed. Keep in mind that reports are meant to persuade as well as inform. Do not dump 10 pounds of activity data on the readers. No one cares how hard you have worked. Instead, give them a few examples of results and the value added by those results.

If You've Never
Measured HR Before . . .

Two Purposes of HR Measurement

Measuring human resources (HR) is a two-phase skill. In the first phase it is necessary to develop data about our performance in a form that is meaningful to our audiences. I say "audiences" because there are several. The first one is the HR department. We should communicate with our people in ways that inform, compliment, critique, stimulate, and reward them, because without them we can achieve nothing. Another audience is the various departments and managers with which we interact to provide a service or to obtain cooperation to carry out our responsibilities. Obviously, informative and persuasive communication is critical in these relationships. Still another audience is senior management, which includes everyone in the system above our level. That is where the power is. If we want to tap into that power, we have to inform and persuade the people who hold it.

This leads to the second phase. There is no getting away from it: We are all salespeople. As we pointed out earlier, more than 70 percent of communications are persuasive in nature. Research has shown that many of the seemingly unimportant comments people make are really attempts to turn others to their way of thinking or make them act according to their wishes. Success at HR requires using numbers to persuade others.

The good news is that at the senior HR level most people have some knowledge of the operations and finances of the organization. This is due to two developments during the 1990s. The first was the arrival of the new types of HR people mentioned earlier in this book. The second is the fact that the competitive pressure on organizations is so great that staff departments have to be more cognizant of their effect on the profitability of the company. This does not excuse government and other not-for-profit HR types because there is steady pressure on those organizations to be more accountable for the public funds they consume. The conclusion is obvious: If we want to be effective communicators in business, we have to build rapport with our audiences. The most direct way to do that is by focusing on the business and using objective data and language to communicate with them.

THOUGHT 4 *We must understand the business if we expect to add value.*

Involving the Staff in Measurement

The first time one introduces the idea of developing a performance measurement system to the staff, one can expect a mixture of reactions ranging from curiosity to apathy to rebellion. The first reaction often is, "I don't need anything else to do. I am already swamped." The next is, "What are you going to do with the data?" The fear is that it will it be used to hurt someone. That concern is followed by, "I don't see any value in doing it," "I don't think it can be done," and finally, "What's in it for me?"

These are reasonable reactions. They reflect the fact that this is a new concept for many HR workers. People are fearful of change unless they see a good reason for it. The introduction of a measurement system often is seen as a radical departure from the norm. It is bound to create fear, suspicion, and opposition. The good news is that there are very plausible answers to these objections as well as compelling reasons for measuring our work. The second piece of good news is that there are now fewer HR types for whom measurement is a problem.

The staff has to be convinced about four points:

1. There is a valid business reason for doing it.
2. It can be done.
3. It won't mean a lot of extra work.
4. There is definitely something in it for them.

Let us discuss these points one at a time.

There Is a Valid Reason for Doing It

The HR department is part of a business organization whether it is a profit or a not-for-profit corporation. HR is not so unusual that it can be run under a separate philosophy, with a somewhat introverted set of objectives and a method of management that does not fit in with that of the larger organization it supposedly serves. HR is part of an organization, derives support from it, and must serve its goals to survive. We operate according to the organization's goals. We use its compensation system and its review and discipline policies. As in most staff departments, our work infiltrates the whole organization, and that body absorbs and sustains us. This is a symbiotic relationship. Therefore, since the larger organization uses quantitative methods, to be in sync with it we need to adopt its methodology for interfacing and reporting results.

It Can Be Done

Objections here are based on the belief that performance cannot be measured. People who have never experienced a successful measurement system stop here. Unfortunately, they still represent a significant, although declining, proportion of HR personnel. Succeeding chapters will provide an in-depth treatment of how the total HR function can be broken down into manageable and measurable pieces. The point is that this is already being done in small and large departments in other organizations. This is true not only in the United States but in many other countries. We know this because this book has been translated and used as a text in universities abroad as well as in many HR departments beyond our borders. There are some techniques to be learned, but a measurement system is much less complicated than a salary structure or a recruitment program.

Once in place, it needs little updating to remain relevant or cope with short-term changes in the market.

It Will Not Mean a Lot of Extra Work

The third objection is difficult to disprove until the system is in place. At first glance it does look like a lot of extra work. Data must be collected from a variety of sources. A collection method must be designed, and a reporting format must be created. And that is only the beginning. Once it's ready to go, somebody is going to have to make it happen. All this is true, but as with any task there is an easy way and a hard way to do it. Technology is coming to the rescue.

The critical element in a measurement system is the collection of data. Once the data are in hand, the reporting system is relatively simple. The secret to easy data collection is to make the data part of the job that generates them. That is, workers are responsible for the development of their own raw data. Software is already on the market, and more is coming in the form of data extraction tools to do the collection job for us. For those who are collecting data manually, there is a template available through the Saratoga Institute into which data can be entered on a regular basis and automatically formatted and calculated. So long as the data are complete, accurate, and turned in on time, it does not matter how the data are collected.

Some people will say that logs get in the way and slow down the work. For 6 years I managed an HR department that ran a system that measured 30 to 40 activities. Almost all our data were collected and recorded manually. We calculated that it took less than 5 percent of our total work time to maintain the system. That was not 5 percent of work time *added* to the day; it was part of doing the job and therefore soon became invisible. Every group, no matter how busy it is, has more than 5 percent of its time lying around. The value of having the data far outweighs the labor. Every consulting firm requires that the professional staff maintain logs of time applied to different jobs. If those people can do it, why can't we?

There Is Definitely Something in It for Them

People have a right to know what the payoff will be for them. Fortunately, there are several rewards for those who make the system work. The most important is knowledge: People will know how well they are doing. This makes them feel their accomplishments. Without accomplishment life becomes a treadmill that leads to burnout. The second major value of having the data is being able to talk in business terms with others. This leads to appreciation for our contribution. As you read this book, look for payoffs from measurement. You will find many.

Requirement For Precision

Whenever the subject of measuring HR work arises, it is interesting to listen to the wide range of perceptions held by our colleagues. Some show no concern for the complexity of the task and seem willing to jump into it without a moment's pause. Others fret over a multitude of minor, solvable issues, apparently looking for reasons why they cannot or should not attempt it.

In the latter case, invariably someone brings up the point of accuracy or precision. There is no question that there is a degree of inaccuracy in all business information. The fact that accounting produces objective data does not guarantee that the underlying assumptions, the raw data available, the decisions about what to report and what to hold back, and the invisible connections among the many steps in a process are included, accurate, or even truthful.

A business is not a research laboratory. There is no such thing as control outside a laboratory. Management does not require accuracy at the .05 level of statistical significance. In research, precision is obviously critical. In pharmaceuticals or medicine, extreme care must be taken with procedures and measurement. Results are often required to be statistically valid beyond the .001 level. That is not what is required in HR measurement. We are operating in the field, with all the problems inherent in field research and experimentation. The marketing department does not have control over the product or the customer, and the finance department does not control the cost of money, yet both are able to evaluate much of their work quantitatively. It is not necessary to introduce heavy statistics to play the numbers game. Performance measurement of the type we are advocating can be handled with the four basic arithmetic functions: adding, subtracting, multiplying, and dividing. Of course, a basic knowledge of statistics is helpful in designing a measurement system that will have the most validity possible. Nevertheless, anyone who has experience in the function, common sense, and arithmetic ability can do an acceptable job.

Any object, issue, act, process, or activity that can be described in terms of observable variables is subject to measurement. A phenomenon can be evaluated in terms of cost, time, quantity, quality, or human reaction. The methods for accomplishing this will be described in subsequent chapters. The only useful question in applying measurement to the HR function is: What is worth measuring? Management will accept progress in lieu of perfection.

THOUGHT 5 *Measurement of business results cannot and need not be as precise as laboratory research.*

Reporting

Most people who make the effort to collect data and measure their activities want to report their accomplishments to management. Report design is an art form. Many people believe that it is simply a matter of arranging data on paper or an electronic medium and presenting the data to an audience. These people seldom succeed in moving their audience in the desired direction.

Reports have two purposes: They inform and persuade. Whether they achieve either purpose depends on the skill of the reporter as much as on the data presented. Reports should tell the story and simultaneously convince the audience that we are professionals who are in control of our function. For this to happen, the audience will have to take the time to read or view the report. To grab and hold their attention we have to speak to them in forms they comprehend and appreciate. Remember, we can do a great job, but if we cannot tell the story effectively, we will never get credit for our accomplishments.

Summary

Many people come into human resources work because they prefer dealing with people rather than things. Many are afraid of numbers. They use every excuse they can find to avoid having to deal numerically. Unfortunately for them, today there are fewer places to hide. It is almost a case of "count or die." Beyond the numbers people fear how the data will be used—perhaps to hurt them. Ironically, numbers can be used more effectively than narrative to demonstrate how well they are doing.

Although accuracy is imperative, extreme precision is not. A business enterprise operates in an uncontrollable environment. There is no way that a person can prove his or her worth numerically. Even salespeople who make sales cannot prove that it was their sales ability that won the orders. Statistical proof is not the point. Management wants to know two things: Are we moving in the right direction, and how do we compare to the competition?

PART II

How to Measure Hiring and Staffing

Trends

If we think of the people in the organization as assets, let's look at our work as being that of "human asset" managers. The subject of this part is acquisition. Just like capital equipment, supplies, and energy, human talent has to be acquired. We can call it hiring, recruiting, staffing, or another term, but in essence it is the acquisition of talent. The value-adding potential of all functions within organizations depends on how effective the talent is that we help them acquire. Everyone acknowledges that people are the key assets in the information age. All other assets are nothing more than inert commodities that can be purchased at market prices. Once purchased and delivered, these resources become depreciating assets. Only the human asset has the potential to learn, grow, and contribute. This part deals with the first step in asset management: acquisition.

Talent Shortage

Everyone knows there is a talent shortage in North America. Whether one is looking for cashiers for a fast-food chain, nurses for a hospital, or systems analysts for a software vendor, there is not enough talent to go around. And at least until the year 2010 there won't be. Population and educational demographics clearly forecast the shortfall. The question is, What can be done about it? The new century is going to be a great battle for talent. Those who are creative in their sourcing are going to be the winners.

A Measured Response

Staffing functions are trying every tactic imaginable to attract talent. From new sources such as job boards on the Internet to new perks such as Bring Your Pet to Work Day, the net is being cast far and wide. Even though the economy softened a bit shortly after the millennium change, there is still a problem filling high-skill jobs. No matter what you try, you are going to have to measure the results or you will have few data to support investing in a special hiring effort. When you keep data on special projects or ongoing processes, you know what worked better and can go to management with confidence as you propose the next investment.

Measuring Workforce Planning

The First Input

Planning is the first formal input in the process of human talent acquisition. As with any other function, the role of planning is predetermined by the style and values of the organization's management. Years ago a computer company president told me there was no need to plan: "We just stay very close to IBM, and whichever way they go, we try to follow and leapfrog them occasionally." I suggested that if that was the case, he should create a spy unit instead of a planning function.

Even in a fast-changing market, planning has several values. One of the central ones is to prepare data that assist management in making decisions about the future direction of the company. Supplying pertinent information about the most likely future scenario lessens uncertainty and risk. Human resources (HR) planning promotes efficiency and effectiveness in the acquisition of human resources. Although planners use numbers to communicate their story, there is more to the job than statistics. More forward-looking HR planners deal with compensation and employee relations in regard to changes in the structure of the organization. Their reasoning is that there is no point in projecting work for jobs that are becoming obsolete, redundant, or inappropriate. This is particularly appropriate in a period when new technologies, team-oriented structures, and knowledge-driven cultures are emerging. Planning could come up with an algorithm to convert the business plan directly into a staff-

45

ing plan. Variations can be offered, based on different assumptions about the future. There are sophisticated HR information systems that incorporate this process.

Planners have talents that are usually unique among HR professionals. A planner can be a catalyst. In the second edition of this book a case was featured that at the time was relatively unusual. In more recent years we have continued to find more examples of analytic work. It is a very positive sign that HR is becoming more business-oriented. In the case mentioned above, Grahn[1] described how a planner converted the sales projection for the coming year into the number of invoices to be processed. Once she learned how many invoices could be processed per person per day, she showed the order-processing manager how many new people would be needed to handle the increased sales. Beyond the discovery of interesting information, she worked out a plan with the manager to increase the productivity of the order-processing function. The result was that the staffing growth curve leveled out in comparison to the sales growth curve.

Another approach to the planning function is to turn a planner into a coordinator. I once gave my planner the task of bringing together people from staffing, training, career development, and organizational development to create a model of effective management. The idea was that once we knew what kinds of skills, abilities, aptitudes, and interests were typical of an effective manager in our company, we would be better able to recruit, counsel, and develop people according to their best fit in the organization and their maximum personal potential. The planner was excellent at this, for she had a better overview of the organization than did most people and was more experienced at handling the types of data that were collected.

Linking HR and Business Planning

Practically every issue of an HR planning journal has an article about tying the HR plan to the business plan. This is so obvious that it hardly needs stating. The key point is that normally HR planning

---

[1] J. L. Grahn, "White Collar Productivity: Misunderstandings and Some Progress," *Personnel Administration*, August 1981, p. 30.

cannot be linked directly to tangible business outcomes. If one looked at the average HR workforce plan, there would be no prima facie evidence that the plan could add value. However, a thorough plan reduces variability and therefore risk. It helps management avoid costs, optimize productivity, and beat the competition to market.

The way to connect HR planning with business results is to start with the strategic vision and business initiatives of the organization. Executives typically set annual targets for productivity, quality, and service that will help the enterprise become more competitive and hence gain market share. The HR plan should list how many of which types of skills are needed to meet or exceed the targets. It can also suggest ways to control headcount growth through automating, reengineering work processes, or outsourcing.

Planners have the tools to make significant contributions beyond planning. Some merely crank out annual documents that quickly find a spot on someone's shelf. The best ones play central roles in business operations.

Profiling and Projecting

One of the difficulties in measuring the work of planners is that their output is primarily a plan for the future. By definition, it will not be known for a year or two how accurate their predictions are. In addition, no one is capable of predicting future events; therefore, it is not fair to blame the planner for the unforeseeable. It is impossible to measure the value of a long-term plan in the short term. Planners thus often feel frustrated because they cannot prove their worth with concrete evidence. Those who work from a value-adding perspective don't have this problem.

Planning does two things. It profiles the current state of the employee population, and it projects future needs or conditions regarding that population. Since it is difficult to measure the effectiveness of projection, it might be better to look to profiling for evaluation purposes.

If the prime output of the planning group is an HR plan, each year it will be possible to measure whether the plan was published on time and whether it met any preset conditions and specifications.

This is simple, obvious, and not very exciting. However, to produce the annual plan, certain data on the employee population must be developed. These data can be used for other projects that have a measurable short-term payoff.

THOUGHT 6 *Planning is effective when it reduces risk and adds value.*

Forecasting through Uncertainty

Forecasting increases an organization's options and reduces the penalties incurred because of inappropriate actions. The success of forecasting depends on the reliability of the data entered into the system, the models and methods used, the linkage between the planners and forecasters and the line organization, and, most important, the insight of those involved. Planning cycles have shrunk from 5 years to sometimes no more than the coming year.

Many factors can skew the results of a forecast. Despite the development of predictive techniques and better data, forecasting is not a precise science. The future is unknown and unknowable. Volatility is the norm. Because of this unpredictability, it is very difficult for the staffing manager to plan. Given the uncertainty, how does a staffing department prepare itself to respond promptly to the demands made on it? Our view of the planning model is shown in Figure 5-1. Planning often focuses on providing bodies; that is the activity. We want planners to focus on how they are adding value.

We have to try to operate with no more, and probably less, than the number of people we need at any given time, and we know from experience that periodically we will be inundated with unplanned and unexpected recruiting demands. In that situation what can we do to mitigate the stress that will be put on our staff while maintaining an acceptable level of recruiting support?

The answer to this question lies in selecting the variables that are most affected by changes in recruiting demand. The most common variables include the requisition inventory, the workload of the recruiters and their assistants (expressed by the number of requisitions they handle), the expected number of hires that can be attained by the recruiters and assistants in a given time period, and the past history of projected openings versus actual openings. All these ele-

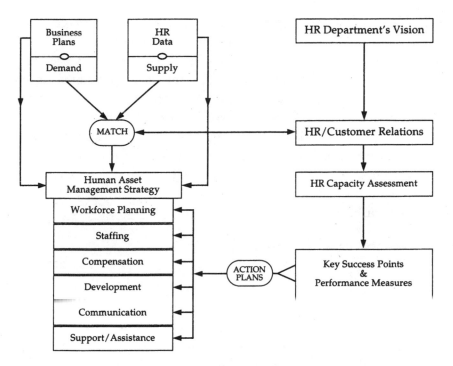

Figure 5-1   Staffing Planning Model

ments are affected by market changes and volatility. They are also influenced by support systems and the nature of management's needs. If we redesign the workflow or automate, it should make a difference in the number of requisitions the staff can handle. If the ratio of exempt to nonexempt or professional to managerial requisitions changes, that may affect our response time and time to fill. The ability to predict the future depends on knowledge of the past, perception of the present, and skills in forecasting.

Requisition Inventories

The first issue that the staffing manager needs to grasp is the size and variability of the requisition inventory. Requisitions are like orders: They come in, they are filled, and they go out. Even in unstable times there are normal fluctuations in the requisition flow just as there are in the order flow. Seasons, competitors' activities, and new product developments all affect staffing requirements and requisition flow. These cycles dictate an uneven load of requisitions.

The staffing manager could predict with some confidence that seasonal cycles will repeat each year. Except when the economy is in a deep recession, these cycles follow their normal patterns—only the amplitude changes. Of late the market has defied traditional analysis. Nevertheless, one has to keep trying. Staffing can track the number of requisitions opened each month and the level of requisitions at the beginning or end of each month. Applicant tracking systems have this capability built in. The three variations on this basic measure are shown below.

REQUISITION RATE

$$RER = \frac{NR}{TR/M}$$

where RER = requisition rate
  NR = new requisitions added during the month (e.g., 27)
  TR/M = total requisitions open at the beginning of the month (e.g., 215)

EXAMPLE

$$RER = \frac{27}{215}$$
$$= 12.6\%$$

Requisitions opened, filled, and in inventory can be monitored as predictors. These three indicators could be displayed on one table. They also could be plotted on a trend chart and shown as three lines, with months on the x axis and number on the y axis. In this example we tracked openings by level. They could also be tracked by department, job group, or other criteria. This information could be recorded on a spreadsheet and updated each month. After 1 year, the business cycle would be complete and cyclical fluctuations, if any, would be apparent. The next two measures would be calculated the same way.

Cost Management

It is obvious that the manager of a staffing department needs to be able to predict the rate of incoming requisitions with some degree of accuracy. Without foreknowledge of the anticipated workload, it would be impossible to maintain a consistent level of service and management of costs. One month the department might be over-staffed, and the next it could be woefully understaffed. If that were the pattern, top management might turn to outside sources to meet recruitment needs.

Requisition flow is only part of the picture, however. Staffing managers also must know how efficient the recruiters are. In the following chapters we shall discuss measures of efficiency and productivity. When we examine recruiter effectiveness, we also shall discuss response time and time to fill. It is also helpful to know how many requisitions a recruiter and the recruiting assistant can effec tively handle, that is, how many requisitions they can work on in an efficient and effective manner. Observation of past performance will show, within a range of values, what the optimum requisition load is for each recruiter and for the overall group in the organization. The manager also will want to have data on the hiring rates for different jobs. Very few jobs have enough applicants. Other jobs go begging because there are more openings than there are applicants. Because the total job market is characterized by a talent shortage as well as variability, the staffing manager cannot maintain an optimum work-force without knowing the profile of the requisition load and the efficiency and productivity levels of the recruiting staff.

Optimum Staff Ratios

After looking at the volume of the incoming requisitions, HR wants to learn how the recruiting staff reacts to that flow. Obviously, people can handle many requisitions if all they have to do is funnel résumés and applications to the requesting departments. However, if the job entails screening incoming résumés, interviewing, checking references, and conferring with the requester, perhaps even 10 requisitions is a full workload.

The perennial question in staffing is, What is a proper ratio of requisitions to recruiters? The Saratoga Institute has studied staffing practices for over 10 years. We found that the ratio of recruiters to requisitions ranged from 1:3 to 1:100, depending on the variables mentioned above as well as expectations of service levels.

THOUGHT 7 *The "right" or "best" number depends on conditions and expectations; there is no absolute answer.*

Since one of the notions underlying the term *productivity* is that the production is long term, let us use that as a working title for the question of optimum staff loading. The only way to arrive at an optimum factor is to track the hiring record of the recruiters and assistants over a long period of time. Fluctuations can distort short-term measures. During demand peaks and valleys the manager shifts people around to meet needs. As a minimum, it takes at least 6 months of production history before we can come to any conclusions. It is better to have the whole year to review, but if we do not have historical data and do not want to wait a year, 6 months is a reasonable minimum.

The fundamental questions are, How many hires did the recruiters produce during each month? and How many recruiters and how many administrative assistants did we have on staff in each of those months? By putting those facts together we can come up with the average monthly number of hires per recruiter and per assistant. This is the basic measure, and a table such as Figure 5-2 could be constructed.

This table shows the average number of hires per month throughout the reporting period. The optimum number is not necessarily the highest number. For example, November produced 38.3 hires per recruiter and 28.7 hires per assistant. This was the highest monthly average for both groups. However, issues of cost, quality, and customer service are also important for a department that is more than a funnel for paper. The staffing manager will take several factors into consideration before deciding which months are the optimum service months. In this case the staffing manager reviews hire quality, cost per hire, and recruiter effectiveness measures and concludes that the months from July through October were the most

Month	New Hires	Number of Recruiters	Average per Recruiter	Number of Assistants	Average per Assistant
January	37	4	9.2	4	9.2
February	40	4	10	5	8
March	57	4	14.2	5	11.4
April	78	4	19.5	5	15.6
May	88	5	17.6	5	17.6
June	79	5	15.8	4	19.7
July	104	5	20.8	4	26
August	114	5	22.8	4	28.5
September	108	5	27	4	27
October	98	4	32.6	4	24.5
November	115	3	38.3	4	28.7
December	61	3	20.3	4	15.2
Averages		3	20.0	4.3	19.2
Total	979	4.5			

New hires planned 682
Attrition* <u>370</u>
Needed for 1995: 1,052

*Turnover projections predict 370 openings resulting from voluntary and involuntary terminations.

Figure 5-2   Staff Productivity Record

effective recruiting period. During those months, the recruiters generated an average of 25.8 new hires and the assistants supported 26.5 hires. Since the projection is for 1,052 open positions in the coming period, the staffing manager divides that by 12 and finds an average of 87.7 openings per month. Dividing that number by the production record of the previous year, the manager finds a staffing level of 3.4 recruiters and 3.3 assistants.

Of course, this calculation is oversimplified because it ignores the variability of the recruitment year. We know that seasonal fluctuations of all types will affect the requisition flow. We have a business plan for the organization that translates this into a projection of hiring needs. We probably have high and low periods of turnover, which imply different levels of openings. All these bits of information go into our estimate of new openings by month. Those 12 numbers would be the dividends, and the hiring production record (25.8) would be the divisor. This set of computations will generate a base staffing level for each month throughout the coming year. By having people cross-trained, we can shift resources back and forth between functions and maintain an optimum level in the recruiting force.

As we track this recruitment function over a period of time, we may find changes occurring that are not seasonal. General business conditions, such as a recession, usually help recruiters improve their time and cost factors because more people are calling, writing in, or coming in off the street to look for jobs. In contrast, the arrival of a new company may create more competition for jobs and make every hire more difficult. This adds time and money to the process and may negatively affect the quality of hires as a result of the scarcity of good labor. A staffing manager has to be aware of these unforeseen factors if an accurate projection for the staff level is desired.

Actual versus Projected Results

It was pointed out earlier that to project the future it helps to know the past. If Shakespeare was right and the past is prologue for what is to come, we could use a convenient vehicle to record the past. The form that we propose illustrates the accuracy of the HR planning system as well as the organization's ability to accomplish its recruitment goals.

The form shown in Figure 5-3 divides the data into two basic categories: additions to staff and replacements for existing jobs. Within those categories we have chosen to look at the data by the subdivisions of exempt, nonexempt, and hourly. As was noted before, the subdivisions are a matter of personal choice. We can do it by any category we choose; it is up to us. The form provides space by category and subdivision to show the projected figure and the actual placement figure.

At the end of a reporting period—monthly, quarterly, or annually—we can check the correlation between the actual figures and the projected figures. Knowing how we have done by subdivision can help us strategize future recruitment efforts. For example, we may

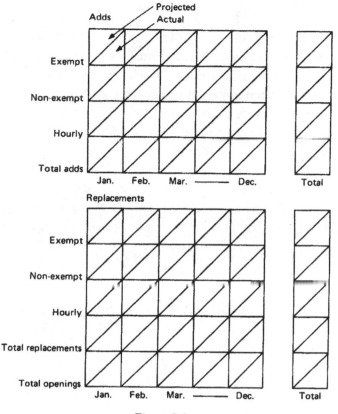

Figure 5-3

find that a department, such as marketing, tends to project its needs either too high or too low. If this is a consistent pattern month after month, we might suspect that we will have to inflate or deflate future projections by a certain amount. The market may change, but personalities seldom do. According to our experience in managing staffing, we could take the annual projections and inflate some while deflating others. The result would be that the actual results would come closer to the projected results than they did before we bothered to study the patterns and make adjustments. This would help us plan staffing levels more accurately. Whenever a new player got into the game, we would start the observations over again.

Summary

Successful people exhibit the habit of planning. It seems that they always have the time to study and plan before they act. By contrast, people who could be classified as moderately successful to unsuccessful seem to spend more time acting and less time planning. They are the personification of the notion that they do not have time to plan, but they do have time to do it over when it goes wrong. There is a lesson to be learned from these two approaches.

Even though it is very difficult to measure the effectiveness of planning until after the fact, planning and its measurement help us learn and avoid problems in the future. Reducing risk and limiting variability are very useful activities in any organization. Measurement plays the central role in this process.

CHAPTER 6

Measuring Recruiting

The hiring decision is often made too lightly; few organizations have stopped to figure out how costly the decision to hire a new employee is. In 1990 UpJohn calculated the career cost and found that it was 117 times the initial year's salary, assuming a 30-year career. The fact that many employees do not stay with a company for 30 years does not lessen the importance of the acquisition decision. The point is that every time the recruitment system cycles, the company incurs a cost and runs the risk of making a poor hiring decision. Even if the new hire is good, there is a productivity loss as the person moves up the learning curve. Any way you look at it, hiring is expensive, and one cannot ignore the importance of the selection process.

When unemployment dropped to the 4 percent range nationally businesses woke up to the fact that people are important. *Talent* is the word now. Organizations are going all out to acquire the talent they need. Sign-on bonuses, unheard of in earlier times, became a common inducement. The Saratoga Institute's annual study of hiring practices and costs revealed that bonuses were being offered all the way down to the supervisory and technician levels.[1]

Acquiring talent is a much more complicated job in the new millennium. Rapidly changing technology and the move to collaborative management models call for individuals with skills and aptitudes, which were not so important in an industrial economy. One must add to this the fact that each job applicant offers a unique combi-

---

[1] *Human Capital Benchmarking Report 2000.* Saratoga Institute, July 2001.

nation of education, experience, aptitudes, skills, interests, needs, values, goals, and qualities. Finally, the desire of many people to balance work and home life and to seek values from work beyond pay makes the recruitment and selection process more difficult.

Internal and External Sources

The staffing process has been thought of as the first step toward finding a replacement for an employee who has recently vacated a job. There are two potential sources of replacement: the outside labor pool and the existing internal workforce. Until the past couple of years the second source was not fully utilized, but the picture has changed in two ways. The most dramatic change has been the rise of *contingent workers*. At the time of the second edition of this book no one was talking about contingents because they were largely invisible. Since that time a few temps here and there evolved into a workforce of permanent temps that grew to such a point that a name was needed for them. According to several sources, contingents now number more than 15 percent of the U.S. workforce.

Since the external labor pool is so shallow, the replacement process starts internally. This is where planners can make a mark. When the skills inventory and succession planning subsystems are operating, by definition they are providing candidates for many openings. The need to look outside is diminished, and the internal reservoir of applicants supplies qualified candidates. Strangely, over the past several years Saratoga's study of hiring costs shows that the cost of internal placements has been higher than that of external hires.[2] This is due to the fact that many internal transfers include relocation costs.

Usually the urge to seek candidates from outside the organization is more prevalent for higher-level openings than it is for lower-level ones. This is more often the case in young, fast-growing companies than in older, slow-growing firms that have a large cadre of experienced internal personnel. Nevertheless, it occurs with enough frequency in both cases to support the generalization. In larger, more established firms the human resources information system (HRIS) database is used to locate available individuals and select those who

[2] *Human Capital Benchmarking Report 1997–2000.* Saratoga Institute, 2001.

most closely match the requirements of the position. In fact, managers often have access to the total workforce to search for potential internal candidates. In the perfect situation the system should be operating at a level of efficiency at which it could provide a fully qualified and interested candidate from the internal workforce for each position. As one job is vacated by an employee moving up to fill a higher-level job, the system would provide a qualified candidate for that job. As the second and lower-level job opened up, the system would yield another appropriate candidate. The process would cascade level by level until only entry-level jobs had to be filled from outside. The only exception would be unforeseeable or cataclysmic events. Examples include an acquisition, which would have to be staffed, and a catastrophe such as a fire, a plane crash, or a mass defection, which would take several key people suddenly.

Stagnation

There is one problem with this scenario: Filling all jobs from within leads to stagnant, incestuous thinking. There has been a good deal of research into what is labeled *groupthink*. Simply described, it is a situation where the individuals who make up a group achieve a state of shared experience and values to the point where they cease to function cognitively as individual minds and begin to accept, without challenge, virtually all the ideas put forth by any member of the group. A high level of comfort, security, and certainty develops within the group. The "not-invented-here" syndrome ("If we didn't think of it, it must be worthless") takes over and blocks any novel ideas not presented by a group member. The amount of stimulus reception drops to a dangerously low level, and the group recycles the thoroughly processed ideas of the past. This situation certainly speeds up decision making, but it completely shuts down the creative process. Recent American industrial history provides several textbook cases of this syndrome.

It is not necessary to repeat here the stories of the many American industries that were severely damaged by groupthink. Their problem did not develop through a lack of capital, material, or equipment. Instead, incestuous value systems would not allow fresh perceptions of a changing world. The lesson for human resources (HR) systems is that they need to do more than project numbers. The systems should be designed so that they can identify the values, aptitudes, and creative abilities needed in the changing market. The current staffing problem is not only a matter of numbers but, more important, a matter of fit. Time frames have shrunk, the impact of decisions has increased, and risk has grown proportionately. Hence, recruitment and selection must become a more scientific process. The move toward competency planning is positive, and the hope is it will not get lost with all the other good ideas HR has had but has not been able to convert into a business value.

No matter how good a job human asset planning does, we will always want to use outside sources for applicants. Everyone knows that we can manage our internal resources to meet some replacement needs. However, many managers don't make any attempt to manage the outside resources. They simply accept what is apparent in the labor market and turn to it as needed. The problem is compounded when there is no central control over the use of outside media or sources. The message of the company goes out in a confusing and sometimes conflicting manner. Then problems over fees develop, public relations suffers, and budgets are overrun. In short, no one is in charge.

Opening of the Sourcing Market

There is a growing trend toward sourcing new hires through whatever channel is most cost-effective. This can entail bypassing the company's internal staffing department in favor of external vendors. Staffing departments, along with other staff functions, have been given warning that they now have to compete for business. One of the remedies for nonexempt sourcing has been what is called on-premise staffing. In this case a staffing agency such as Manpower, Kelly, Adecco, or Spherion will take space inside the company and put its staffing professionals to work filling job requests. This is appealing to senior management because the staffing agency presents a business case of how to do it more cheaply. Since management views HR as an expense center, it likes the idea of doing things more cheaply. This is the perception that this book will help you to change.

Since the financial markets have put top management under pressure to control operating expenses and at the same time to grow the top line, many staff functions have been outsourced and more will be. This trend will not be reversed in the foreseeable future. Several of the large consultancies, such as Accenture, PriceWaterhouse-Coopers, and its spinoff Unifi, are moving into the outsourcing business. A newcomer, Exult, within 14 months of its founding had booked several long-term HR outsourcing contracts with Bank of America, BP-Amoco-Arco, International Paper, Unisys, and Tenneco that were worth several billion dollars.

The Make or Buy Decision

Organizations have two choices in acquiring human assets. They can train internal people for greater responsibility (make it) or go to the market and hire someone (buy it). One of the fundamental variables in the make or buy decision is cost. It takes money to run an organization whether it is a profit or a not-for-profit business. Money has to come from somewhere, and it is usually in finite supply. The principle of most businesses has been: The less we spend on acquisition of resources, the more we can put into products or services. Ironically, the acquisition process has a wider range of effects on the organization than is generally realized. The cost-effectiveness of any given hire does not stop when the offer is accepted. That's actually when it starts, and it can be traced all the way through the new employee's career until the day that person becomes a turnover statistic. The issue of turnover cost really starts with selection. Turnover is as much a problem of making the right hire as anything else. Some companies with historically high turnover rates have cut them by 50 percent or more by working on improved selection programs. Changes in an organization after the fact can hurt the best selection efforts, but a system that employs modern hiring tools and techniques can have a long-term positive impact.

Employees should be treated as investments, not as expenses. They provide a return on the money spent to sustain them and thus qualify as an investment. Later we will look at a way to calculate the return on investment of pay and benefits. Managers spend a great deal of time studying potential returns on investment in capital equipment. However, they do not take the same care in scrutinizing a job candidate, whose cost may be many times the cost of a new machine. A basic change of attitude toward the selection process is the first step in managing hiring costs.

The First Measure

To make an intelligent decision regarding the trade-offs between promoting from within and hiring from without, it is necessary to know the relative cost of each choice. In this chapter we will start with what is often thought of as the first measure: cost per hire (CPH). Cost per hire applies whether one is talking about internal or external sources. Internal placements do not require all the types of expenses that external sourcing does, but there are still costs, and they need to be calculated.

At first people tend to think of CPH as the direct cost for advertising and agency fees. However, when one digs deeper, one begins to realize the multitude of expenses generated by the replacement process. There are several types of replacement expenses, and they fall into the following categories:

Type	Expense
Source cost	Advertising, including job boards and on-line ads, agency fees paid to generate applicants, and hire and/or referral bonuses.
Staff time	Salary, benefits, and standard overhead cost of the staff to meet with the manager to discuss sourcing; work with the media and/or agency to begin the search; screening applications; calling applicants in for interviews; interviewing applicants and checking references; reviewing candidates with the manager and scheduling interviews; making or confirming the offer.
Management	Salary, benefit, and standard overhead cost of the requesting department, time management to plan sourcing, discuss and interview candidates, and make a hiring decision and an offer.

Type	Expense
Processing cost	Manual and automatic data system cost of opening a new file, cost of medical examination, cost of employment and record verification (mail or telephone), security checks, and so on.
Travel and relocation	Travel and lodging costs for staff and candidates and relocation costs.
Miscellaneous	Materials and other special or unplanned expenses. The cost of new employee orientation may be included or considered part of training expenses. Reference checking, physical examinations, drug screening, and bonding checks are other examples.

In its simplest yet most complete form, CPH can be expressed as shown in the equation below.

COST PER HIRE

$$CPH = \frac{AC + AF + RB + TC + RE + RC + NC}{H} + 10\%$$

where AC = advertising costs
    AF = agency fees
    RB = referral bonus
    TC = travel costs
    RE = relocation
    RC = recruiter costs
    NC = unsolicited no-cost résumés

In 1986, the first Society for Human Resource Management (SHRM)/Saratoga Institute Human Resource Effectiveness Report was published using this formula. Over the next 8 years the formula proved to be accurate within 1.5 percent; that is, the sum of all other costs was between 9 percent and 10.5 percent. From this experience has come the knowledge of how to collect valid and reliable data with a minimum of effort. The 1.5 percent represents the cost of all other activities. This may sound low, but compared to all the other activities, about 10 percent is typical.

The two examples that follow show the equations for calculating external and internal cost per hire (ECPH and ICPH). External costs are for employees hired from outside the organization; internal costs are for current employees hired to fill an open position. The difference between the two is the inclusion or exclusion of agency fees, which are not applicable for an internal hire.

EXTERNAL COST PER HIRE

ECPH
$$= \frac{E/AC + E/AF + E/RB + E/TC + E/RE + E/RC + NC}{EH}$$

where E/AC = external advertising costs (e.g., $55,000)
  E/AF = external agency fees (e.g., $43,000)
  E/RB = external referral bonus (e.g., $7,000)
  E/TC = external travel costs ($6,000)
  E/RE = external relocation (e.g., $20,000)
  E/RC = external recruiter costs (e.g., $9,000)
  NC = unsolicited no-cost résumés
  EH = external hires

EXAMPLE

E/CPH
$$= \frac{\$55,000 + \$43,000 + \$7,000 + \$6,000 + \$20,000 + \$9,000 + 0}{16}$$
$$= \frac{\$140,000}{16}$$
$$= \$8,750$$

INTERNAL COST PER HIRE

$$ICPH = \frac{I/AC + I/RB + I/TC + I/RE + I/RC + I/NC}{IH}$$

where I/AC = internal advertising costs (e.g., $1,000)
  I/RB = internal referral bonus paid (e.g., $15,000)
  I/TC = internal travel costs (e.g., $21,000)
  I/RE = internal relocation costs (e.g., $60,000)
  I/RC = internal recruiter cost (e.g., $9,000)

$$I/NC = \text{internal no cost}$$
$$IH = \text{internal hires}$$

EXAMPLE

$$I/CPH = \frac{\$1,000 + \$15,000 + \$21,000 + \$60,000 + \$9,000 + 0}{25}$$

$$= \frac{\$106,000}{25}$$

$$= \$4,240$$

Source costs are divided into four types: advertisements in all media, agency fees, employee referrals, and no-cost unsolicited résumés. We will ignore the last category, but hires from this source are included in the denominator of the formula given above. Hiring costs are rather straightforward, since the invoices from the advertisements, Web costs, and the fees from agencies are unequivocal and fees paid to employees are well known. When we run one advertisement for one position, it is easy to ascribe the cost of the ad to that hire. However, often combination ads that showcase two or more jobs are run. Sometimes a blanket ad calling for an unstated number of applicants is placed. An example of the first type of ad would be one that calls for a supervisor of accounting, senior accountants, and accounting administrators. A sample of the second would be an ad stating simply, "Assemblers Wanted." In both cases we are hoping for multiple hires from one ad. The problem can be further complicated when there are entire company postings on an Internet job board or the company's Web site.

In an assembler advertisement it is fairly simple to divide the ad's cost by the number of assemblers hired to obtain an average ad cost. However, an accounting ad is a more complicated decision. If one supervisor, one senior accountant, and three accounting administrators were hired from this ad, how would we apportion the cost among the five hires? Is it fair to divide the cost of the ad by five? That would imply that it is as easy to hire supervisors as it is to hire accounting administrators. We could weight the charges by the salary level of each hire. In that case, should we use actual salary, entry-level salary, or the midpoint of the salary range?

Questions such as these become important in attempting a detailed analysis of the CPH. They are also issues if the cost of the advertisement must be charged back to user departments. There are occasions when two or more departments agree to pool their resources to place a large ad for people who could be employed in several departments. A common example of this is the job of programmer; often a programmer may be able to function in several departments. If we are looking for junior and senior programmers for several departments, the problem of cost allocation is compounded. It is important to establish the ground rules ahead of time, because when dollars are on the line, manners disappear. Also, we do not want users to think that they have been treated unfairly. If they think that, they are not likely to be as cooperative the next time we want to optimize our return on the corporate advertising dollar. The issue in cases like these is not, What is the right way? There is no prescribed rule to follow. The question is, What is the best way for all concerned at this time? If we are going to calculate CPH over an extended period, which is the only worthwhile way, we must have some consistency in our methodology. If we allocate costs one way this month and another way next month in an effort to keep everyone happy, the month-to-month results will not be comparable.

Agency fees cover all types of outside agency sourcing. Executive searches, retained and contingent searches, employment agencies, and even temporary workers who are converted to permanent workers are all applicable agency costs. In the case of executive and retained searches, the fee can run to tens of thousands of dollars. This, along with relocation, is usually one of the highest costs. This is why so many companies have strict controls regarding the use of executive search firms.

Some companies have employee referral bonus programs that pay current employees a bounty if they bring in qualified applicants who are subsequently hired. When the labor market became very tight in the second half of the 1990s, many organizations started offering sign-on bonuses to people who came in directly without going through an agency. In the second edition I posed the question of whether this was a short-term phenomenon. Now, in the twenty-first century, it is clear that it is not. Besides examples such as this, there will always be some kind of special expense that eludes the best plan. The point is to keep one's eyes open and make sure it is included.

Expenses associated with travel and relocation are significant. A managerial candidate flown from the midwest to either coast, fed and lodged for a day or two, and flown home can easily cost the company a couple of thousand dollars, and that's only for the first trip for one candidate. By the time we do that for two or three visits, bring the finalist's spouse out to look over the territory, and top it off with a few house-hunting trips, we have watched several thousand dollars disappear, and we haven't even considered the cost of relocation. In the 10 years between the first and second editions of this book the average relocation cost quintupled. In the last 5 years it has continued to rise, although much more slowly. Often management positions are filled without incurring significant travel or relocation expenses. Then, all of a sudden, we may spend $50,000 on one hire. If we throw that one in with the ones preceding it, for which we may have spent less than $5,000 total, the ensuing average CPH will be skewed. The number will be misleading and not indicative of what has happened over the whole range of hires.

The $50,000 must be added to the total cost of hiring for the month. However, it probably will be appropriate to report two sets of figures. One would be the hires that did not require relocation. The other would be those for which there were relocation costs. Not only is this more truthful, it provides management with an appreciation for the impact of relocation expenses on the bottom line. Our job involves more than showing management how effectively we are managing our department; it is also imperative to show management how the job could be done better. If we can develop a staffing and costout plan that will prevent having to hire people who require relocation, we probably can get support for it.

The Saratoga Institute's studies have shown that the recruiters' salary and benefits cost multiplied by the number of hours spent per job is the sixth important cost variable. All other staff time—clerks, hiring department staff, and management—is part of the 10 percent miscellaneous cost variable. Thus, we don't recommend spending a lot of time working it out. However, if you feel you must, here are some tips.

The calculation and allocation of staff time can quickly become an indecipherable mess unless you establish an accounting method and stay with it. The simplest way to reduce this problem to a manageable and understandable variable is to introduce standard labor costing. By borrowing a leaf from manufacturing's book, it is possible to determine the normal cost of an employee hour of work and set that as the standard rate. For example, a staffing assistant's standard rate could be determined in the following manner:

Salary (converted to hourly rate)	$14.25
Benefits (30% of salary)	4.28
Overhead charge (space, equipment, etc.)	8.65
Total	$27.18

The standard hourly rate applied to all staff time calculations where a staffing administrative person is involved is thus $27.18. The recruiter's standard time can be calculated in the same manner.

In time we will be able to develop an average number of hours that an administrator and a recruiter put in on a given class of hires. Let us say, for example, we find that the administrator spends 1.5 hours on average per direct labor hire. If we multiply $27.18 by 1.5, the product is $41.77, which becomes the standard cost of staffing administration time for each direct laborer the clerk assists in hiring. Multiply $41.77 by the number of hires that month and we have one component of the total month's cost of hiring. The same process is then applied to recruiters, receptionists, assistants, and anyone else in the department who is involved in hiring. We may even choose to allocate a portion of the staffing manager's time.

The process may have to be recomputed for different types or levels of jobs. Usually it takes more time to hire managers than to hire assemblers. Hence, although the standard labor rates will not change, the amount of time each person devotes to the hire may change by job. Therefore, the multiplier will change. The most dramatic changes are usually with the recruiters. At the nonexempt level, recruiters may have to spend on average half an hour per applicant interviewing for each hire. At the exempt level, that could jump to two or three hours per applicant. In addition, the number of applicants seen per hire may vary significantly. This will strongly influence the CPH when calculated by job level. It takes time to set standard rates and establish a realistic time multiplier. It is up to us to use what is most appropriate to the situation. We are free to choose as long as we are consistent. Try to keep it as simple as possible; a few points either way is not critical.

The last thing to keep in mind in employing standard labor rates is that rates change over time. The average cost of a person in the staffing function today is at least 30 percent higher than it was in 1994, when the second edition of this book was published. We need to check costs periodically. It is usually sufficient to do this on an annual basis. Doing it more frequently would cause confusion in the monthly comparison of CPH statistics. Remember, the real reason for measuring is to find out if we are doing an effective job of managing the function. This is not an exercise in statistical precision but a tool for managing.

The allocation of employee orientation costs is a process for which there is no standard rule. Some HR managers think it is a cost of hiring because it usually occurs before the person assumes the job. Even if it comes a week or a month later, they believe it should be charged to hiring because the information presented is aimed at easing the induction of the new person into the organization. Another opinion is that orientation takes place after the hire and therefore is part of an individual's training. This argument has not been resolved. In my opinion, until we adopt a generally accepted set of accounting principles for the HR field, it is a moot point. Account for it on either side and let it stand by itself. When we fold it into the total cost of a hire, it is insignificant. The only rule that always applies is to be consistent.

Breaking It Down

The true value of the measurement system becomes apparent only when we examine a dependent variable such as cost per hire. The bottom-line number, CPH = $X for a given month, is the starting point for what can be a very enlightening tour of the staffing function. Whether we have an automated or a manual data entry system, we can divide CPH by any of the types of expenses discussed above.

Furthermore, we can mix and match those independent variables in almost any combination. The net result is a chance to discover in great detail where we are being effective and where we can improve.

It is easy to measure CPH by source. We can compare the average CPH by using the cost of advertising versus the cost of agencies. We can throw in other sources, such as employee referrals, and make multiple comparisons. Another fundamental cut is level. We can look at CPH for exempt, nonexempt, and hourly employees. We can cut it finer by combining level with job groups; we can look at the difference between the CPH of entry-level, junior, and senior programmers, for instance. Of course, to be able to make those cuts, we have to remember to collect those data at the time of hire.

There are many subsets of CPH that are obtainable. When a database program or simplified spreadsheet is used, the CPH for a given type of employee, by department or source, can be tracked. For example, looking at hiring costs by source and by department will show how extensive the use of agencies in certain departments is in comparison to departments that hire more from employee referrals. Most of the software companies, such as PeopleSoft, SAP, Lawson, and SAS Institute, have come out with workforce analysis programs. At the beginning of 2001 they were still in the first generation, but they will certainly become more robust quickly. The key is to break the reasons down into the various components.

Source Analysis

For the following analysis, standard costs for staff and management time, travel, relocation, and other costs are taken as givens. The outcomes are only the sourcing costs. The process of holding certain costs constant and calculating certain others is a good way to isolate and emphasize trends. The basic equation is as follows:

SOURCE COST PER HIRE

$$SCPH = \frac{AC + AF + RB + NC}{H}$$

where AC = advertising costs (e.g., $48,000)
AF = agency fees (e.g., $29,000)
RB = referral bonuses (e.g., $17,000)

NC = no-cost hires, unsolicited résumés, nonprofit agency, referrals, etc. (e.g., $0)

H = total hires (e.g., 41)

EXAMPLE

$$SCPH = \frac{\$48,000 + \$29,000 + \$17,000 + 0}{41}$$

$$= \frac{\$94,000}{41}$$

$$= \$2,292$$

The basic formula can be varied by changing total hires (H) to include only exempt hires (EH) or nonexempt hires (NEH):

$$SCPH = \frac{AC + AF + RB + NC}{EH}$$

or

$$SCPH = \frac{AC + AF + RB + NC}{NEH}$$

Once we have the basic formula, we can change the denominator to any group of hires and recompute cost per source for that group. For example, we could look at source costs for exempts versus nonexempts or for the technical, administrative, sales and marketing, and equal employment opportunity (EEO) classes.

For reporting purposes it is enlightening to show the comparative costs of each source of hire. To do that, simply separate the variables in the numerator and do separate computations:

$$SCPH = \frac{AC}{H} + \frac{AF}{H} + \frac{RB}{H} + \frac{NC}{H}$$

A sample report based on this type of cost analysis is shown in Figure 6-1.

Special Recruiting Programs

It can be useful to evaluate the costs and outcomes of ongoing programs on a periodic basis. For college recruitment programs or national recruiting campaigns, the costs can be identified and separate calculations can be performed. Staff time (ST) and management time (MT) may be included or not, depending on the objective:

(a) April: Cost of Hires by Source, in Dollars

	Agency			Advertising			Referral Bonus			Unsolicited No-Cost	
	Number	Total Cost	Cost per Hire	Number	Total Cost	Cost per Hire	Number	Total Cost	Cost per Hire	Number	Cost
Exempt	6	47,500	7,916	8	24,375	3,047	5	1,500	300	1	00
Nonexempt	1	624	624	24	10,078	420	24	2,400	100	9	00
Total	7	48,124	6,875	32	34,453	1,077	29	3,900	134	10	00

	Total Number Hired	Total Cost	Cost per Hire
	20	73,375	3,669
	58	13,102	226
	78	86,477	1,109

(b) Year to date: Cost of Hire, by Source, in Dollars

	Agency			Advertising			Referral Bonus			Unsolicited No-Cost	
	Number	Total Cost	Cost per Hire	Number	Total Cost	Cost per Hire	Number	Total Cost	Cost per Hire	Number	Cost
Exempt	21	83,512	3,977	28	43,282	1,546	16	4,800	300	3	00
Nonexempt	8	2,843	355	91	26,270	289	69	6,900	100	17	00
Total	29	86,355	2,978	119	69,552	584	85	11,700	138	20	00

Total Number Hired	Total Cost	Cost per Hire	Year to Year
68	131,594	1,935	1978: 712
185	36,013	195	1979: 662
253	167,607	662	

Figure 6-1 Source Cost per Hire Report: (A) April. (B) Year to Date.

$$SCPH = \frac{AC + AF + TC + RE\ (+\ ST + MT)}{H}$$

The result can be compared to other methods of recruitment as one input in a cost-benefit analysis.

Interviewing Costs

We already know how to calculate standard labor costs for the staff and for outside management. Observations will disclose how long on average each interview takes. Computing the cost of interviewing (CTI) as a component of the total cost is a simple two-step process:

STEP : INTERVIEWING COST

$$CTI = \frac{ST + MT}{I}$$

where ST = staff time, total staff time spent interviewing (e.g., $43.10 per hour standard cost × a half hour per interview × number of interviews)

MT = management time, total management time spent interviewing (e.g., management time based on an $87.90 per hour standard labor cost × one hour per interview × number of interviews)

I = number of interviews, total number of applicant interviews (e.g., 237)

EXAMPLE

$$CTI = \frac{\$5,107 + \$20,832}{237}$$
$$= \frac{\$25,939}{237}$$
$$= \$109.45$$

STEP : SOURCE COST PER HIRE (PER INTERVIEW)

$$SCPH = \frac{CTI + AC + AF + RB + NC}{H}$$

where CTI = total monthly interviewing costs determined by using the formula for cost per interview to calculate total interviewing costs (e.g., $25,939)

    AC = advertising costs (e.g., $56,000)

    AF = agency fees (e.g., $63,000)

    RB = referral bonuses (e.g., $7,600)

    NC = no-cost hires, nonprofit agencies, etc. (e.g., $0)

EXAMPLE

$$SCPH(P/I) = \frac{\$25,939 + \$56,000 + \$63,000 + \$7,600 + 0}{74}$$

$$= \frac{\$152,539}{74}$$

$$= \$2,061$$

This example reflects the cost of the fact that although there were only 74 hires, it was necessary to interview 237 applicants or conduct 237 interviews.

Additional Costs

Although not included in the basic formula for CPH, sign-on bonuses can represent a substantial increase in the basic hiring costs. Since these costs are most often given only to certain job groups, it is best to measure them independently. The equation is a very simple process of dividing the sign-on bonus costs by the number of people hired who received a sign-on bonus.

SIGN-ON BONUS FACTOR

$$SBF = \frac{SBC}{HS}$$

where SBF = sign-on bonus factor

    SBC = sign-on bonus costs (e.g. $48,000)

    HS = hires who received a sign-on bonus (e.g., 4)

EXAMPLE

$$SBF = \frac{\$48,000}{4}$$

$$= \$12,000$$

This example shows that the average sign-on bonus was $12,000. A second and more revealing calculation is by level. For example, we could include only executive sign-on bonus costs and executives hired or manager sign-on bonus costs and managers hired. We then would be able to allocate those costs correctly.

Special Event Analysis

In the second half of the 1990s, as the labor pool began to dry up, most staffing managers found themselves in a position of having to perform recruitment magic. Today there are growing and immediate needs for large numbers of certain types of employees, such as electronic technicians and programmers. In fact, almost all job applicants from fast-food servers to nurses and other professionals and managers are in short supply. Whatever the particular need, staffing managers often have to conduct some type of special event designed to recruit a relatively large number of people in a very short period. This may take the form of an open house. Open houses are often daylong or evening events where both recruiters and line managers are on hand to expedite interviews and offers. The recruiters and managers may go into a city after a weeklong media blitz. Refreshments are often served, and favors may be given away. Essentially, the manager marshals all the company's resources and concentrates them on this one important day or week, hoping that it will attract a large number of qualified candidates and fill most of the open requisitions.

When the event is over, the staffing manager will want to evaluate its effectiveness, based on the return on investment (ROI). There is a simple four-step method for calculating that. It is so simple, it can be done by hand on a piece of paper with a handheld calculator. If we want to retain the learning from this analysis, we can put it on an electronic spreadsheet and compare future similar events with this one.

1. Make a list of all expenses on the left-hand side of the paper. These expenses include ad costs, management time costs for both the HR staff and the involved line department, refreshments, space rental, prizes and incentives (if used), and all the

other types of costs shown in the basic CPH formula. Total these expenses at the bottom of the column.

2. Write the number of people hired (assuming in this case that they are all of one type, for example, programmers) on the right side of the page. If we are looking for several unrelated job groups, such as accountants, technicians, and administrative assistants, it may be difficult to divide the costs precisely among the different types. If separate ads for each type are run, their costs could be assigned to each group. General expenses, such as refreshments, could be prorated according to the number of applicants for each job group. Therefore, we may have to prepare more than one analysis.

3. If we can break out costs by category, great. If we have an automated system, this will be a simple process. Divide the total expenses by the total number of hires to obtain CPH for this event overall or by category. This tells the manager what the absolute ROI was, but it does not indicate if it is better or worse than the cost would have been using conventional means. To answer that question one more step is required.

4. Referring to the most current data on CPH for similar jobs, compare the open house CPH to the staffing department's monthly report on CPH. This step tells the manager if the open house hires are less expensive or more expensive than hires obtained by the other method. We can even compare the costs to those in Saratoga's database. Normally, well-planned and well-executed special events yield a better CPH than do standard methods. Focused attention and high levels of cooperation usually yield high ROIs. Even if the event's CPH is higher, there is a trade-off in time spent. In a few days of preparation and action such an event usually fills more open positions than weeks of standard recruiting. If there is a premium for quick results, a special event almost always delivers.

On the question of hire quality, we have found that special events produce applicants of at least equal caliber to those obtained through conventional methods. Ways of assessing the quality of hires will be discussed in the next chapter.

THOUGHT 7 *The value of anything becomes clear when we understand its purpose, even if it takes several steps to find the purpose.*

Summary

Evaluating the cost-effectiveness of the employment process is one of the easier judgments to make. Costs are mostly visible in the form of invoices for advertisements, fees, and travel. The less apparent expenses, such as the cost of someone's time, can be determined quickly. The primary thing human resources staffs consistently complain about is their inability to get their hands on the cost data. In some companies the bills are sent directly to the hiring manager for approval and then to accounts payable for payment, bypassing the HR office completely. When that is the practice, a deal can be made with the accounting department.

Sometimes the accountants receive bills about which they have little or no information. They spend a good deal of time tracking down the source of the bill or the person who submitted it in order to get an explanation or an approval signature. If we are being bypassed, we can tell the accountants that if they will pass all employment-related bills to us, we will verify the amounts, relate them to a given event, and obtain the necessary approvals. The controller will thank us for taking an onerous, time-consuming task off the accounting staff's back, and we will then be in control of the process rather than being passive spectators.

No HR department can claim to operate efficiently if it does not know how much it is spending to hire people. Acquisition costs are important whether we are talking about machines or employees. Fortunately, these costs are easily obtainable and are powerful tools for proving that we are maximizing the organization's recruiting ROI.

CHAPTER

7

Keeping Management (Your Customer) Satisfied with the Hiring Process

There are other staffing considerations besides cost. Issues of timeliness, completeness, and quality may be more important in the eyes of the hiring managers, our customers. Customers are focused on achieving their operational objectives. The decision point may shift among time, cost, and quality as outside pressures change. In a fast-growing company, having a warm body in place may be the key requirement. Without sufficient staff, managers cannot meet their production and service objectives. As growth slows, managers can take more time, be more selective, and opt for quality. Knowing where the customers' priorities are or are likely to be will enhance our service. This is another example of the value of establishing customer partnerships.

All performance measures, whether direct or indirect, can be used for at least two purposes. The first is to help us understand, manage, and control the organization; the second is to work with people outside the group. We want to develop a database that can be used in several ways. Here are a few examples:

- *Watch how the internal requirements are changing.* Which jobs are more in demand than others? Which business units have the biggest or most urgent requirements?
- *Watch how the external labor market is changing.* In general, are there more or fewer people available and qualified for work? Which skills are in shortest supply?
- *Look for trends.* By observing our own experience as well as labor market statistics we can foresee where there might be a shortfall of talent coming.

The second use for the database is to report activities and results. Periodically, we should report to management on the state of the acquisition process. By not only reporting headcount or jobs filled but also describing the implications of the results and anticipating near-term talent availability, the staffing function moves from being a transaction center to being a strategic partner.

Someday we may be required to defend our processes and results. By maintaining a database, we will be able to demonstrate that criticisms are unfounded. Some managers are indecisive. When they are criticized for poor performance, they may claim that the problem is a lack of support from staffing. By keeping track of the quantity and quality of candidates, we can prove that the problem does not lie with us. Conversely, if it does, we will see where we have flaws and can improve the process. Automated applicant-tracking systems have many features that can be used to reveal the true performance of the staffing function. Unfortunately, research by the Saratoga Institute for several of the applicant-tracking software vendors has revealed that the customers are not using the capability for which they are paying.

Once we have dealt successfully with managers' criticisms regarding timeliness and quantity, we may have to answer for the quality of our candidate referrals. Indecisive managers may concede that we have met the tests of time and volume. Then, in an attempt at face-saving, they may "yes, but" us and accuse us of referring inferior or unacceptable individuals. There is only one way to deal with this, and our position must be absolutely inflexible. We refer only one type of applicant: a qualified applicant—period! We can prove it by recording in our system how well we have matched the specifications on the requisition to the qualifications of the applicants. We do not send out teasers, loss leaders, straw men, shock troops, or any other quasi-qualified or unqualified individuals. If we ever admit to offering management anything but a suitable candidate, we will destroy our credibility and undermine our position forever. There is no other stance to take.

By far the most important use of the database is for continuous process improvement. By keeping track of what's going on internally and externally we can manage rather than just oversee staff activity. By knowing trends and market forces related to costs, time factors, and labor availability we will run a more efficient and cost-effective shop. We will also be able to counsel our customers regarding changes in and possible effects of the workforce market on their operations.

Time Factors

Basically, there are three time issues in the recruitment process. The first issue has to do with how long it takes to develop qualified candidates and refer them to management for an interview. This is called response time, and it is the period over which we have the most control. The second issue is how long it takes to fill a job requisition (have an offer accepted). This is called time to fill. Once we refer an applicant, our degree of control begins to lessen. I will discuss the recruiter's responsibility after a referral when we return to this issue. The third issue is time to start. This ends when the new hire actually shows up for work. We have little control here, but as far as the customer is concerned, until this happens everything else is activity without results.

Response time is defined as the cycle time from the day we have a signed, approved job requisition in hand to the day on which we call or forward to the requesting manager at least one qualified candidate ready to be interviewed. This is an important issue. Although it does not mean that we have completed the assignment, it does show how quickly the procurement system works. The response time formula below shows the calculation. In this case it is not a ratio, as we are accustomed to working with in cost measures, but a subtraction problem.

RESPONSE TIME

$$RT = RD - RR$$

where RT = response time

RD = date first qualified candidate was referred for an interview (e.g., September 22)

RR = date of receipt of job requisition (e.g.; September 4)

If the referral date is in a different month than the requisition date, one simply counts the intervening days. For example,

RT = August 20–September 4

   = 11 days until the end of August + 4 days in September

   = 15 days

EXAMPLE

$$RT = 22 - 4$$
$$= 18 \text{ days}$$

Adding total days to respond and dividing by total hires gives an average response time.

This formula came in very handy when I was managing the human resources (HR) department and was therefore responsible for the results of all of its functions, including staffing. I received a call from a high-ranking person in the company who chewed me out for the alleged slow response time of my recruiters. Since I did not know offhand what our current rate was for the job classification he was angry about, I told him I would look into it and get back to him. After he hung up, I went to the lady who maintained our manual applicant-tracking system (in those days we didn't have personal computers) and asked her for the log she used. I was concerned that there might be some justification for the complaint because the jobs he mentioned were for computer programmers, and programmers were a very scarce commodity in our marketplace. I was hoping that we had at least maintained a reasonable response rate over the year. The worst situation would have been one in which each month our time to respond had increased. Within a few minutes I was able to draw out of the log the average response time for programmers over the past 10 months. I constructed a simple chart and plotted the results on it (Figure 7-1).

As you can see, it showed unequivocally that the recruiters were doing a superb job. In a lean market they were managing to respond more quickly each month throughout the year. It was gratifying to call the man back and say, "John, I don't know where you are getting your data, but my records show that our current response time is only about 14 days. Over the year it has gotten better, not worse." He replied that he found my numbers hard to believe, and so I suggested that he come to my office and look at the data. To make a long story short, he came, he saw, and he stormed out of my office, vowing vengeance on his managers. I learned later that he went back to his department and verbally assaulted his managers for lying to him. The problem had been that the managers were not meeting their schedules and were blaming staffing unfairly for not filling the numerous open requisitions.

The managers were claiming that for a wide variety of highly imaginative reasons, they did not have time to see the candidates we were referring. By the time they came back to us and said they were ready, the candidates had found jobs in other departments in the company or in other organizations. The recruitment process had to start all over again. This resulted in jobs being open for many weeks and work not getting done. When put under the gun by their boss, they sought a scapegoat in the staffing department.

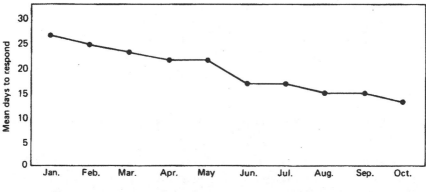

Figure 7-1   Response Time for Programmers (January to October)

This is an example of how a service function, in this case the HR department, can be blamed for a line department's problems. The lesson is clear. If I had not had the data to set the record straight, I probably would have had to take the blame for the problem. I call that bag holding: One manager will walk into another manager's office and make an accusation. In effect, the accused is handed a bag of garbage. Unless the accused can muster a defense based on facts, he or she will have to accept the bag. Human resources staff members have more than their share of garbage bags tossed through their doors. When we have a measurement system that demonstrates our performance, we can tell the bearer what to do with the garbage.

Internet Effects on Response Time

Job boards are both a blessing and a burden when it comes to rapid response time. For lazy recruiters this is a quick way to bury hiring clients in paper. They can scan the boards and download any résumé remotely related to the requisition. They also can pull applications from the internal database and quickly overwhelm the hirer. Of course, we refer only qualified applicants, ones who have a chance to become bona fide job candidates. By taking the first route we might be able to show a rapid response, but we would leave ourselves open to criticism about the quality of the referrals. The lesson is simple. The fact that technology has given us access to massive databases of applicants does not mean we can turn our desks into little more than mail transfer points.

THOUGHT 9 *Technology is a tool, not a crutch.*

Time to Fill

The second time issue is time to fill. Line managers used to have a mistaken notion of the recruiting process as a relatively simple matter. The perception was that a requisition is delivered to staffing, an advertisement is run, applicants are screened, and a few are selected for interviews by management. The good news is that the labor shortage in the United States has existed for a number of years and managers realize that finding qualified candidates is not an easy job.

The staffing process has about 30 separate steps. Time to fill measures the total number of days between the delivery of an approved requisition to staffing and the date on which an applicant accepts the job offer. The calculation is exactly the same as it is for response time. The only difference is that the referral date (RD) is replaced by the offer (accepted) date (OD). The formula for time to fill is shown below.

TIME TO FILL

$$TTF = RR - OD$$

where TTF = time to have an offer accepted
RR = date the requisition is received (e.g., September 4)
OD = date the offer is accepted (e.g., October 20)

EXAMPLE

$$TTF = September\ 4 - October\ 20$$
$$= 46$$

Time to Start

The third time measurement is time to start. It is calculated exactly as is time to fill except that it shows the additional number of days between acceptance and start. The start date is the day the new hire reports for work. Thus, the formula for time to start is start date minus requisition receipt date.

TIME TO START

$$TTS = RR - SD$$

where TTS = time till the new hire starts
RR = date the requisition is received (e.g., September 4)
SD = date the new hire starts work (e.g., November 10)

EXAMPLE

$$TTS = September\ 4 - November\ 10$$
$$= 67$$

A staffing manager who is looking for opportunities to improve the time to fill or time to start record does not have to look hard. There probably is no need to monitor all 30 steps in the recruitment and selection process. Besides, an automated applicant-tracking system naturally monitors several of them. If there are others that we need, we can add a module or run a separate application and combine the two periodically. Any large-volume recruitment function should have an automated applicant- and requisition-tracking system. With such a system in use, an efficiency audit is easy. Figure 7-2 shows how one might look.

We start by selecting the key checkpoints we want the system to record. In this example I have chosen 10 checkpoints. This system can be programmed to run as part of the core function of an applicant tracking system. Spreadsheet or database software can be used to define checkpoints and calculate them automatically.

There is another way to record these events. In the event date cell put the number of days or elapsed time since the last event. For example, on the first requisition from manager J. Jones the line would read as follows:

Event	1	2	3	4	5	6	7	8	9	10
Date	9/1	1	7	5	6	9	6	1	7	33

Requesting Manager	Event* and Date									
	1	2	3	4	5	6	7	8	9	10
J. Jones	9/1	9/2	9/9	9/14	9/20	9/29	10/5	10/6	10/13	11/15
F. Koontz	9/2	9/4	9/11	9/17	9/22	9/30	10/7	10/9	10/10	11/1
L. Smith	9/7	9/8	9/16	9/22	9/30	10/9	10/20	10/21	10/30	11/15
G. Mack	9/7	9/9	9/19	9/30	10/15	10/25	11/10	11/12	11/18	12/7
E. Kieffer	9/8	9/9	9/15	9/30	10/9	10/16	11/5	11/7	11/14	1/2

*Event numbers:

1–Requisition received; 2–Sourcing started; 3–First applicant responds; 4–First screening; 5–Follow-up contact; 6–First management interview; 7–Hiring decision made; 8–Offer made; 9–Offer accepted/rejected; 10–New employee starts work.

Figure 7-2   Hiring Track

Event numbers: 1, requisition received; 2, sourcing started; 3, first applicant responds; 4, first screening; 5, follow-up contact; 6, first management interview; 7, hiring decision made; 8, offer made; 9, offer accepted or rejected; 10, new employee starts work.

Event 1 is the receipt of the requisition, the starting date for the process. We could put 0 for elapsed time. However, the starting date is more worthwhile. Since event 2 took place on 9/2, there is 1 day of elapsed time and the number 1 is entered. Event 3 was on 9/9, which is 7 days later, and so on across the line. This approach has the advantage of showing immediately how much time has been lost between steps. For a manager who is looking for places to cut response time and time to fill, the delays are apparent. The largest opportunities are at events 3, 6, 9, and 10.

In place of "requesting manager," the job title can be entered. In a computerized system there can be both because we do not have the space limitations of a manual log. When there is too little space, the best solution is to show job title and department number.

Time is the enemy of an ambitious recruiter. By keeping track of response time, time to fill, and time to start, the recruiter and the manager can know how they are doing. They will also be able to defend themselves if necessary. Finally, they will be able to go to line management with the facts to obtain cooperation in speeding up the process.

Referral Rate

One large company in the northwest was for many years the major employer in its region. The staff members had become accustomed to taking their time in recruiting and enjoyed the luxury of having many applicants for each vacancy. As a result, managers developed the habit of looking at as many as 10 candidates before making a hiring decision. Late in the 1970s other organizations around the country began to see the advantages of locating plants in that area. Within a year or two several large and medium-size plants had been built within 15 miles of the large company. Suddenly there was competition for qualified personnel. However, the managers of the first company maintained their habit of waiting for staffing to produce 7 to 10 candidates. When they began to go for weeks without filling jobs, they complained loudly to staffing. After viewing the evidence, they finally accepted what they had been told before: The game had changed. They could no longer expect more than two or three candidates for most positions. For certain jobs they would be lucky to have one. Today, after more than a decade of market turmoil, people are more amenable to the notion that they have to change.

As market conditions change, referral rates generally change accordingly. In the case just described, management's expectations and practices had to change if it wanted to fill the jobs. One of the ways the staffing manager can keep on top of the change is to compute a referral ratio. To avoid confusion with the RR acronym from the response time formula, we use RF to stand for the referral ratio and call it the referral factor. The ratio is shown below.

REFERRAL FACTOR

$$RF = \frac{R}{O}$$

where RF = referral factor, relationship of candidates to openings

R = number of candidates referred for an interview (e.g., 134)

0 = number of openings (e.g., 19)

EXAMPLE

$$RE = \frac{134}{19}$$

$$= 7.4\%$$

These data can be collected by job group or work unit to show how many qualified candidates on average are being developed. A variation on this formula is to substitute hires for openings. Not all openings result in hires. Sometimes conditions change between the time an approved job requisition arrives and the time a hire can take place. The difference is subtle but may be meaningful in some situations. A realistic referral factor will always be a combination of management demand and market conditions. No matter which factor predominates, the staffing manager should know what the ratio is; otherwise, it cannot be improved.

Job-Posting Career Development System

In the chapter on career development we will deal with the job-posting system as part of the career development effort. Here we look at it solely from an administrative standpoint.

Three perspectives of job posting are the employees' use of the system, the rate of hire generated by the system, and the role of the system in the total hiring scheme. Each perspective provides opportunities for measurement.

Periodically jobs are posted for employees to see and apply for. In terms of this discussion, it does not matter which job levels are posted or how long jobs are left on the list. Posting systems vary widely among industries and in different parts of the country. Management philosophy, union status, intranet capabilities, and other factors dictate how a system will be run. As long as the system rules do not change, valid measurements can be conducted over time. No matter what the style of the system is, the first questions to ask are, How are people responding to it? When we post a job, what happens? Are we flooded with employees eager to transfer? Does anyone at all show up? The basic measurement is the job-posting response rate (JPR), which indicates how many responses are received per job posting. The formula below shows how the JPR is calculated.

JOB-POSTING RESPONSE RATE

$$JPR = \frac{A}{PJ}$$

where JPR = job-posting response rate
A = number of applications received at the job-posting desk (e.g., 212)
PJ = number of posted jobs (e.g., 43)

EXAMPLE

$$JPR = \frac{212}{43}$$

= 4.9 applications per posting

People may apply for several jobs simultaneously, realizing that they can obtain only one of them. Nevertheless, one should count applications rather than applicants, because this indicates what the system is generating. The fact that some people are chronic applicants or have other idiosyncratic reasons for applying is an issue outside the system. Sorting through hundreds of applications in search of multiples from one person is not worth the effort. Pulling those few out of the pile probably will not make a significant difference in the numbers.

Job posting, if monitored, can yield much more than a list of applicants for open positions. Assume that there is a flood of applicants for a particular job or for all jobs. What could that mean? The answer can be found somewhere among the reasons people apply for transfer. A few are as follows:

- Desire for advancement
- Escape from a bad supervisor
- Lack of interest in the current job (boredom)
- Escape from a bad interpersonal situation (coworkers)
- Better pay
- Movement to a new location (geographic)
- Change in job responsibilities
- Family or health problems

An analysis of the source of applications and the reasons given by applicants often helps pinpoint an organizational problem. If the people who run the posting system develop a rapport with the employees, they will tell the job counselors the real reasons for their applications. Poor supervision, boring jobs, an unsafe or unhealthy environment, inequitable pay, and other sources of employee unrest will surface. Then we will have a chance to investigate and decide whether the complaints are reasonable.

Assume that very few employees respond to postings. What could that imply? It may mean one or more of the following:

- There is a consistent history of internal rejection in favor of outside applicants.
- There is no visible support from management.
- There are threats from supervisors about applying for other positions in the company.

- The department has done a substandard job of dealing with applicants.
- Only low-level jobs are posted.

All of these things occur, but unless we monitor our responses, we will never become aware of potentially serious organizational problems. Consider the consequences of supervisors threatening people who apply for posted jobs. Immediately we recognize the possibility of charges of unfair labor practices or discrimination suits. Besides playing the traditional role of a transfer mechanism, the job-posting system can also be an early warning device. If we have our antenna up and scanning, we may see something coming over the horizon in time to intercept it.

There are variations on the basic JPR formula, one of which is to calculate how many posted jobs are responded to, as in the following formula.

JOB-POSTING RESPONSE FACTOR

$$JPRF = \frac{PJR}{PJ}$$

where JPRF = ratio of jobs posted to jobs responded to
   PJR = number of posted jobs responded to (e.g., 43)
    PJ = number of posted jobs (e.g., 212)

EXAMPLE

$$JPRF = \frac{43}{212}$$
$$= 20.3\%$$

The maximum percentage can never exceed 100 percent.

This gives a picture of the spread of responses. In the formula we may have a large number of applications per posting, but they may be for only certain jobs. Averages can be deceiving, and so there is a measure in statistics, called the standard deviation, that indicates how broadly the numbers are spread from the mean. In a sense, that is the type of function this measure performs. It indicates whether all the jobs are being applied for. If the number is less than 100 percent, we can note which jobs are not drawing applicants. If those jobs continually fail to turn up any interest, we can look into the reasons for that and do whatever is appropriate.

Another way to track responses is by job type. It may be worthwhile to know which jobs are drawing the largest number of applicants. This is not discovered through the use of a formula; it is a tracking task. We can set up a spreadsheet, either manually or automatically, that tracks the number of applications for specific jobs. Applications are tallied by job, and the story tells itself. Again, follow-up will uncover the reasons for abnormally high or low responses.

The second test of the job-posting system takes the process a step further by dealing with the number of hires or placements that result from the system. The formula used here is called the job-posting hire rate (JPH).

JOB-POSTING HIRE RATE

$$JPH = \frac{H}{JP}$$

where JPH = percentage of jobs filled through job posting
   H = number of hires made from internal applicants (e.g., 36)
   JP = number of jobs posted (e.g., 212)

EXAMPLE

$$JPH = \frac{36}{212}$$
$$= 17\%$$

This measure follows the same logic as the job-posting response ratio and carries the process to its conclusion. If a high rate of response is coupled with an equally high rate of hire, the system would appear to be fulfilling its mission. If both factors are not in an acceptable range, it is a sign that the system should be reviewed for defects. This is what people in business like to call the bottom line. After all is said and done, what is the result? Obviously, the objective is to fill a large percentage of the posted jobs. We may not want to fill every position from internal sources because this could lead eventually to organizational incest. Fortunately, most industries have learned their lesson and no longer expect or want all hires to come through the system.

Some companies set targets or goals for internal replacement rates. This is probably a healthy thing to do. It lets everyone know what the expectation is. If it is communicated well, employees will understand and support it. A formula for measuring these targets is called the internal hire rate.

INTERNAL HIRE RATE

$$IHR = \frac{IA}{H}$$

where IHR = percentage of jobs filled internally
IA = jobs filled by internal applicants (e.g., 36)
H = total hires (e.g., 76)

EXAMPLE

$$IHR = \frac{36}{126}$$
$$= 28.6\%$$

There is a company that encourages supervisors and managers to support the job-posting program through a cost transference mechanism. It works like this. Department A decides to accept the transfer request of an employee from department B. A then must pay B, through a cross-charge, $X to cover the cost incurred by B to recruit a replacement. The amount is determined at the beginning of the year and is based on the average cost of hiring an exempt or a nonexempt employee. If B replaces the lost employee from another internal source, the charge passes to that department. Eventually, whoever has to go outside for a replacement is compensated for that expense. If the last department in line does not choose to replace, it still gets the money as a reward for having developed a good employee and for having found a way to operate more efficiently. In light of the drive to operate more cost-efficiently, this method can be a stimulant for managers to practice continuous improvement.

Job-posting measures are a good example of the inherent value of measurement. These seemingly secondary issues yield information well beyond what appears on the surface. In the process of obtaining data on one subject, the procedure and the results cause another set of questions to be asked. Gradually the holistic, interrelated systems nature of the HR function is revealed. Time and again we see how one process connects with another. In this small series of job-posting measures we have discovered how job counselors are connected to affirmative action, employee relations, compensation, and labor relations. As we work through each of the main HR functions, the many rewards for measurement will become overwhelmingly clear.

A second perspective on the organization's internal hiring process emerges from calculating the percentage of internal hires that are promotions versus those which are transfers. By understanding these results, one can uncover other career development issues.

CAREER PATH RATIO: PROMOTIONS AND TRANSFERS

$$\text{CPR/P} = \frac{P}{P + T} \quad \text{or} \quad \text{CPR/T} = \frac{T}{P + T}$$

where CPR/P = career path ratio/promotions
      CPR/T = career path ratio/transfers
          P = total promotions (e.g., 15)
          T = total transfers (e.g., 82)
    P + T = number promoted plus number transferred (e.g., 97)

EXAMPLE

$$\text{CPR/P} = \frac{15}{97}$$
$$= 15.5\%$$

or

$$\text{CPR/T} = \frac{82}{97}$$
$$= 85\%$$

Recruiting Efficiency

To describe the performance of a recruiter it is necessary to look at more than how many applicants the recruiter has helped turn into hires. Some recruiters believe that hires are the sole criteria of their efficiency. However, recruiters work in a group as part of a team. How they handle their total job responsibilities is as important as the number of hires they effect.

It is better to measure recruiters as a team than as individuals. This principle holds true, wherever possible, for other functions as well. If people feel they are under the gun to come up with good numbers, they are liable to succumb to the temptation and give us what we seem to want: numbers rather than results. When employees start to manufacture numbers, the system becomes worse than useless; it is fraudulent. Treat recruiters as a team. Pool their data and report their results as a group. Since we started talking about human resources as a system, we have emphasized the team aspect. Teaching the staff to work together and report results collectively takes away individual threat and promotes cooperation. When we set team objectives and team rewards, we get teamwork.

Let's start by looking at recruiters' efficiency. How productive are their interviewing techniques? What is the average length of interview for given types of jobs? How many interviews does it take to develop a list of qualified candidates? How many does it take to achieve a quality hire? Ratios for all these issues can be created if that will be useful. The most basic measure is average length of interview.

INTERVIEW TIME

$$AIL = \frac{HO}{I}$$

where AIL = average length of interviews*
HO = total hours spent interviewing (e.g., 6.8)
I = total number interviewed (e.g., 3)

EXAMPLE

$$AIL = \frac{6.8}{3}$$
$$= 2.3$$

---

*AIL is computed by determining the total amount of time a recruiter spends interviewing and dividing by the total number of people interviewed.

This ratio can be accumulated for all recruiters and measured on a daily, weekly, or monthly basis and by exempt, nonexempt, or hourly job classification. This figure is needed as an input to other equations. It is a prerequisite to cost of hire measurement when staff time is involved, and it is necessary for measuring the cost of interviewing. It is also used in other indirect measures of recruiter efficiency and effectiveness.

Along with interviewing time, some staffing managers like to know how much time recruiters spend on administrative duties. There is no clear definition of administrative time. Is it all activity other than application screening and interviewing? Does calling on sources of applicants, such as schools and not-for-profit agencies, count as recruiting time or administrative time? Some managers insist that their recruiters spend at least 15 percent of their time out of the office cultivating low-cost sources of applicants. Usually they consider this administrative time, but we can call it whatever we like. The point is that recruiters should be doing that kind of work, and we may want to track it occasionally. A simple spreadsheet kept by the recruiter or the recruiter's assistant will provide the data.

There is another efficiency measure that yields information about both the recruiters and the sources of applicants. It is called hire ratios. At first glance this looks very complicated. Although it is complex in appearance, it is quite simple to follow, since there is a natural sequence to it. The hire rate formula that follows lays it out.

HIRE RATE

$$HR = \frac{I}{A} \; \frac{R}{I} \; \frac{H}{R} \; \frac{H}{A}$$

where HR = hire rate
  I = interviews (e.g., 30)
  A = applications received (e.g., 120)
  R = referrals (e.g., 10)
  H = hires (e.g., 4)

EXAMPLE

$$HR = \frac{30}{120} \quad \frac{10}{30} \quad \frac{4}{10} \quad \frac{4}{120}$$
$$= 25\% \quad 33\% \quad 40\% \quad 3\%$$

Hire ratios trace the process from the point of application to the point of hiring. They show how the original pool of applicants is cut at each step. These computations can be made for all hires or can be done separately by source for different levels, job groups, or locations.

The first issue to look at is the ratio of applications to hires. Hypothetically, one could say that an advertisement that produced 120 applications was very effective. However, if we obtained only four hires, was it really effective? Consider the time, and therefore the cost, of processing those 120 applicants. Thirty were interviewed after someone plowed through 120 applications. Ten got a second interview by the line manager. Several other people in the requesting department might have repeated the second interview. When the process was finally completed, with four hires, probably 60 to 80 hours of labor had gone into it. Is that satisfactory?

I recall the occasion when one of the field sales forces of the computer company where I worked started a new sales training program. Without seeking advice from the staffing group, they placed an advertisement and got over 300 responses. At that point we received a panicked cry for help. They wanted to hire only four people initially. As they plowed through the ever-growing number of résumés, it was evident that anyone who had ever considered a sales career was applying. One might say that 300 résumés was a great response, but it was only a large response. The first screening eliminated over 280, and that was being generous. It took four people more than a day to accomplish the first cut. That is not my idea of a productive ad.

The second issue that the hire ratio brings out is the efficiency of the recruiters' selection criteria. In the example above, they screened out 75 percent of the applications, and after interviewing 30 people, they referred 10 to management. Management selected four. That means that only 3 percent of the applicants were hired.

None of these numbers has an intrinsic "rightness" or "wrongness." As we read the numerators, the denominators, and the percentages from left to right, we begin to get a feel for how the selection process is working. We may know how acceptable the numbers are at first glance, or we may have to collect the data for a period of time until we can develop norms for acceptable practice. Either way, this measure can be a very helpful part of the criteria for recruiting efficiency.

Another measure that says something about how productive recruiters are is called the offer acceptance rate, better known as the *hit rate* (HO). Simply stated, the hit rate is the ratio of job offers made to job offers accepted.

OFFER ACCEPTANCE RATE

$$OAR = \frac{OA}{OE}$$

where OAR = percentage of offers that result in a hire
OA = offers accepted (e.g., 48)
OE = offers extended (e.g., 60)

EXAMPLE

$$OAR = \frac{48}{60}$$
$$= 80\%$$

It is helpful to have an acceptable standard for this ratio. Under normal circumstances perhaps three or four out of five offers should be accepted. College recruiting typically is an exception to this rule.

If a recruiter knows the client manager's idiosyncrasies, comprehends the subtleties of the requesting department, does a good job of screening and interviewing, and sees to it that the right salary and conditions are offered, it is not hard to reach at least an 80 percent hit rate. As the job market shrinks, the acceptance rate will increase. This is a direct reflection of supply and demand. With few job opportunities available the candidate is more likely to accept the offer.

None of the criteria mentioned above are unreasonable. They represent the knowledge and skills a competent professional recruiter must have. The value of having a standard is that at a glance the staffing manager can tell how it is going. It is not necessary to wait for someone to complain that we can't seem to hire people.

There is probably nothing more irritating, frustrating, and wasteful than an employment offer that is rejected. After the staff and the hiring department have spent many hours talking with candidates, checking references, comparing strengths and weaknesses, and preparing an offer, it is very disheartening to be turned down. If it happens, often we will have very unhappy customers and a demoralized recruiting staff.

The purpose of tracking acceptance rate is to generate a signal that indicates that performance is unacceptable. When the signal flashes, we can investigate and take steps to remedy the problem before the client senses it. For that reason it is important that the standards of performance be set higher than the client would demand. If, for example, the line managers feel that a 70 percent hit rate is acceptable, we will want to set our goal at 80 to 90 percent. This way we can drop to 75 percent, catch the signal, identify the problem, and act on it before the rate drops to 70 percent. We always want to solve our problems before they become visible to the client. Our professional image depends on a high standard of performance.

Average acceptance rates in the Saratoga Institute Human Capital Benchmarking Report typically have been about 80 percent for the past 12 years, and they haven't moved more than a few percent either way from year to year. Typically, we will find a low acceptance rate isolated in one group. This makes it easy to correct. If it is widespread, this usually means the pay or benefits packages are not competitive or that there is another general organizational problem (such as a negative reputation).

Two Ways to Quantify Quality

Up to this point we have been looking at ways to measure efficiency and productivity in the recruiting corps. But what about effectiveness? Effectiveness implies something beyond productivity; it embodies an expectation of desirability. It is not only doing something well; it is doing the important thing well. This issue of importance brings up the subjective nature of quality, which makes it more difficult to measure than productivity. The fundamental struggle in organizations has been between HR people, who see their work as purely qualitative, and management, which wants hard data to analyze. The key to closing this values gap depends on the ability of HR to describe qualitative results with quantitative data.

Usually, when people think about quantifying HR work, they look at the total function, which may encompass nearly a hundred seemingly discrete tasks, and wonder how they can ever measure it. There are ways to attack this problem. Quality is a function of use over time. When an employee joins the organization and begins to work, we can assess performance, but that requires waiting. How do we approach quality rating in the short term?

We have already explained that the way to do that is to break down the function into those individual tasks which are quantifiable. The process of dividing a complex issue into identifiable parts is one way to determine the quality of new hires. The only difference is that we will build a quality measure not by defining tasks but by selecting specific results that reflect the quality of a new employee. As always, the objective must be results, not activity.

Surely one of the most critical indexes of a recruiter's effectiveness is the quality of the individuals who are hired. Recruiters may do many tasks well, but if they cannot produce good candidates, they must admit failure. The new hire is the end product of everyone's labor. The staffing manager, the recruiter, the administrative assistants, and the line manager are all involved in the process. Ultimately, the recruiter is the one who is held accountable for the quality of the end result.

The path to assessing the quality of a new hire runs down two tracks. First we must acknowledge that quality is time-bound. We do not know how good something is until we have contact with that person over a period of time. Therefore, the problem is, How do we judge the quality of a new hire at the time of hiring—before the person starts working? We'll give the answer to that shortly.

The second path to quality assessment is easier. It is found when we answer the question, How do we describe a good employee? Performance is the first indicator that comes to mind, but that is not the only criterion. Promotability and stability also come into play. There may be others to add to the list, but for now let us work with these three. Recruiters deal with many applicants and generate many hires. To have a fair measure of the results of their labor, we should do a periodic evaluation of all hires. A semiannual review is a fair system to use for this purpose. There is usually enough activity in 6 months to smooth out any uncontrollable factors.

Patience is a prerequisite to measuring quality. We want to avoid flash-in-the-pan assessments. As everyone knows, some new employees look great for the first few months, until they feel secure. After about 6 months the true nature of the individual becomes visible, and evaluations made thereafter are normally more reliable.

Performance on the job, promotion to higher levels, and stability are all issues that cannot be measured for a minimum of 6 months. Only if an employee leaves in a short time can we assess stability. From a management standpoint, this may be disturbing. However, quality is inherently a long-term issue. Whenever we think about product quality, we expect that the product not only will do what it is supposed to do but will last. We have a right to expect a product to perform its function for a long time before we allow the manufacturer to proclaim its quality. Likewise, it is unreasonable to expect a qualitative assessment of a new employee in less than 6 months, and a full year is an even better appraisal period. With this as an assumption, let us look at a quality of hire (QH) measure.

QUALITY OF HIRE

$$QH = \frac{PR + HP + HS}{N}$$

where QH = quality of the people hired
       PR = average job performance ratings of new hires (e.g., 4 on a 5-point scale, or 80 percent)
       HP = percentage of new hires promoted within 1 year (e.g., 36%)
       HS = percentage of new hires retained after 1 year (e.g., 70%)
       N = number of indicators used (e.g., 3)

EXAMPLE

$$QH = \frac{80 + 36 + 70}{3}$$
$$= \frac{186}{3}$$
$$= 62\%$$

The resulting percentage, 62 percent, is a relative value. It is up to the person constructing the equation to decide if that number represents high, medium, or low quality. The decision can be based on a historical comparison, preset performance standards or objectives, or management mandates.

Having said all that, we are faced with the reality that performance ratings, promotions, and turnovers are beyond the control of the recruiter. A perfect hire can be driven out by a poor supervisor, lack of promotional opportunity, job market conditions, and many other phenomena that have nothing to do with the recruiter or the recruiting process. Business, whether it is profit or not for profit, is an influenceable, not a controllable, activity.

A less objective but more valid procedure for establishing a quality criterion is to ask the receiving department; we could ask the hiring manager to rate a new hire at the time of hiring. Before the person goes to work, the hiring manager rates, and ranks if we like, this hire against all other hires during a given time period. The rating can be along a scale, say, 1 to 5 or 1 to 10. The ranking procedure is based on a comparison. A list would have to be maintained, and the receiver would insert the newest hire into the list in the appropriate slot. There are problems associated with establishing the validity of these types of opinions. Nevertheless, the measures are arrived at systematically, which implies some degree of reliability and objectivity.

That is the most complete and arduous way to measure quality. It works, but probably the best measure is the simplest. Compare the specifications on the requisition—education, experience, required skill levels, special abilities (language), and the like—to the qualities of the new hire. If they match, you have a high-quality hire. What happens after that has nothing to do with the recruiting and selection process, with one exception. Success on the job depends on fit as well as skills. If the recruiter knows the hiring manager and the department in which the new person will work, a good fit should occur.

Recruiter Effectiveness

To answer the broader qualitative question of recruiter effectiveness, we will follow the same procedure but employ different indexes. The way to start is to ask, What do recruiters do that makes the most difference? Effective work does not consist of performing one task. It is the sum of many important things done well. If we want to know how effective a recruiter is, we have to talk about several key tasks. As an example, let us say that an effective recruiter sources, screens, recommends, and assists management in the hiring of good employees. Beyond that, effective recruiters respond quickly, fill jobs promptly, cut hire costs to a minimum, maintain a high hit rate, and find quality candidates. Effective recruiters may do a few more things that make a difference, but for now let's stop there.

The following is a list of important issues for recruiters:

- Response time
- Time to fill jobs
- Cost per hire
- Acceptance rate
- Quality of hires

When we do this, we are free to select our own list. There are no mandatory tasks or results that add up to effectiveness in all situations. Qualitative terms are by nature open to subjective definition. All we have to do is agree on the variables with the other people who are going to judge recruiter effectiveness. Assuming that we agree on the sample, the next step is to put the variables together so that they add up to effectiveness, as shown below.

RECRUITER EFFECTIVENESS

$$RE = \frac{RT + TTF + CPH + OAR + QH}{N}$$

where RE = overall recruiter effectiveness
  RT = response time (e.g., 9 days)
  TTF = time to fill (e.g., 34 days)
  CPH = cost per hire (e.g., $884)
  OAR = offer acceptance rate (e.g., 80%)
  QH = quality of hire (e.g., 71.7%)
  N = number of indexes used (e.g., 5)

We can decide to take the resulting numbers at face value and make a judgment of relative effectiveness. This is often sufficient, but if we want more objective data, we can compare each number with a predetermined goal. If we perform the percentage test on all indexes, we will have converted the data to a common base. Then we can add all the percentages and divide by N to come out with a percentage of effectiveness, as shown in Figure 7-3.

Proceed carefully in calculating the percentage of goal achievement. In response time, goal is divided by result because the objective is to respond in 8 days or less. For time to fill and cost per hire, the objective is to fill in 45 days or less at a cost of $1,000 or less. In both cases this was achieved, and so performance exceeded 100 percent. In quality of hire, the result was divided by the goal because the objective was to exceed 75 percent. The question of which is the divisor and which is the dividend depends on whether we want the result to be a higher or lower number than the goal.

Measure	Result	Goal	Goal Achievement, Weighted Percentages
Response time	9 days	8 days	88 × 1.0 = 88
Time to fill	34 days	45 days	132 × 1.5 = 198
Hit rate	80%	80%	100 × 1.0 = 100
Cost per hire	$884	$500	113 × 2.0 = 226
Quality of hire	71.7%	75.0%	96 × 3.0 = 288
			900 ÷ 8.5 = 105.9

Figure 7-3   Percentage of Recruitment Effectiveness

If we believe that one measure is more important than another, we can weight the measures to correspond to our evaluation. We might say that time to fill is 1.5 times more important than response time or hit rate. We might also say that cost per hire is two times and quality of hire is five times more important. Then we can multiply these factors by the percentages, add all five products, and divide by the sum of the weights. Mathematically, this is better than averaging simple percentages. The result is a weighted evaluation of recruiter effectiveness. This is probably the most thorough computation we would consider. One step less would be to eliminate the weighting and simply compute an overall average percentage of effectiveness. The simplest and most common procedure would be the first one, a face-valid check of the actual raw data result.

Whichever method we choose, the fundamental principle is the same. Any subjective issue can be quantified by collecting and calculating data on a few key activities or results. Quality is an issue that requires more than one criterion, and it can be quantified.

THOUGHT 10 *A little useful information is more valuable than a mountain of irrelevant data.*

The Staffing Structure

In times of instability planning for new or replacement staff is a precarious art. Growth plans have come down from 5 years to sometimes no more than a few months. Everyone recognizes that the long-term planning routines practiced from 1950 to the 1990s are extinct.

Human resources plans deal with the internal and external sources of people needed to make the current business plan. The HR plan profiles the existing workforce, predicts the turnover rate, and projects the company's staffing needs by type, place, and time. However, a number of external and internal factors affect the plan. Internal factors affect availability and utilization of current staff; external factors affect the recruitment of new employees. All affect the results and skew the plan. Despite the development of predictive modeling techniques and better sources of information, it is clear that staff plans and forecasts are anything but a precise science. The future is still unknown and unknowable. Stable industries and stable economic conditions increase the ability to predict, but stability is a thing of the past. Volatility is the norm for the foreseeable future. Because of this unpredictability, it is very difficult for the staffing manager to plan even for the staffing department. The issue is, Given the uncertainty, how does a staffing department prepare itself to respond promptly to the demands made on it? Our view of the planning model looks like Figure 7-4. The guiding principle is that each step should be connected to some type of identifiable and measurable value. Too often planning focuses on providing bodies; that is the activity. We want planners to focus on how they are adding value.

Most companies will not allow the staffing department to carry excess employees. That is, we're one in a million if we have the luxury of maintaining a 110 percent staff complement in order to be ready for any emergency. Since we have to try to operate with no more, and probably less, than the number of people we need at any given time, and because we know from experience that periodically we will be inundated with unplanned and unexpected recruiting demands, what can we do to mitigate the stress that will be put on the staff while maintaining an acceptable level of recruiting support?

The answer to this question lies in selecting the variables that are most affected by changes in recruiting demand. The most common variables are the requisition inventory, the workload of the recruiters and their assistants (expressed by the number of requisitions they are handling), the expected number of hires that can be attained by the recruiters and assistants in a given period, and the past history of projected openings versus actual openings. All these variables are affected by market changes and volatility. They are also influenced

Month	Opened			Filled			Remaining		
	E	SNE	h	E	SNE	h	E	SNE	h
Jan	35	104	128	21	95	126	14	9	2
Feb	41	109	136	35	107	131	20	11	7
Mar	43	101	95	52	104	100	9	8	2

Figure 7-4   Requisition Activity

by the support systems and the nature of management's needs. If we redesign the workflow or automate, it should make a difference in the number of requisitions the staff can handle. If we choose to source through agencies versus advertising, it will affect the workload. If the ratio of exempt to nonexempt or professional to managerial requisitions changes, that may affect response time and time to fill. The ability to predict the future depends on knowledge of the past, perception of the present, and skills in forecasting.

Summary

We have looked at the staffing function and measured it with the five basic indexes: cost, time, quality, quantity, and customer service. It was pointed out that the most important measure is customer satisfaction. Without it, we are out of work. The examples given were not meant to be all-encompassing. Rather, they were samples of what we consider the most important tasks to measure, based on decades of designing, managing, and consulting on human capital measurement systems.

Do not use all the sample formulas. Instead, choose a couple that have particular value for your situation. Furthermore, feel free to modify the sample to fit your needs. The way these formulas are expressed is not the only acceptable form. There is no national standard system, such as accounting enjoys—i.e., the Generally Accepted Accounting Practices (GAAP) protocol. Therefore, you are free to design any measure the way you need to in order to fit your organization's requirements.

There may be special needs within the company. Consider the environment, the staff, line management, business conditions, organizational objectives, and anything else that may affect the staffing function. Then design a set of measures and reports that will help meet the twin goals of effective management and persuasive reporting.

PART III

How to Measure Compensation and Benefit Values

Trends

There have been significant changes in the operating environment that organizations have faced during the last few years. Very few companies have escaped the need to downsize the workforce to meet the demand for efficiency and cost reduction. Simultaneously, the increasing rate of technological change and the greater emphasis on quality and customer service require repeated upgrading of employee skills. As skills grow and promotions are made, there is an expectation of increased salaries and bonuses. All this is occurring at a time when cultural values in many organizations are changing from the traditional management-worker role to a more flexible type of structure that encourages teamwork and increased employee involvement.

Compensation = Pay + Benefits

Compensation can be thought of as the total package: pay plus benefits. We will describe wage and salary systems as pay programs. The pay systems of the past and many that are used today do not measure up to the challenges presented by these vast changes. Smart compensation professionals are learning that their future rests in looking past a compensation program that is simply an exercise in conducting salary surveys and positioning pay along a regression line. The compensation system must be managed for its value to the organization. Therein lies the problem. There is a new mental model for compensation systems. Traditional pay systems need to be viewed, designed, and measured in terms of their effectiveness and value to the organization. How can they be constructed so that they serve the organization's need for increased productivity, quality, customer service, and other organizational performance indicators? Can we see how they are directly adding value?

Pay programs can be reactive (designed according to current market needs) or proactive (configured as a strategic tool). In general, the pay difference between top performers and bottom performers has not been made great enough. Take-home differentials of a couple of percent are demotivating. Managers have not faced up to dealing with employees who do not perform as well as others. It's far easier to grant the usual increase than to confront an employee. True pay for performance still needs improvement. A highly competitive global market calls for flexible pay programs. Management has to get over the fear of losing poor or even average performers and focus on rewarding the performance required for organizational success.

Rather than being treated as an ongoing process, pay for all employees above the entry level should be more flexible both upward and downward. Paying for exceptional performance requires a reliable measurement system and a fresh look at the effects of individual effort on business outcomes. Employees want to see differentiation in pay and have little tolerance for poorly performing coworkers. They end up resenting an organization that allows those workers to continue working and pays them the same as highly productive employees. Experience has shown that productive people would rather not have the nonproductive people around and would willingly pick up the extra load. When the better performers complain about minimal performance pay differentials, they are often rebuffed with the managerial response that "they should be happy to have a job." This avoidance mechanism is two generations out of date.

The Role of Benefits

Benefits are an important but secondary part of the total compensation program. For the most part they need to be competitive, but having the best package will not guarantee that everyone will want to work for a company. Benefits change as the workforce and the family change and as the government responds to those changes. Management uses benefits to shield the worker from catastrophic health problems as well as to promote fitness, provide recreation, and offer security. In unusual times new benefits appear to help companies attract or retain talent. As pressures change, so does the benefits package.

The Total Package

Effective compensation practices are specific to the organization. The values and ethics of the organization drive them. The Chief executive officer and management's philosophy in regard to the value of people, the ability to pay, competitive position, and the business structure and focus, plus other factors, comes into play in establishing compensation programs. It isn't going to get easier, and a measurement system is essential to knowing where the value is coming from and rewarding it accordingly.

Compensation: Connecting It to Revenues and Expenses

The Most Popular Topic

Compensation is the one subject within human asset management that everyone wants to talk about. It is sometimes difficult to involve managers in studies of planning, training, recruitment, or employee relations programs. But if you are going to review or revise the compensation system, you will find people knocking down the door to get on the project team. This is reasonable. Everybody, no matter how talented or limited, understands two factors in life: pain and pleasure. People view their pay as one or the other. Most people can use more money, and when someone brings up the subject, they usually are eager to talk about it. People want to lobby for a bigger share of the pie or, in the worst case, protect what they have. The challenge for a compensation manager is not to get people interested but to develop and manage a system that is equitable and is used rather than subverted.

If I ask you how you determine whether your compensation program is doing its job, what would your answer be? The correct answer, of course, is, "It depends." What does it depend on? It depends on what the program is supposed to be doing. What is the purpose of the compensation system? Whenever that question is asked, the usual reply is something like, "Compensation's mission is to assist in attracting, retaining, and motivating employees." That is almost correct. Technically speaking, motivation is an inherent trait of human beings. One cannot motivate a person; one can only stimulate or provide incentive for employees. This is a small point, but for the sake of precision and the education of managers, it is worth noting. The implication of providing an incentive versus motivating is profound when applied to managing people. However, this is not the place to go into it in depth; we need only the notion that motivation is internal and incentive is external.

Compensation's Challenge

Designing compensation programs is a complex process. There is much more to it than doing a salary survey and spreading numbers across a form. In the past compensation professionals had to understand the processes for planning, projecting, and administering. They also had to be comfortable with statistical procedures. In addition, they needed to be able to synthesize data from many sources and shape the data into a structure that everyone could understand and use. That structure had to meet the reasonable needs and demands of employees and managers as well as mesh with the philosophy of the organization and its ability to pay. All this could not be attained through haphazard methods. It required the development of a system. As was pointed out earlier, people understand the value of money in their lives. They will put up with a lot of managerial ineptitude except when it comes to pay.

In today's more fluid and informal organizations, job structures are changing. Traditional heavily structured compensation systems are falling out of favor because they do not suit the times. Compensation professionals are feeling the pressure to be more responsive and flexible. It is becoming clear that jobs as we've always known them are being replaced by competencies. The new organizational forms are requiring people to spend more time on teamwork and projects. Thus, old job descriptions linked to pay grades are becoming obsolete. When old systems give way to new ones, the need to monitor and objectively measure the emerging system's performance and value becomes critical.

By tracing the processes indigenous to a compensation system and the results that the system yields, one can find points to assess. The potential trap lies in measuring the usage and outcomes of the system and implying that this equates with the productivity or effectiveness of the compensation department. In one sense it does, and in another it does not. This point is important, and the issue is complex enough that we need to spend time now to establish the rationale for different measurement criteria.

First, referring to our definitions of *productivity* and *effectiveness*, you recall that we said that productivity relates to levels of performance in valued activities. Effectiveness is doing the right thing— getting the desired result. The two issues are semantically discrete but pragmatically inseparable. It is hard to imagine effective performance that is carried out in an unproductive fashion. Nevertheless, I will offer a way of looking at the compensation department from both a productive viewpoint and an effective viewpoint.

The compensation department attempts to fulfill its organizational role of assisting in attracting, retaining, and incenting employees by doing the following:

1. It builds a system of performance management and pay that suits the evolving needs of the organization.
2. It controls the cost of the pay program not just by monitoring the dollar cost but also by influencing how managers use the program.
3. The compensation staff tries to communicate the pay and performance management system to the employees so that they will understand how and why it works the way it does.
4. The compensation department strives to convince employees, by monitoring management pay practices, that the system is just, equitable, and competitive.

The way to judge the compensation department's productivity or effectiveness is to look at each of the focal activities separately, starting with system design. The question is, Does the pay system serve the changing organizational structure and management philosophy? As markets and organizations change, pay systems have to be redesigned. Many alternative pay methodologies are missing. Skill-based pay is one approach that has the potential to address the shortfalls of traditional pay systems and meet current pay system challenges. It is also one of the fastest-growing compensation innovations as more and more organizations look for ways to build direct links between organization performance, individual contribution, and pay. Incentive pay and broadbanding are two other methodologies that are still in vogue. New approaches are being tested in many organizations; employees are even being put in charge of their own pay determination. The message here is that compensation professionals will have to acquire new and creative skills to design the pay systems of the future and meet the continued challenges of business competition and economic survival.

Cost control is an activity of the compensation department. However, the results of that activity are external to the department. Costs are, to be sure, a function of how system components are handled. For example, writing job descriptions and leveling jobs affect salary expenses. You can measure productivity by calculating how long it took the compensation analyst to write a job description or level a group of jobs. You can also outsource the activity and resource the productivity similarly. However, the effectiveness of the work is measured by what happens when managers use those descriptions and pay grades. The work is performed effectively if managers can attract, retain, and provide incentive for people, while staying within the salary budget. By definition, if a system meets its objectives and does so with an acceptable level of employee satisfaction, it is effective. The second part of that definition leads to the third focal point of measurement in compensation.

Employee satisfaction is a phenomenon totally external to the compensation department, yet it depends in part on the work of the compensation staff. A number of vehicles are available to the department for explaining the system to employees. The most direct methods are meetings and written communiqués, both electronic and on paper. However, the method that ranks above all others is the manner in which an individual's manager utilizes the program. The role of the compensation manager is to make sure that those in supervisory positions are handling the system in the intended manner. The best way to determine that is through employee surveys and exit interviews. When it comes to pay questions, people are seldom reticent about telling you what they think and feel. A less formal but easily accessible source of effectiveness data is daily feedback. Your staff usually knows how people feel about their pay. They hear about it all the time if they are maintaining contact with the employees as a whole. If employees understand and feel good about the pay program, it is fair to claim that the staff has done an effective job. They also hear about it from the staffing group. If they are unable to hire new employees because of a low salary offer, you will surely know.

In summary, it is relatively easy to measure the compensation staff's productivity. Primarily, this requires a judgment of how efficiently they and/or the external vendor are carrying out their tasks. Effectiveness, since it is a subjective term, is more ambiguous. To have a good measure of effectiveness, it is necessary to create a composite consisting of several external outcome variables. Although composites are not as neat as a single unequivocal measure, they are the only way to generate a useful indicator.

Maintaining a Moving System

One of the truest statements about salary structures is that they cannot stand still but must be dynamic. In the past that usually meant an annual review of pay grades. Structures changed only if a significant event occurred. Today, and in the foreseeable future, structures are less permanent. With organizations attempting to manage pay costs, experiments are in vogue. It is interesting to watch organizations move to new methods, such as broadbanding, and then gradually modify them.

With the trend toward more teamwork, the components that hold a salary structure together must be monitored constantly. Since jobs change, jobs have to be broadened. A proactive manager thinks ahead to see structural changes and trends.

The auditing of job descriptions is only part of the process. Job descriptions help recruiters who need up-to-date information to fill jobs. However, unless they are followed by job evaluation and leveling, the salary structure does not benefit. Thus, regular system maintenance is a two-step process. Once job descriptions are rewritten, job evaluations are conducted and the structure is releveled. Maintenance goals can be set for descriptions, evaluation, and leveling. The following formula generates the job evaluation factor.

JOB EVALUATION FACTOR

$$JEF = \frac{JE}{J}$$

where JEF = percentage of jobs evaluated and leveled
   JE = number of jobs evaluated and leveled (e.g., 207)
    J = total number of jobs in the system (e.g., 238)

EXAMPLE

$$JEF = \frac{207}{238}$$
$$= 87\%$$

  Another way of looking at the vitality of the system is to approach it from an exception standpoint. How many exceptions exist within the structure, or how often is it necessary to make adjustments to achieve a worthwhile objective? Two examples of this are pay increase exceptions and salary adjustments, usually for a group of jobs.

  In the first case it is worthwhile to know what percentage of employees have salaries that exceed the maximum for their grade or salary band. The calculation is simple, as shown below.

Salary Range Exception Factor

$$SRF = \frac{EX}{E}$$

where SRF = percentage of employees over salary grade maximums
   EX = number of excesses (e.g., 6)
    E = average number of employees (e.g., 140)

EXAMPLE

$$SRF = \frac{6}{140}$$
$$= 4.3\%$$

A growing incidence of excesses may reveal an aging and stagnant employee population. With early retirement programs and recent earnings that is hard to imagine. But whatever the reasons, a number of people may have "maxed out." Besides being a structural problem, this creates an abnormally high labor cost. In today's intensely competitive marketplace companies must maintain and manage pay programs to aid in controlling its labor costs. Another question that may surface is poor salary management. Managers sometimes use salary dollars to try to solve interpersonal problems. For example, they may have employees who should be counseled about lack of effort to qualify themselves for promotion or a pay increase. Instead of facing the issue, the manager requests a salary increase above the maximum. Keeping track of the excesses is one means of monitoring the system. This also pays off by pointing out organizational or managerial problems.

A second example of exceptions involves requests for a salary adjustment. Even with the pressure to keep costs down, market penetration may force an unplanned adjustment in a specific job group. What if you suddenly learn that a competitor is now paying programmers 20 percent more than your company does? You can choose to hold the line, and it will be more difficult to recruit programmers. You also might begin to experience unwanted turnover in that group as the employees learn what is being offered elsewhere. If jobs are truly available, more often than not management will choose to adjust the salary range and the salaries of the current programming staff.

That kind of a situation can and does come up in every organization from time to time no matter what the organization's needs are. However, if it seems to be happening with great frequency, it may signal the need to completely audit the structure and pay program. Sometimes a company forgoes a structural review because it believes that it can safely go another few months without increasing the ranges. Then it begins to experience a constant stream of requests to make adjustments. In this case it had miscalculated or ignored information that might have predicted the need to adjust or redesign. Adjustments for a specific group may have an unsettling effect on the larger organization. If another group hears about it, those employees will begin to look for reasons why they too deserve an unscheduled raise. Soon a ripple spreads out across the organization, and the compensation department finds itself under severe pressure to meet both supportable and unsupportable demands. In such cases the management of the system has been taken away from the department.

There is no need to create a formula to track the frequency of adjustments. The point is to note that adjustments are exceptions to a system; if there are too many exceptions, this implies that the system is no longer functional.

Cost Control

Periodically, all employees are entitled to a review of their performance. In a study of organizational communications, it was found that employees were much more interested in performance and career opportunity information than in any other topic. There probably has been as much research and speculation on performance reviews and appraisals as there has been on any managerial subject. Operating philosophies have been created to inform and support managers so that they can do a more credible and constructive job. Elaborate procedures have been developed to help managers review their employees. However, very few companies are happy with their review systems.

As a last resort, some organizations have set up a standard profile for managers to use when distributing performance appraisals in their groups. Some still insist on using a bell-shaped curve. They are saying in effect that most issues, activities, and outcomes are naturally distributed on the curve; therefore, we would expect that the performance scores you give your group will be more or less normally distributed. That is, a very small percentage will receive the highest possible rating, a slightly larger number will receive the next highest rating, most of the people will be about in the middle, and the remainder will be spread down the bottom of the curve. Management sometimes may become very specific and say that no more than 10 percent of employees can receive the top rating, the second level should include about 20 percent, 40 percent should get a middle rating, 20 percent should get a low one, and 10 percent of employees should be on probation. A word of caution, however. There has been a recent surge in discrimination lawsuits over this issue. Both men and women over age 50 are claiming age discrimination because of their placement in the low end of the curve, with their salaries being in the upper end of their range. If there is a performance problem, one should deal with it instead of using a forced distribution as an easy way out.

One way to display the distribution data for several groups is to put the information on a table. On the y axis list the departments and the number of employees. On the x axis, place the performance levels. It is helpful to show both the number of people appraised at a particular level and the percentage of the whole which that represents. Figure 8-1 is a sample performance appraisal table.

It is relatively easy to see how each department did against the goal and how the departments compared to one another. Was one consistently high? Was another consistently low? Either way, if the differences are significant, they can be precursors of organizational problems.

A quicker evaluation can be made if those percentages are plotted as curves on a graph. Using various colors, five or six groups can be shown on the same chart without confusion. If you have set a desired distribution curve or percentage, you can also plot that. Then everyone can quickly see the correlations and deviations between the standard and the actual situation.

Salary increase patterns can be handled in the same manner. Many organizations now set increase standards; for example, they may decide that the average increase should be 8 percent in the coming year. Within that parameter they allow managers to distribute increases as they see fit. Other organizations may structure the process by dictating minimum and maximum increases throughout the system.

No matter how the system is set up, the results can be displayed to show how they compare to the standards. The principle is the same for salary increase displays as it is for performance appraisals.

Division	Number of Employees	Performance Level 5		Performance Level 4		Performance Level 3		Performance Level 2		Performance Level 1	
		#	%	#	%	#	%	#	%	#	%
A	885	15	1.7	566	64.0	231	26.1	71	8.0	2	0.2
B	565	42	7.4	329	58.2	168	29.7	26	4.6	0	0
C	590	38	6.4	220	37.3	272	46.1	60	10.2	0	0
D	260	20	7.7	113	43.5	95	36.5	32	12.3	1	0.3
E	178	22	12.4	110	61.8	38	21.3	8	4.5	0	0
F	134	24	17.6	86	64.7	20	14.7	4	3.0	0	0
Corporate total	2612	161	6.2	1424	54.5	824	31.5	201	7.8	3	0.1

Figure 8-1. Performance Appraisal Distribution

When a tabular format is used, the vertical axis shows the departments, set in a column along the left side. The elements to be reviewed are placed across the top as column headings. The columns may be levels—for example, nonexempt and exempt—or job groups—for example, programmers, engineers, and accountants. The average salary increase percentage is then indicated in the appropriate position on the table.

Increase patterns can also be shown in a bar chart format. The percentage increase is placed on the vertical y axis from 0 up to a chosen maximum. The groups to be viewed are arranged across the horizontal x axis. However, the larger the y scale is, the less the differences between groups will appear to be. For instance, a percentage range of 20 points will make the differences between measured groups smaller than a range of 15 points. A wide range lessens the visual impact. If the maximum recorded increase is 14 percent, it is best to use a 15 percent scale. The difference between the lengths of the bars will be more dramatic than if a 20 percent scale is used. Always keep in mind the fact that a report is supposed to both inform and make a point; design a chart that tells your story as effectively as possible.

Another goal-type measure is quite common, and most organizations use it: the salary budget. Budgets are constructed from different perspectives, but they all end up at the same point: they tell managers how many total dollars can be spent on salaries. Most budget systems kick out a monthly or quarterly report that shows the variance between actual and budgeted figures. Somewhere in the finance system the salary account is subtotaled by department and then totaled for the whole organization. Simply divide those numbers by the budgeted figure and see what the variance is. If you do this on a month-to-month basis, you can see loosening or tightening trends across a range of departments. The results can be presented in either dollar or percentage variance.

Distribution Patterns

The last section, where we looked at increase patterns, was a precursor to a discussion of distribution patterns. The underlying issue in both cases is, How are managers using the system? It was pointed out earlier that we cannot design systems and then disavow how they are used. Our job is to guide management in the proper utilization of the programs we develop. This is not always easy, but it is our obligation not only to design the tool and teach people how to use it but also to monitor its use and point out faults. This is where the concept of effectiveness comes in. Inappropriate and improper use of a salary program can be unfair to employees and dangerous for the organization. When pay is distributed incorrectly, some employees will benefit and others will suffer. Furthermore, the organization will be jeopardized. Poor pay practices usually lead to increased turnover, low morale, and, as just described, legal actions against the organization.

Compensation managers have a mechanism that they can use to study the distribution of individual salaries within a salary grade. If a salary structure is set up so that there are four subdivisions to each salary grade, it is called a *quartile structure*. The method that is used to calculate the distribution pattern reveals how many people have a salary within each quartile of a given grade. When those figures are plotted, the result is called a *maturity curve*. From a technical standpoint this is a very valuable measure for the compensation department because it shows how well the structure is aging. That is, are there too many people in the upper portion of the grade? That could mean that the employee population is stagnating and an excessive number of people are "maxing out." This shows up vividly when organizations move to broad-banding.

It is important to look at salary distribution from an equity point of view. There are two ways to be certain that there is no intentional or unintentional discrimination. The more precise method is to use a variation of the maturity curve described earlier. In this case you would look at salary distribution across quartiles of each grade for each of the groups you wanted to examine. Obviously, this can be a complex calculation that cannot be performed easily without the ability to access and query the HRIS database. To calculate the distribution, you would set up a query for each category. You would then set up the table with salary grades in the first column. Quartiles 1 to 4 would constitute the next four columns. Each quartile position on the table would display either the number of people or the percentage of people from that category whose salary fell into that position. To know whether the resulting distribution profile was equitable, you would have to do the same thing for categories of employees.

A simpler way to obtain a sense of whether there was a problem would be to use average salaries or employee cost factors for each group, as shown in the next Formula. Using an average cost eliminates the task of spreading individual salaries across a grade. This approach also allows you to display data on all categories in one report. When the results are compared, you can scan for any obvious or serious disparities. This is the simplest way to do the job, though you could convert actual salaries into percentiles. I do not see the value of the extra labor, however. Many people have difficulty dealing with percentiles, and actual average salaries do not really need interpretation.

There is a hidden danger in dealing with averages, though. Averages lump together all salaries and ignore the differences among them. As a result, the average may look fine, but there may be a few people who are a long way from the mean. A standard deviation indicates how wide a spread there is between individual salaries and the average salary. Although the average salary across groups may be similar, the standard deviations may indicate a large difference. Many programs and calculators can run a standard deviation.

Distribution studies can be made for a variety of issues. Besides certain categories, you could look at pay patterns across departments, locations, or any other classification you thought might be hiding or breeding a problem. Compensation managers are responsible for monitoring the systems they design. Conducting a distribution study once a quarter goes a long way toward ensuring equitable pay practices.

Cost Analysis

In most organizations payroll costs are the largest or second largest single expense item. The two most common calculations are total cost of payroll and average salary cost per employee. There is no mystery to the whys and hows of these measures. The simpler of the two measures is the average cost per employee, as shown below.

Employee Cost Factor

$$\text{ECF} = \frac{\text{TC}}{\text{FTC}}$$

where ECF = employee cost factor: average salary per full-time equivalent (FTE)

    TC = total compensation

    FTE = number of FTEs

EXAMPLE

$$\text{ECF} = \frac{\$686,000}{15.2}$$
$$= \$45,131$$

This measure can be shown by exempt, nonexempt, or equal employment opportunity (EEO) groups and for contingent employees. The latter measure is very useful in the determination to hire contingent versus regular employees.

Variations on the basic measures are also useful. An often overlooked cost item is payroll taxes. An organization not only pays its employees an hourly rate or a monthly salary, it also pays a significant amount of money to the government. These funds go for Social Security, income taxes, unemployment insurance, and in some states disability insurance. To appreciate how much this can amount to, compute a payroll tax factor, as shown below.

Payroll Tax Factor

$$\text{PTF} = \frac{\text{PT}}{\text{C}}$$

where PTF = portion of total salary or wages (including bonus and incentive pay) absorbed by payroll taxes

    PT = sum of payroll tax deductions for Social Security (FICA), federal income taxes (FIT) and state income tax (SIT), unemployment insurance (UI), and state disability insurance (SDI) where applicable (figures will vary by state and income level)

    C = total compensation (salary, bonus, and/or commission)

EXAMPLE

$$PTF = \frac{FICA + FIT + SIT + UI + SDI}{Salary + bonus + incentive}$$

Both the magnitude and the rate of growth of this expense item have become critical operating concerns for management. Compensation departments should keep total dollars as well as percentages in front of management. The executives who run organizations owe it to their stockholders and employees to be cognizant of this cost and to be active in dealing with the various governmental bodies to slow the inexorable rise in these job-killing taxes.

Management Reporting

Management's attention should be focused on strategic macro-level data. Rather than filling a report with counts of jobs leveled and salary actions processed, you should show how pay relates to other expenses as well as to sales, number of employees, and benefits. These variables are the basics of a business whether it is profit or not for profit. One matchup that many firms monitor is employees and revenues. By dividing total revenue by total employees they obtain a number that they track as a marker of efficiency. If revenues equaled $200 million and there were 1,400 employees, the ratio would be $142,857 per employee. If this number improved significantly, it would be a sign that gross productivity was increasing. The improvement may not necessarily be all in factory productivity. It might be the case that salespeople are becoming more efficient, engineering had simplified a design, or manufacturing had automated a procedure. The reason was not necessarily obvious, but the result is clearly positive. Of course, a decrease in the number would indicate a deterioration in performance somewhere. An equation for revenue per employee is shown below.

REVENUE FACTOR

$$RF = \frac{TR}{FTE}$$

where RF = revenue per employee
    TR = total organizational revenue
    FTE = number full-time equivalents

EXAMPLE

$$RF = \frac{200,000,000}{1,400}$$
$$= 142,857$$

A second measure that further defines productivity is income per employee, or income factor, as shown below. This measure illustrates the dollar income or profit generated per full-time equivalent and provides an integrated picture of productivity and expense control efforts. It measures organizational efficiency, the success of corporate strategies, and the achievement of corporate objectives. Because this measure combines both revenue and expenses, it is best rendered over time.

INCOME FACTOR

$$IF = \frac{TR - TE}{FTE}$$

where IF = income per employee
    TR = total organizational revenue (e.g., $200,000,000)
    TE = total operating expenses (e.g., $105,000,000)
    FTE = number of FTEs

EXAMPLE

$$RF = \frac{200,000,000 - 105,000,000}{1,400}$$
$$= \frac{95,000,000}{1,400}$$
$$= 67,857$$

A similar measure of cost and efficiency is the employee hourly cost factor (average hourly rate). Similar to the employee cost factor, this measure provides a finer screen of labor costs. It is calculated as shown below.

EMPLOYEE HOURLY COST FACTOR

$$EHF = \frac{P}{EHW}$$

where EHF = employee hourly cost factor

        P = total wages and salaries paid (e.g., $107,320,000 annually)

  EHW = total employee hours worked times number of employees (e.g., annual = 2,080 × 1,929; monthly = 173.33 × 1,929)

EXAMPLE

$$EHF = \frac{107,320,000 \text{ (annual)}}{4,102,000 \text{ (annual)}} = \$26.16$$

Adding the hours worked variable refines a gross compensation number into an hourly one. This is more workable. It is difficult for a person to deal with an eight-digit number. The figure $57,017,000 is useful in rallying support for an efficiency or productivity drive, but $26.16 is a human-scale number. Employees can say to themselves, "If I can find a way to save just 10 cents an hour in labor cost, that will save the company almost $300,000." It is this type of micro thinking that contributed to Japan's strong position in the world market. Most people can think of ways to save a dime, but they do not deal with $300,000 often enough to know where to start.

We have looked at cost from several perspectives. The last one is the cost by function. The workforce can be divided into many groups, such as level, job group, department, and location. Another is supervision and management. Few people consider what it costs an organization to manage itself. Consider the portion of the organization that is populated by supervisors and managers. This category includes everyone from the first line supervisor to the chief executive officer. All these people exist in the organization, yet they are not producers. Their job is to manage the work of others. The question is, "How much does that service cost?" The simplest way to find out is to compute a cost to manage. Two methods are shown below. The first, management investment, shows total management cost per employee. The second, management cost factor, shows the average manager's pay.

MANAGEMENT INVESTMENT FACTOR

$$MF = \frac{MC}{FTE}$$

where MF = management investment factor
MC = total management compensation (e.g., \$150,462,000)
FTE = total employees (full-time equivalents, e.g., 10,500)

EXAMPLE

$$MF = \frac{150,462,000}{10,500} = 14,330$$

MANAGEMENT COST FACTOR

$$MCF = \frac{MC}{M/FTE}$$

where MCF = management cost factor
MC = total management compensation (e.g., \$150,462,000)
M/FTE = management employees (full-time equivalents, e.g., 1,929)

EXAMPLE

$$MCF = \frac{150,462,000}{1,929} = \$78,000$$

A metric that fully covers workforce costs includes the organization's benefit costs. After all, benefit cost is a per-employee charge and is part of an employee's total pay. The method used to calculate total labor costs is shown below.

TOTAL LABOR COST FACTOR

$$TLF = \frac{TC + BC}{FTE}$$

where TLF = total labor cost factor

TC = total compensation (e.g., $483,000,000)

BC = benefits cost (not including pay for time not worked, e.g., $144,900,000)

FTE = numbers of FTEs (e.g., 10,500)

EXAMPLE

$$TLF = \frac{483,000,000 + 144,900,000}{10,500}$$

$$= \frac{627,900,000}{10,500}$$

$$= \$59,800$$

There are other questions that compensation can also address. We made a case earlier in this chapter for the interrelated nature of human resources (HR) functions. By looking at hiring and employee relations issues, we can find evidence of the compensation program's effectiveness. Where there is effect we may be able to identify cause. Here are a couple of questions that could be asked of other HR departments:

1. Are we able to consistently hire below midpoint? Within range? The answer tells us if our structures are staying competitive. New hire information will show starting salaries.
2. Are people leaving for the same level of job and getting substantially more money? This is another approach to the competitive structure question. The answer can be found in exit interviews.
3. If there are incentive programs, such as piece rates and bonuses, do the employees feel that they are challenging and fair? Surveys and interviews will provide the answer.
4. Do supervisors and managers find the system easy to understand and, more important, explain to their staffs? Again, surveys and interviews will tell the story.

There are many more questions like these that can be asked about the system. In every case answers are available. When they are put into the mix with the more quantitative issues, a well-rounded evaluation of the compensation function emerges.

Employees' Pay Attitudes

Tangential to the pay system and its utilization is the reaction of employees to their pay. Whether the job market favors the employees or the employer, the employees' attitude is the same: they get angry when they feel they're being cheated. They will find ways to obtain equity for themselves even when they have to stay in a low-paying job. Since behavior is based largely on perceptions of the environment and since pay is part of the perceptual field, it follows that employees' view of their pay must correlate with some aspects of work behavior. What has not been proved is exactly how, when, and how much attitudes affect behavior on the job. For the compensation department to be effective in terms of optimizing the organization's return on its salary dollars, attitudes toward pay have to be addressed. The concensus from studies over the last two decades shows that

1. Money is a general means to satisfy needs.
2. Money is a basic incentive.
3. Money may be an anxiety reducer.
4. Money keeps workers from being dissatisfied but does not motivate them.
5. Money is an instrument to attain a valued goal.
6. Money is not the primary reason people stay at or leave an organization.

Whether you agree with these views or not, you probably would agree that pay is an important issue in the minds of your workforce.

I believe that people fundamentally ask themselves two questions about their pay. First, Am I paid fairly? Is the amount of money I make appropriate for the effort and responsibility I put into the job? Second, Does the ratio of my input to my outcome compare favorably with that ratio for other workers in my company, locale, and industry? Remember, employees have extensive information at their fingertips. The Internet is full of job-specific salary information.

Since pay is important to employees, you want to know as much about their attitudes toward your system and its utilization as you can. The most common ways of obtaining that information are interviews, focus groups, and surveys. Structured and unstructured interviews at orientation, during a person's employment, and at the time of termination can elicit a good deal of useful information. Surveys are much more complicated and time-consuming. They also can cause more harm than good if they are not administered properly or if the findings are not responded to. There are many surveys available commercially. Some are offered on-line and include extensive computer-based analyses as well as national and regional norms. It is not the purpose of this chapter to review them. The objective in mentioning surveys is to point out that they are probably necessary in some form if you want to find out how effective the pay program is in the eyes of the recipients. Also, those who have not used surveys extensively must realize that they are not as straightforward as they seem. I firmly believe that surveys should never be conducted with large groups of employees without professional assistance. A significant percentage of surveys backfire on the user because of lack of knowledge about how to design or conduct them, rash judgments of the results, or inappropriate or nonexistent follow-up with those surveyed.

Many organizations conduct exit interviews with employees who have quit with the hope of learning the reasons behind their decisions to leave. Interviews held on-site, generally on the employee's last day of work, rarely tell the true story. Employees don't want to leave with an unfavorable opinion toward them. They are smart enough to know that they may need to come back to the employer for one reason or another. Overall, the easiest answer to give is "more money," but often the true answer is much more than that. All things being equal, if employees feel they are being paid fairly and equitably, they will not leave solely for higher pay. There will be deeper reasons that drive them to that decision. It is these reasons that the employee rarely shares with the employer. Only when an external third-party service conducts the interviews and maintains ex-employees' anonymity will you be able to find the true story.

The fundamental question is, Before you lose an employee, what can you do to keep that person and keep him or her productively?

Our conclusion is that it is important to know how your employees perceive their pay. Also, it is important to be proactive. Understand their perceptions before they become a turnover statistic. Pay may or may not be the most important issue for employees, but few issues are more sensitive.

The Strategic View

The focus up till now has been principally on administrative or micromanagement issues. The compensation group needs this type of data to monitor the performance of the system. The other side of the coin is the macro or strategic perspective.

Top management is not interested in the arcane technology of compensation administration. The senior team views compensation as an expense that, it hopes, retains and provides incentives for the workforce to perform at a high level. We never know how much of a person's performance is influenced by monetary rewards. Nevertheless, management accepts the premise that pay can be a stimulant. Compensation managers should point their management reports toward two issues: expense trends and correlations to performance.

Figure 8-2 shows a simple yet powerful display that can be presented to management. It shows the trend over time of payroll and benefit costs as a percentage of operating expenses. These are two of the items tracked in the annual Saratoga Institute Human Capital Benchmarking Report. By comparing your data to data from other companies of your size, type, region, or revenue growth rate, you can establish an ongoing competitive analysis. This is the level at which top management can and should focus its attention. Presenting this type of data on a regular basis causes the compensation manager to be viewed as someone who transcends administration. The compensation manager becomes part of the executive team that manages the cost-effectiveness of human capital. The formulas used to calculate these data are shown below, followed by a summing of the two basic formulas.

COMPENSATION EXPENSE PERCENT

$$CE = \frac{TC}{TE}$$

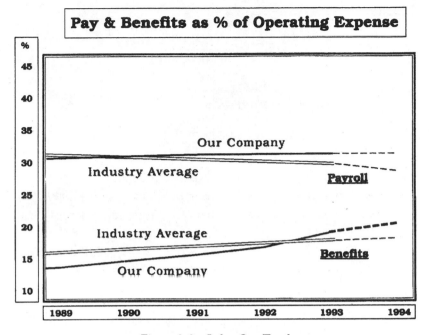

Figure 8-2   Labor Cost Trends

where CE = compensation expense percent
    TC = total wages and salaries paid out (e.g., $43,000,000)
    TE = total operating expenses (e.g., $105,000,000)

EXAMPLE

$$CE = \frac{43,000,000}{105,000,000}$$
$$= 41\%$$

BENEFIT EXPENSE PERCENT

$$BE = \frac{TB}{TE}$$

where BE = benefit expense percent
    TB = total cost of all benefit program expenses, employees'
        share only (e.g., $29,000,000)
    TE = total operating expenses (e.g., $105,000,000)

EXAMPLE

$$BE = \frac{29,000,000}{105,000,000}$$
$$= 27.6\%$$

TOTAL COMPENSATION EXPENSE PERCENT

$$TCE = \frac{TC + TB^*}{TE}$$

where TCE = total compensation expense percent
TC = total wages and salaries paid out (e.g., \$43,000,000)
TB = total cost of all benefit program expenses (e.g., \$11,000,000)
TE = total operating expense (e.g., \$105,000,000)
*Not including pay for time not worked: vacations, holidays, sick time, etc.

EXAMPLE

$$TE = \frac{43,000,000 + 11,000,000}{105,000,000}$$
$$= \frac{54,000,000}{105,000,000}$$
$$= 51\%$$

In choosing one measure over another for reporting to management, it is important to select metrics that represent management's concern and interest. If the organization is focused on controlling costs, the compensation expense metrics are important. If the focus is on improved sales and total revenues, it is better to report compensation as a percentage of revenue. This metric shows the amount of salaries and wages paid to all employees on the payroll as a percentage of revenue generated. Over time this metric can show if the organization is obtaining a higher or lower return on dollars invested in people. The basic measure of compensation to revenue, compensation revenue percent, is shown below.

COMPENSATION REVENUE PERCENT

$$CR = \frac{TC}{TR}$$

where CR = compensation revenue percent
TC = total wages and salaries paid out (e.g., $43,000,000)
TR = total organization revenue (e.g., $200,000,000)

EXAMPLE

$$CR = \frac{43,000,000}{200,000,000}$$
$$= 21.5\%$$

Of course, you can continue this process by adding in the benefit costs and calculating benefit revenue percent and total compensation revenue percent. These formulas follow the same algorithm used for compensation revenue percent. Compensation can monitor its costs and effectiveness in a multitude of ways. The important thing is to report them in a way that is meaningful to management and focuses on business objectives.

A third strategic compensation issue is the return on investment of incentive plans. Sales personnel have long worked on incentives. When used judiciously, incentives can be very powerful. There is a fast-growing trend to put more pay at risk in positions other than sales, and this has become a key component in many salary plans. This can be very difficult to administer if a sound individual and group performance measurement system is not in place. A simple way to measure the cost of at-risk pay is shown below as variable compensation percent.

VARIABLE COMPENSATION PERCENT

$$VC = \frac{TV}{TC}$$

where VC = variable compensation percent
TV = total variable pay; includes pay in addition to regular pay and not given on a regular basis, i.e., overtime, pay premiums, commissions, performance bonuses, and profit sharing (e.g., $6,000,000)
TC = total wages and salaries paid out (e.g., $43,000,000)

EXAMPLE

$$VC = \frac{6,000,000}{43,000,000}$$
$$= 14\%$$

You may find it advantageous to break down variable pay to its four main components and calculate each one as a percentage of total compensation. By looking at each one individually, you can then measure its effectiveness. The four are

- Overtime and pay premiums
- Commissions
- Performance-related bonuses
- Profit sharing

Incentive plans are only as good as the performance measures on which they are based. If you want to introduce pay at risk or other incentive programs, you must first implement a system to measure and report performance objectively. Most important, the workforce must be able to understand the program and believe in it. Incentives can be very immediate, as with weekly or monthly payouts. Or, as is often the case, they can be longer term, with quarterly or annual rewards. You can pay for individual or team performance. Payouts can be based on productivity, quality, service, or sales and completion targets, using cost, time, quantity, quality, or human reaction indexes. Long-term plans most often are based on profit goals. There are so many variations that one could write a book on their pros and cons. For our purposes the issue is that performance measures are the foundation.

One of the best performance systems I have seen starts by focusing everyone's attention on the four strategic imperatives of the organization: quality, customer service, employee relations, and financial responsibility. Then each person develops a set of objectives within these four categories. The performance levels are all described in quantitative terms. There are both individual and team objectives, and pay is based equally on individual and team performance. In addition, the company sets an annual corporate profitability target with monetary rewards tied to it. The program was developed participatively with the supervisors and managers of the company. Its impact on operating effectiveness and morale has been outstanding.

The key to top performance is to be able to connect an individual's or group's actions with a desired result. If you refer to the value chain in Chapter 4, it will give you an idea of how to apply the logic to link action to value added.

THOUGHT 11   *We get exactly what we pay for.*

Summary

Compensation management is like overseeing an oil pipeline. It is a continuous, seemingly endless flow with a few interruptions to repair leaks. There are few checkpoints to determine how we are doing. Although the compensation function deals mainly with quantitative issues, there are relatively few measures of the compensation group's efficiency and productivity. Staffing lends itself more to that type of evaluation because it is basically project work. Each opening is like a project, with a beginning and an end. Compensation has maintenance tasks whose efficient accomplishment can be evaluated. However, the results are of interest only to compensation and human resources management.

In light of the shortage of talent and the constant drive for competitive advantage in the marketplace, we suggest shifting the focus from process or system maintenance to a strategic effectiveness perspective. The compensation program has a purpose that is far-reaching, important, and complex. To achieve its mission it must establish and maintain a structure, and we can audit how well it is attending to that responsibility. Another task for compensation is to meet the needs of the organization fairly and equitably for all employees. We can track system utilization to see how well it is operating against preset standards and goals. Since the creation of pay equity is a fundamental mission, we can look at the results of the use of the system to determine whether pay is being distributed properly across all groups. We can also measure the cost of wages and salaries and check to see if it is within acceptable ranges. We also can measure employee attitudes toward the pay and performance appraisal system. Employees' behavior probably will correlate with those attitudes. Finally, we must deal with strategic issues of expense management and return on investment of base pay and incentive programs. This is where top management should focus its attention. At this level compensation shifts from an administrative function to a strategic partnership.

By evaluating how well the organization is doing across this wide range of indexes, we can make a judgment about the effectiveness of the compensation department. Compensation designs and develops systems. Wage and salary actions take place endlessly. The sheer volume of pay actions make it nearly impossible to prove individual causal connections between the compensation staff's activities and unit outcomes. Nevertheless, overall the department should be able to show that it has strongly influenced the utilization practices and cost outcomes of the system as well as the employees' satisfaction with their pay. In addition, if compensation data are presented to management and move it to make effective strategic decisions, the compensation department can put together a strong case for its having contributed to lowering turnover, increasing morale, and affecting operating ratios in productivity, quality, service, and sales.

Perhaps the most compelling reason for monitoring the compensation system comes from the Saratoga Institute's exit interviewing service results. Over many years we have consistently found that people cite poor pay administration as a reason for leaving. They are more concerned with the equity and timeliness of pay than with the amount. Pay is one of the three most important issues for every employee. The other two are the work itself and relationships at work. Pay is a very personal issue. It is like an individual scorecard. When it is believed that pay planning and administration are off, people get very upset. The loss of key personnel is intolerable in today's market. It behooves compensation professionals to make certain that supervisors and managers are making the most of the compensation system.

CHAPTER

9

Benefits: Measuring Plan Effectiveness

Managing the Trend

Benefits are a phenomenon of the second half of the twentieth century. In 1940 the cost of the typical benefit program was approximately 5 percent of payroll. After World War II "fringe" benefits became common. A U.S. Chamber of Commerce survey showed that the average cost per employee for benefits rose by 297 percent between 1969 and 1980. During that period average weekly earnings rose by 223 percent. Throughout the 1980s the cost of benefits continued to rise, although at a slower rate.

This was driven by a combination of accelerating health care costs and a lengthening of the list of social welfare benefits provided by organizations. Today the Saratoga Institute's annual Human Capital Benchmarking Report shows that benefits commonly amount to 30 to 40 percent of salary, depending on the industry.

Before 1990 employees developed an expectation that the organization had to do more than pay them a salary. It also had to

- Provide a security blanket in the form of health and life insurance
- Establish some sort of retirement security because the Social Security system is uncertain

- Pay tuition assistance or otherwise invest in employee skills and knowledge

Starting with the economic slowdown and downsizing of the 1990s, the benefits profile changed. Employee cost sharing and leaner benefits began to appear. Conversely, as the population demographics shifted from baby booming to baby aging, the organization was called on by the employees to help with child and elder care and provide recreational and fitness facilities and programs. In short, the employer is expected to play a multifaceted role in the life of the employee. This is taking the place of family support. The demographic and political realities are as follows:

- There are more one-parent families.
- In two-parent households both the mother and the father need to work outside the home to earn enough income.
- At the local level extended families and community and church support organizations are declining.

Accordingly, it appears that employers' involvement in the lives of their employees can only grow.

The purpose of the benefit program is to augment the salary program in an attempt to attract, retain, and provide incentive for employees. The question is, How can we tell if the benefits department is operating efficiently and effectively? By nature, benefits probably help attract and sometimes retain employees, but are not the primary reason for most people to join an organization and have never been proved to stimulate performance. Benefits play a background role. They are there when an employee needs them, and when they are not in use, they tend to be forgotten. The job of benefits is to make sure that when employees need to use a benefit, they find it readily accessible and able to provide a satisfactory solution to their problem. How well the benefits department accomplishes this objective is the subject of this chapter.

Costing and Communicating Benefits

Management tends to look at almost everything involving employees from a cost rather than a value investment standpoint. This is why most conversations about benefits begin with a cost aspect. However, benefits have an impact on the organization's effort to attract and retain employees. The question is, How can we know which benefits do that most effectively? One way to answer that is to survey the employees. The best way is to study employees' participation and usage patterns. It seems logical that a program that addresses the needs of many employees will receive heavy usage. There are other, less important issues in benefits management. Plan maintenance report filings and timely responses to employees' requests are part of the job.

Because benefits quickly fade into the background in the mind of the employee, communication is important. We shall look at what and how benefits communications can take place. Finally, cost containment is one of the easiest measures. Because of the high cost of benefits, cost control has become a primary aspect of a benefit manager's job.

Everyone who works on benefits programs knows what percentage of payroll these programs represent. It is important to keep that number visible because of its magnitude. No one can say what the number ought to be. It is a direct reflection of the employer's perception of its relationship with the employees as well as the ability of the employer to purchase a benefit for the employees. There are two primary benefit cost measures from which all others emerge; total cost and support cost.

Total Cost

Most of the time when I ask people what benefits cost their company, they give me a number that represents the direct expenses associated with the various plans and programs: insurance premiums; vacation, holiday, and sick leave pay; tuition reimbursement; profit sharing; thrift and pension plans; and recreation programs. That number also includes legally mandated programs such as FICA, unemployment insurance, worker's compensation, and short-term disability. In addition, discounts on the employer's goods or services; separation pay and moving expenses; paid breaks; jury duty, voting, and bereavement time; service and suggestion awards; and other programs specific to the organization are incorporated.

When all the numbers are combined, the sum can be impressive, as seen in the calculation of the benefit factor.

BENEFIT FACTOR

$$BF = \frac{TB}{TE}$$

where BF = benefit factor

TB = total cost of benefit programs, employer's share only (e.g., $21,000,000)

TE = total headcount employees (e.g., 1,400)

EXAMPLE

$$BF = \frac{21,000,000}{1,400}$$
$$= \$15,000$$

As impressive as this is, it represents only part of the expenses associated with benefits. The missing piece consists of the staff costs, overhead costs, and computer costs necessary to maintain the programs. When insurance claims are outsourced, the cost of that processing is included. However, if the company brings the work in-house, hires a staff, and gives them space and equipment to do the job, usually the cost is forgotten. If the benefits program were shut down, people, space, and equipment costs would be eliminated immediately. By the same logic, as long as the program exists, the support costs should be included.

Based on the forgoing analysis, the computation for total benefit costs is illustrated below.

TOTAL BENEFITS COST

$$TBC = ST + OH + PC + PP + Misc$$

where TBC = total benefits cost

ST = staff time: staff hours spent on benefit planning and administration multiplied by salary and benefit hourly rates (e.g., $480,000)

OH = overhead expenses for space, furniture, equipment, etc. (e.g., $145,000)

PC = processing costs associated with benefit program administration (e.g., $560,000)

PP = plan payments, insurance and retirement, and payments for government-mandated programs, including charges by external plan administrators, trustees, etc. (e.g., $21,000,000)

Misc = vacation, holiday, sick leave, education, recreation, etc. (e.g., $10,000,000)

EXAMPLE

TBC = 480,000 + 145,000 + 560,000 + 21,000,000 + 10,000,000
= 32,185,000

Two additional calculations produce the two most commonly discussed numbers: cost per employee and percentage of compensation.

TOTAL BENEFIT FACTOR

$$TBF = \frac{TBC}{TE}$$

where TBF = total benefit cost per employee
TBC = total cost of benefits (e.g., $32,185,000)
TE = total headcount employees (e.g., 1,400)

EXAMPLE

$$TBF = \frac{32,185,000}{1,400}$$
$$= \$22,989$$

BENEFIT COMPENSATION PERCENT

$$BCB = \frac{TB}{TC}$$

where BCB = benefit compensation percent
TB = total cost of benefit program (e.g., $21,000,000)
TC = total wages and salaries (e.g., $43,000,000)

EXAMPLE

$$BCB = \frac{21,000,000}{43,000,000}$$
$$= 48.8\%$$

The last metric we will show to measure benefits is the one recognized and used 97 percent of the time by both employees and employers: health program cost. The results are watched more closely now than ever before.

Employers caught by the recent tight labor market were reluctant to pass on these costs to the employees. However, because of ever-increasing rates and fewer costs covered, employees are now being asked to take on a larger portion of the health care tab.

Employers are busy altering plan design and contracting with less expensive insurers in an effort to control health care expenses. We feel this will continue with more cost controls over the next few years. In conclusion, keep a close watch on your health program costs and benchmark to remain competitive.

HEALTH CARE FACTOR

$$HCF = \frac{HCC}{PE}$$

where HCF = health care factor
   HCC = health care program cost (e.g., \$4,900,000)
    PE = participating employees (e.g., 1,400)

EXAMPLE

$$HCF = \frac{4,900,000}{1,400}$$
$$= \$3,500$$

Participation Patterns

Benefit packages offer employees some choices. Beginning in the 1990s with the restructuring of benefit plans, there has been a trend toward more flexibility in offerings. Employees today are better informed about and more focused on retirement and budget management than they were a decade ago. Since the advent of the World Wide Web they have been better equipped to make their own decisions about which benefits they want and need. Most plans are designed to provide a security core of health and life insurance while leaving many other options to the employee's discretion. Late in the last century child and elder care became common and much needed options. Savings and profit-sharing plans, employee stock purchase plans, sabbatical leaves, and educational reimbursements are other benefits from which employees can choose.

The usage rates are probably the best data source for benefits managers. The percentage of participation, or the usage rate, can be computed for a given benefit across different groups of employees. For example, one could look at the usage of a particular benefit, such as an employee stock purchase plan, by exempt versus nonexempt employees. Or one could calculate usage by department or division. Age, sex, race, job groups, and other cuts are also possible. This type of analysis yields patterns that could help design or redesign the benefit package to a more cost-effective system. Knowing usage patterns also helps us decide where to put our money when we decide it is time to change the package.

The main problem that can arise from an analysis of usage patterns involves employee understanding. Plans and options are so complicated that many people have trouble making the right choice. For most this is a matter of trial and error. When employees make their annual choices and find out later that they misunderstood them, they then must wait until the next enrollment period to make another change. From a benefits management standpoint we have to make sure we are doing an effective job of communicating each benefit. There are many formal and informal ways to find out how well we are communicating. A focus group session with a representative group of employees will show why they misunderstood the program, if that is the case. Then a new communication program can be launched with a subsequent pattern audit and feedback session.

Some legislation-based programs require broad usage of a plan by people at all levels across the organization. If we don't watch for that, the organization may be rudely reminded of it by an auditing agency. Not only does this cause embarrassment for the company, people in some contributory programs, such as income deferral plans, may find that their tax deferrals did not turn out to be what we told them to expect in the beginning. Effective benefits managers consult use and participation studies before they recommend changes in or additions to the current package and make sure that everything is running the way it should.

> **THOUGHT 12** *We learn more from watching what people do than from listening to what they say they want.*

A good way to analyze usage is to look at the number of participants by specific benefit component, participant demographics, and component cash per employee, both participating employees and total organization employees. The last two are shown below.

BENEFIT COMPONENT COST

$$BCF = \frac{BCC}{PE}$$

where BCF = benefit component factor for (e.g., retirement and savings plan payments)

    BCC = benefit component cost (e.g., $3,570,000)

      PE = participating employees (e.g., 1,100)

EXAMPLE

$$BCF = \frac{3,570,000}{1,100}$$
$$= \$3,245$$

TOTAL BENEFIT COMPONENT FACTOR

$$TBCF = \frac{BCC}{TE}$$

where TBCF = total benefit component factor

     BCC = benefit component cost (e.g., $3,570,000)

       TE = total headcount employees (e.g., 1,400)

EXAMPLE

$$TBCF = \frac{3,570,000}{1,400}$$
$$= \$2,550$$

Maintenance

As benefits have become more complex, support activity has become not only more time-consuming but also more important. Local and federal governments require a plethora of periodic reports. Both welfare and retirement plans must have reports prepared and mailed out to regulatory bodies. Account status updates must be sent to plan participants. The accounting standards change periodically, requiring changes in the way companies account for retiree benefits.

Government agencies require that reports be mailed to them on schedule. Maintaining a master calendar is an effective way to ensure that reports are filed on time. Each filing should be listed on the calendar by title and receiving agency on the date it is due to be mailed. By referring to this tickler each week, the benefits manager can see what is due for preparation and mailing. The fact that plans may be administered by an outsider does not take accountability away. We have to monitor the outsiders to make sure they are keeping us out of trouble. When we are thinly staffed, everyone has a constant batch of brushfires to deal with, and it is very easy to miss a filing date. With the use of a reminder system the chances of that happening are greatly reduced. Maintenance is an important activity in benefit systems. The manner and timeliness with which it is handled provide an indication of the staff's efficiency.

Employee Communications

Another important and often underemphasized activity is the employee benefits communication program, the aim of which is to improve return on investment (ROI) for benefits. I use the term *ROI* because of the passive nature of benefits. It was noted at the beginning of this chapter that benefits very quickly become background.

People always know how much their salaries are and know exactly when they are due for the next increase, but they usually forget about the benefit package until they need to use part of it. As a result, the organization does not receive a very healthy return from its considerable investment in benefits. To improve that situation, the benefits manager needs to develop an active communications program.

There are many opportunities to communicate with employees. Here are some methods that are commonly used:

1. Orientation of new hires is the first opportunity to explain the package in detail.
2. Handbooks are given out at orientation, and intranet sites are listed and explained.
3. Brochures can be used in a variety of ways to describe individual plans or present an overview.
4. Summary plan descriptions, which are mandated, explain the nuts and bolts of the various plans.
5. E-mail announcements along with traditional posters and bulletin boards are visible means of keeping employees aware of the features of various benefits.
6. Articles or a benefit column can be written for the employee newspaper.
7. If employees do not have automatic deposit of their paychecks, paycheck stuffers can be included in pay envelopes to remind them about something that is timely.
8. Letters about issues such as changing coinsurance provisions can be mailed home, where the employee's spouse will see them.
9. Information meetings during which employees can ask questions or receive updates can be held at convenient times and places.
10. All-employee meetings can be scheduled to announce major changes and improvements.
12. Social Security Web sites can be put on the intranet for those who want to check the status of their accounts.
13. Open enrollment periods provide periodic opportunities to review plan provisions or highlights.

14. Benefit fairs can be set up at times that are convenient for employees so that they can inquire about a benefit or refresh their memory about what is available.
15. The annual benefit statement is considered by most people to be the most powerful communication tool.
16. Videotapes can be produced and run during lunch periods in the corner of the cafeteria, in a conference room, or on the intranet.

The list is not all-inclusive. There are other things that can be done.

Gaining Control

From the end of World War II until the mid-1980s there was un-interrupted growth in benefit programs. I can remember operating under the mandate from management that we would improve our benefit package in some way at least once each year. With the slow-down starting in the early 1980s and the realization of how expensive benefit packages had become, many organizations halted the 30-year trend and began to look seriously for ways to cut back plans or save money through administrative changes. With the low growth and profitability of the first half of the 1990s, benefit reduction efforts continued. However, when the economy strengthened, new benefits, some of them quite faddish, were launched. As the economy softened in the first decade of the new century, we watched some of the fad benefits go away. This is a good lesson. Everything runs in cycles, so keep in mind that we can and will change benefit plans to respond to changing economic forces and employee values

There are four general opportunities for organizations to reduce benefit costs. They are found in

- Plan design
- Plan administration
- Plan communication
- Plan financing

Before we launch into major changes in the design, administration, or communication of the benefit program it is wise to consider what we are trying to achieve with benefits. Some companies have benefits simply because their competitors have them. Others know precisely why they have a certain mix of programs. It may save a lot of grief later if we can get management to reconsider the rationale for benefits. When we know why we have certain benefits and what we hope to achieve by spending more or less money on one program versus another, we will know where to look for reductions, eliminations, modifications, or enhancements.

Plan Design

Practically speaking, it is very difficult to eliminate a long-standing benefit completely. Union contracts notwithstanding, employees come to expect a benefit as their right after it has been offered for a while. Although it is not impossible to drop a benefit, we usually have to come up with something to replace it or face a morale problem that could cost more in lost productivity than the expense of the benefit. The other side of the issue is what to do when the company is running consistently in the red. There are methods that can directly reduce the cost of a benefit. First, we can introduce employee cost sharing. On medical plans we can increase the employee's share of dependent coverage. We may be able to show employees that to maintain the same level of coverage they will have to contribute a couple of dollars toward their own coverage this year. The Internal Revenue Service has helped in this regard by permitting employees to convert their sharing to pretax dollars. This makes it somewhat more acceptable.

So-called cafeteria approaches have added flexibility to benefit plan design. We can offer choices of two or more types of medical plans. Health maintenance organizations and preferred provider organizations serve the needs of different populations by offering the best ratio of care to cost based on individual need. If your plans are experience-rated, the result should be stabilized or the cost should be lowered.

Wellness plans have been introduced in some organizations, in which employees who do not use the medical benefit can get a refund of some of the cost. These plans come in several variations with differing degrees of success. The main concern with them is that people may not seek healthcare when they should because of the cost. The result could be a severe problem later that might have been avoided if they had sought help in the early stages.

Another way to reduce costs and discourage unnecessary use of benefits is to tie the whole health–vacation–sick leave program together and cost it out to a total that is acceptable. If people use less than that total, they get some form of reward. However, this is a sensitive matter, and a good deal of thought would need to go into the design of such a program.

The bottom line is that there is a strong trend toward individualism in designing plans these days. No longer do you have to have a benefits package that is a mirror image of another organization's package. This calls for a new level of creativity, but it also offers an opportunity to demonstrate effective management of the benefits program.

Plan Administration

Beyond bookkeeping tasks, there are other ways to assess our administration from the standpoint of cost containment. With the periodic changes in accounting and government regulations it is not fruitful to write about the details. The point is that whether we maintain the plan internally or outsource it, we have to be creative in working for the benefit of the employees.

One of the most effective activities you can get involved with is an employer group that lobbies and negotiates down the cost of health care. Hospitals and clinics need to control costs too. If we can find ways to work with them to provide health care at a lower cost to everyone, they are likely to be receptive. They know they cannot continue escalating the cost of medical services. The first edition of this book predicted that "if they [the medical profession] do not find ways to contain expenses, there will be a successful move by Congress to set up a national health plan." In 1994 President Clinton's unsuccessfully attempted to push through a national health care program. There will certainly be periodic attempts by social lobbyists to establish some type of national health plan. If the health care industry, including the American Medical Association, acts in the interest of the public, it will avoid such a plan. When an industry does not take care of its problems, the government comes in, usually with a solution that businesses don't like.

Plan Communication

There are many vehicles for communicating benefits to employees. Through constant communications with employees about their benefits, we can involve them in the program. It becomes something they participate in, not something that is done to them without consideration for their perceived needs or interests. Besides informing them, the communication program should educate them. We can teach employees something about how to deal with health care providers. Some companies hold a "health day." They bring in health care professionals to teach employees how to ask questions and give them the confidence of knowing that they have a right to the answers. We can also train supervisors in some of the rudiments of benefits. By having supervisors answer basic questions on the line, we can save staff time and employee time. Also, the employee-supervisor bond improves and organizational productivity increases. However, this is somewhat risky because supervisors have a lot of other things on their minds and may give the wrong answers. In the worst case someone will take their advice and get hurt.

The intranet has made communications much easier. Everyone who is hooked into the network periodically receives an e-mail message that talks about some aspect of the benefit program. It can be a reminder of open enrollment time, a notice of a change in the plan, a call for feedback, or any other message that needs to be transmitted. There are many ways to communicate benefits beyond the traditional methods.

There is a trend toward health education in many organizations. Physical fitness programs, smoking cessation, first aid, cardiopulmonary resuscitation, nutrition, and stress reduction are now part of the employee health program in many organizations. However, some companies spend time and money on stress-management programs and then send employees back into units where the organizational philosophy and operating practices create unnecessary physical and emotional stress.

Plan Financing

Alternative plan financing offers many opportunities to reduce benefits costs quickly and directly. For decades almost all organizations carried standard full-cost insurance programs for health, disability, worker's compensation, and life coverage for their employees. They paid their premiums and hoped that the rates would not rise too much. In the late 1970s more companies started to experiment with alternative financing arrangements. Minimum-premium contracts, self-insured plans, and outsourcing administration became more widespread. In almost all cases these procedures for funding insurance programs have proved to be money savers. They eliminate pre-funding of reserves for claims. Self-insured plans eliminate state premium taxes as well as the risk and reserve charges of the carrier. In the early years only the larger companies tried these options. More recently organizations of every size have been finding alternatives to the old full-premium approach. The risks of self-insuring can be covered by an inexpensive stop-loss policy that provides coverage for extraordinary claims. Insurance companies have become much more creative in the last decade. They are vulnerable, and they know it. Today we can usually find ways to get the benefits we want at something less than the sticker price.

In many companies the cost of pension plans has become a burden. There are several ways in which burden has been reduced. Here benefits consultants earn their fees by helping management choose among funding methods. Depending on the growth profile of the company, funding alternatives can save a lot of money now and in the future.

There are many ways to manipulate the financing of various plans. New approaches come to the market continuously. Choosing the alternatives that best suit current and future needs can significantly affect the organization's bottom-line profits. With changes in retirement plan funding we have a chance to manipulate the cash flow of the organization. Today there is no question that benefits management is a core issue in organizational profitability.

Summary

Organizations spend a great deal of money on benefits. Management finds itself pulled in two opposing directions. On one side there is a strong push to expand the private sector's involvement in benefits. This probably will happen even more as the federal government finds itself less able to provide services without additional deficit spending. The on-again, off-again driving force for a national health program indicates that some type of plan will pass eventually, although it may be a long time coming. On the opposite side is the drive to control costs to stay competitive in the world market. It is incumbent on benefits managers to be cost-effective directors of the program. Beyond controlling cost there is an even more important issue: showing the top executives how the organization can improve its ROI in benefits. If we change our mental image of benefits from a cost to a return on investment, we probably will find new ways to make benefits worthwhile for the organization as well as the employees.

The real effectiveness of benefits management will not be found in efficiency ratios. Although those ratios help, the important values are found in benefits strategy and macro-level management reports. Top executives need to see benefits data that will help them use a benefit as a lever to attract and retain key employees. The twenty-first century opened to a shortfall of human talent in almost all positions from entry-level jobs. Benefit packages that are flexible and go beyond health and life insurance can give us an edge in recruiting that scarce talent.

PART IV

How to Measure Training and Development Values

Trends

Two phenomena of the latter half of the twentieth century have had a profound effect on training and education: the need for lifelong learning and electronic technology.

Need to Learn

With knowledge becoming the key to economic survival at the personal, organizational, and national levels, continual lifelong learning has become imperative. The accumulation and availability of information have spawned an obsessive drive for change and improvement. It is human nature that when something becomes easy to obtain people want more and more of it. Granted, there are some people who go through life largely comatose. They are not even aware of what we are talking about. We are focusing on people who are trying to learn, grow, advance, and get more out of life.

Computers and the Web

As often happens, a need finds a solution. Computers have been used in education for over 40 years. First they were large mainframes locked in an operations center and accessed through batch processing using punch cards. Later, the desktop dumb terminal and then the personal computer put the power of computation in the hands of the user. Finally, the World Wide web came along and gave everyone the ability to access educational material from anywhere at any time. Now individuals and companies are using the power of the computer and the Internet to fulfill their information and learning needs.

Organizational Training

The growth of the services side of the economy has accelerated the need for information and employee development. Companies and not-for-profit organizations are increasing their investments in both content and delivery mechanisms. This is not a decision brought about by some type of enlightened altruism. The hard fact is that without a workforce that is constantly increasing its knowledge and skills, a company cannot remain competitive. For decades management has believed that employee education and training were a good thing, but the commitment to it waned every time there was a slowdown in business. That is still true, but not as much as in the past. Before wiping out training, management is taking a long look at what effects that might have. Conversely, as executives invest more in training and educational programs, they are beginning to look for some assurance that there is a return on this investment. That is the focus of the next chapter.

e-Learning: Distance and Self-Paced Learning Measures

Each form of human experience has strengths and weaknesses, and learning is no exception. There are many ways to learn. It starts at the mother's breast and continues for most people throughout their lives. People learn from direct experience, from the behavior and words of others, and through contact with media that convey the great works of literature, arts, science, religion, politics, and even athletic activity.

Practical versus Popular

The training and education programs produced and delivered by organizations for the benefit of their employees and customers take many forms and use many media. The argument over classroom versus self-directed versus on-the-job experience is pointless. Each topic has a medium through which it is best encountered. However, it is a truism that distance consumes value. This is a way of saying that the farther the learning experience is from its application, the less it is relevant and retained. As we select and design development programs, we need to keep in mind that in all cases except direct on-the-job exposure, the learning medium should be as close as possible to the skill being taught.

A very expensive developmental fad is survival or outdoor team-building programs. The assumption is that people learn teamwork by building rafts and climbing cliffs together. They probably do, in that environment. It is a lot of fun for the fit but embarrassing and agonizing for the unfit. In either event the vendors of such programs are enjoying a good income. The problem with this approach is that there are no conclusive, consistent data suggesting that these wilderness-based team-building experiences are carried back to the office or plant. Sending people into the wilderness is not a cost-effective way to teach them how to behave in a business environment. It is the classic example of how distance from the application limits the value of the exercise.

If we want to measure results, we must provide skill training in the context of the job. Raft building doesn't have any of the risk factors that corporate performance has. In short, it is fun, but float or sink, the employees still have their jobs when they get back to the company. Building a raft or scaling a tree might show people the inherent value of teamwork, but when they return to the office, a new set of dynamics kicks in. No longer are they playing a game. This is the real thing. Their livelihoods—pay, promotions, position, careers—are on the line every day. When a decision point is surrounded with that set of factors, it is extremely difficult to transfer the lessons from the forest to the office or factory.

e-Based Learning

There is a strong body of evidence showing that adults learn best by doing rather than by listening or watching. Hands-on experience is the way to go, whenever possible. Yet sometimes distance does not allow people to personally experience a skill. In those cases one can turn to the computer for an effective learning medium. The computer is a marvelous teaching tool. Practically any type of material can be converted into a format that can be presented on a computer screen. However, this capability does not mean that all learning is done best with a computer. Every topic has its most effective medium. As Marshall McLuhan[1] pointed out, each medium has an effect on the message. The computer certainly delivers material differently than does a workbook or an audiotape. Computers have the advantage of being able to combine audio and video in a real-time feedback process. Computer simulations, graphic presentations of how to do it, and even simple text can be linked to deliver and test material and to test comprehension.

Once we have chosen the medium we want to employ for the learning experience, we can design and distribute the material in the appropriate forms. Take a self-paced learning experience. People have used books and manuals to learn at their own speed for hundreds of years. Computer courses offer more flexibility and graphics as well as an interactive experience that can go back and forth at the click of a key, asking, answering, and checking. The computer is one of the most efficient measurement mechanisms because as the learner responds to the programmed questions, the computer can record a wide range of information. From the learner's side it can keep track not only of the answers of the learner but also of how the person used the program. How many times did the learner have to recycle before she or he gave the right answer? From this we might decide that the material was too easy or difficult for this person. Perhaps we need to set prerequisites for classes so that the person does not waste time or become frustrated and demotivated by failure. We might learn from studying the learner's responses that the material was not well presented or that the questions were confusing or ambiguous. Electronic technology can be a great teaching medium, but it does not replace direct contact with the topic.

Measuring Training Effects

We could go on exploring the many different ways in which material can be presented and the pros and cons of each method. However, this is not a train-the-trainer manual or a treatise on adult learning theory. The objective here is to discuss how to measure the effects

---

[1] Marshall McLuhan, *Understanding Media*. New York: Signet, 1964.

of any type of organizational training or education. We are not going to focus on the learning process but on the results of that process:

- How well did someone learn?
- How effectively did he or she apply the learning, most importantly from a business standpoint?
- What difference did it make to the business imperatives?

The rest we leave to the training professionals' knowledge of methodology and learning theory. However, it is important to understand that the act of measurement yields more than proficiency scores. Review of the measurements of learning is one of the best ways for trainers to choose the most effective teaching methods. Obviously, if students score well but are not able to apply what they have learned, there is a problem. If they can practice a new skill but there is no improvement in productivity, quality, or service, there is a problem. If the skill improves performance but the improved performance has no effect on organizational initiatives, there is a problem. Measurement is more than an exercise in collecting and reporting data. It has the power to identify problems by type. Once experience with reading the data is gained, we can begin to see how to prevent a repeat performance. Eventually we gain insights from reading the results to find solutions to adjacent, previously unseen problems. For instance, if we are training someone with the purpose of improving that person's level of output, test scores may point out quality as well as productivity problems. This is the reason for measuring from as many angles as possible: cost, timeliness, quantity, quality, and human reaction. Every problem at work is usually definable from more than one of these five perspectives.

Organizationally sponsored training and development is one way people build knowledge and skills and even change attitudes. The theory is for that investment of time and money there should be a return that is greater than the investment. Some firms believe that any type of education is useful, and they are probably right. Learning French cooking may have no direct effect on an employee's job skills. However, the fact that the company sponsored it and the person gained some degree of accomplishment, enjoyment, or self-esteem from it may translate into greater motivation, higher levels of collaboration, and more effective job behavior. It would be very difficult to verify this, but common sense might support the premise.

Methodology

Rather than bore you with repetitious samples of measures, we are going to refer to the formulas and examples in Chapter 12. The key is to measure learning in terms of changes in attitudes, skills, and/or knowledge. Although the teaching medium has an effect on the learning experience, that is not our focus. In this book we are interested primarily in learning how to measure the various outcomes of any teaching method. In that sense the formulas are generic and apply in almost all cases across various teaching media.

Knowledge Management: Linking with Organizational Learning

State of the Art of Knowledge Management

Knowledge management (KM) is a spin-off or outgrowth of the intellectual capital (IC) movement. Launched in the mid-1990s, IC became a synonym for *intangible assets*. Thing's from process mapping to customer relationships to employee skills are forms of IC. As organizations became intrigued by this management nostrum, the demand to make it practical emerged. For many people this is still a problem. They can discuss it only in broad, nonquantitative terms. Others have moved toward KM as a first step in operationalizing IC. As of the turn of the millennium KM had its own set of definitional problems. The prime question is, Can people really manage knowledge? Follow-on issues are, What is the difference between knowledge, wisdom, and information? When does information become knowledge? Can we see it happen or do we have to accept it as a mysterious human process?

Transformation of Organizational Learning

Until the late 1990s learning meant training to most people. However, formal classroom training is useful but has limited value. Studies consistently have shown that people attribute the greatest learning to hands-on projects. Learning by doing is more powerful than learning by listening.

Today organizational learning encompasses all forms of knowledge and skill acquisition. This is why knowledge and learning are colliding. With technological advancement and organizational change coming at revolutionary speed, people need all the tools they can get to keep up. As a result, formal classroom training has been augmented with many forms of distance learning and experiential opportunities. The growth in project teams has made it apparent that a great deal of valuable knowledge is gained in the process of working. Without a method for capturing it and pushing it out to those who can or should use it, we are missing a great opportunity to build a competitive edge.

The Foundation

The basis for any knowledge management and organizational learning (KMOL) program is the corporate culture. Most organizations need to develop a new culture that is driven by trust and sharing. The first requisite for leveraging investments in training and development is a culture that promotes and reinforces the sharing of information. The commitment to this type of culture goes beyond writing new policies and procedures. It is a signal that management is serious about getting everyone at all levels and across all functions to work in new ways.

There is consensus that KMOL only works when there is buy-in at all levels of the organization from the top executives down. There is a natural symbiotic relationship between knowledge and learning. It is the most effective way to transform an organization from the old economy to the new, e-based network. As yet there is a dearth of broad-based quantitative and qualitative evaluation systems. To sustain KMOL it is imperative that there be a demonstrable connection between the investment and a financial return.

CODE

KM can be broken into four steps identified by the acronym CODE, which stands for

> Collect information
> Organize it
> Disseminate it
> Evaluate its utility

Well-designed systems provide better access to content. This reduces query time and increases the accuracy of the output. It allows companies to find the right person quickly.

Information turns to knowledge as a human being acquires it, applies his or her experience base to it, and has the insight to see broad and new uses for it. When it comes to helping people do this we can say we are on the road to creating a KM system. The challenge of measurement is in the final stage, when we look at what people are doing and try to determine what role, if any, the systematic use of knowledge acquisition and application had on the product of their work.

The following are a few examples of the value of codifying and disseminating knowledge:

- Sales associates who can get questions answered quickly, accurately, and completely report that they build credibility with their customers, which leads to increased reliance and less of a tendency to go to competitors as well as increased sales.
- Being able to pull data from multiple sources reduces the time needed to respond to requests for proposals and structure bids. Decreases of 30 percent or more in response time are common. Concurrently, requests for information have been reduced by a factor of 10 (i.e., 20 hours to 2 hours) as a result of direct access to relevant data. This leaves more time for prospecting and sales calls.
- General managers find that their time to respond to escalated problems has dropped by as much as 40 percent because fewer information problems are occurring.

- Companies report increased sales of "new" products as a result of learning and knowledge sharing. New products can be defined as those anywhere from less than 1 year old to less than 5 years old, depending on the industry. Some industries have such benchmark data available through marketing or sales associations.
- Some companies have adopted the Saratoga Institute's Human Capital Value Added (HCVA) metric as a way of tracking their profitability. The HCVA formula is revenue minus operating expense minus pay and benefits (including contingent pay) divided by full-time equivalent employees. It is a profit per employee metric. This feeds into the KMOL system because it cuts out nonhuman investments and shows gain only from investments in employee pay and benefits.

KMOL Practices

Surveys of successful KMOL programs show that communities of practice are the most effective learning process. They yield four types of improvements:

Cost reduction by reducing time away from work to learn
Improved quality through finding errors earlier in the process
Reduced risk and uncertainty by focusing investment in activities with a higher probability of success
Improved technology transfer by sharing insights within the community on how to do something and thus cutting time to learn on one's own

One company reported a return of 20 to 40 times the investment in a community of practice. The actual gain was 400 times the investment. However, assuming that people would have found the answers to their questions and learned through trial and error, the multiple was discounted. The resulting figure can be argued up or down depending on how much one discounts for traditional learning methods. Nevertheless, no matter how much one discounts it, there was clearly an extraordinary return on the investment.

Distance learning consists of more than formal training opportunities in an electronic format. Through KM systems everyone gains the ability to learn what he or she needs to know from wherever and whoever holds the information. This is a form of distance learning that is extremely pragmatic.

As organizations become more team-driven, the sharing of knowledge and skills is essential. The value is found in the outputs of the team. Projects are finished with better results than in the past.

Qualitative Methods

The testimony of employees and customers can be used to evaluate the effects of KMOL. Climate surveys indicate how current employees feel about the knowledge-sharing aspect of the culture. When conducted by a neutral third party, exit interviews also produce reliable information on the culture. In both cases we can set up the methodology to cluster responses into predetermined categories, including collaboration, responsiveness, reliability, empathy, respect, and any number of other factors that relate to the corporate culture. The benefit is the feedback received on the human response to the investment. This is important because it can support and extend the quantitative benefits or offset them. An offsetting example would be an increase in turnover of key personnel who feel that there is insufficient sharing of knowledge. This inhibits their near-term performance and long-term personal growth. In an economy that depends on continual learning for competitiveness, a high turnover of professionals is extremely dangerous.

Expert Advice

Although KM is still in its infancy, there has been significant learning about how to go about it. The following is a synopsis from a number of early experts on how to make it happen.

1. *Understand the existing culture.* What are the attitudes toward sharing knowledge and promoting learning? What is the basic belief about intellectual capital? This is the playing field on which we must engage the organization.

2. *Have a clear vision.* The initial success will depend on our ability to clearly articulate the reasoning and values behind a KMOL system.

3. *Acknowledge the power.* Every organization is an exercise in power. We need to understand where the power lies and what type of politics rules. It is naive to ignore these realities and thus lessen our ability to gain top management support.

4. *Build the team.* Recruit the key power brokers to the team, including senior managers and professionals. These individuals often include lower-level personnel who have a good deal of credibility at the first and second levels.

5. *Make a success.* People gravitate to success. Everyone wants to associate with a winner. Make certain that the first visible project succeeds. This might mean scaling it down to ensure that it will meet or exceed its objective.

6. *Demonstrate value.* From anecdotal testimony to quantitative data, build an evaluation system. Stories are sometimes more powerful than hard data, especially in the early stages in the project.

Stages in Developing a KMOL with Evaluation of Each Stage

Vision

Someone decides that KMOL is necessary and beneficial. This is the selling stage, in which others must be recruited to share the vision. The selling point can be current problems and/or future opportunities. The objective is to convince others that there can be improvements in productivity, quality, or service. Benchmarking within the industry or region can be an effective tool for making the case.

The only measure at this point is whether others can be recruited to the cause.

Strategy

At this point the process for turning the vision into reality takes place. The basic question is, What is the best way to make this happen? One way is to solicit interest in a community of practice. Offering people an opportunity to come together around a common interest is usually appealing. If the community is open and free of bureaucratic encumbrances, people will want to participate. From the community we can begin spreading information through electronic bulletin boards, chat rooms, or other methods that require little funding. As the value becomes visible, requests for funding a pilot project or a communication channel can be made.

As these efforts play out, they usually are evaluated in anecdotal stories. Sometimes limited qualitative or quantitative data begin to surface. The most common outcome is cost reduction. Other data might be time saved or a quality metric such as error elimination.

Expansion

Based on the first limited successes, the effort can be expanded to include larger-scale projects. Now funding is essential. This is a test of management's commitment. Faith is necessary at this point because typically the results of these larger-scale initiatives take longer to appear. When they do, the data can be compared to previous internal performance levels as well as to external benchmarks.

At this point it is necessary to show quantitative returns on investment. Clear reductions in cost, improvements in customer retention, increased sales, and the like, are essential metrics.

Institutionalization

At this point the culture must support sharing. If it does not, the project will not survive. It will be viewed by employees as another management fad. Here top management must be very visible in its support. Funding, as well as personal involvement, is necessary. Some of the most successful programs have senior-level managers acting as instructors and group leaders. As the system matures, measures of knowledge management can be incorporated into managers' performance evaluation.

Measures now are more qualitative. Financial benefits have been proved in the third stage. At this stage climate assessment is appropriate. What do the employees think about the emerging culture? Factors may include the ones listed above in "Qualitative Methods." We can develop a "balanced scorecard" approach that would be composed of a small number of qualitative and quantitative measures (see Figure 11-1). Measurement is less important than it was in previous stages. Management has bought in and is pushing culture change.

IC CAPACITY METRICS

Learning: Hours of training per Headcount
   Percent of staff in company sponsored education
   Invested dollars per Headcount in T & D

K Containment Rate: Percent of Key staff with more
   than X years in position

Organizational Capacity: Average number of years
   of education per employee

Diversity: Percent of exempt positions held by
   members of affected classes

KM MACRO METRICS

HCVA: Revenue - Purchased services per FTE

HCROI: Ratio of Profit to Remuneration per FTE

HEVA: NOPAT - Capital Cost per FTE

HMVA: Market value - Book value per FTE

KM PROCESS METRICS

Innovation: Percent of revenue from new products
   R&D expenditure as percent of sales

Drag: Span of control (employees per supervisor)
   Cost to supervise
   No. employee self-services on intranet
   G&A cost as a percent of sales

Team Effectiveness: Percent of team projects that
   achieve their objectives

Outsource Factor: Percent of G&A services
   outsourced (payroll, maintenance, IT, etc.)

Figure 11-1   Qualitative and Quantitative Measures

Summary

Knowledge management and organizational learning are here to stay. They are the mill that grinds the organization's intellectual capital and turns it into flour. The evolution from manually operated to computer-driven machinery and from a product-dominated to a service-dominated economy has replaced muscle with brains. Well over half of all work now is driven by computer programs. This starts at fast-food registers and flows all the way to space launches. The importance of knowledge, and consequently learning, can only grow exponentially.

To manage any high-growth investment one must be able to gather and understand the data that underlie it. This implies measurement systems and analytic skills. KMOL measures will be developed and applied as a product of the workforce analytic programs that are now being offered to human resources professionals.

Leadership and Management Development: Measuring the Effect

Education versus Training

For people who are interested in measuring the results of development programs there is a single driving question: What is the central purpose? Do we want to educate people, or do we want to train them? Education is the presentation of concepts and information to people for the purpose of imparting knowledge. Although we certainly want to build the learner's knowledge base, training is and should be more of an interactive exercise whose goal is to develop skills and competencies. It is one thing to know; it is something else to be able to do.

In the first edition of this book (1984) it was estimated that about 75 percent of supervisory and management programs were more educational than training-oriented. This has been changing steadily over the last several years. The trend is now more toward skill building than it was through the 1970s. Still, much time is spent dealing with concepts of communication, motivation, leadership, and the like. The student-worker is better informed about these principles of management but can seldom apply them unless there is an experiential phase in the training. Even when programs appear to deal with specifics, they are still presented in an educational manner. A good example is a class in conflict resolution. These programs usually start by covering the research findings, which are the current theoretical basis of the topic. Then they turn to a case study or a game simulation so that the subject can be viewed in some kind of context. It is hoped that this exposure will give the student-worker a thorough understanding that later can be transferred to the workplace.

That method is satisfactory if the objective is to educate someone. However, it is impossible to measure the results of a development effort at a level beyond attitude or knowledge. Since the pressure to make training more practical and to get a return on the investment is growing, it would be suspect to infer that something happened in the workplace as a result of a "training" experience if the program was conducted as described above. We cannot claim to have made someone proficient at something if we have presented only concepts.

Proficient is defined with one word: *skilled*. To become skilled one must have more than knowledge; one needs to apply that information. If we wait for employees to apply learning on the job after the class is over, they have trained themselves; we have educated them. The bottom line is that cause-and-effect relationships cannot be proved in educational programs. In other words, if we educate, we cannot prove that the program was the causal force in a person's new behavior. The danger for the training function is that as business slows, training will be dropped as nonessential.

Skill Building

To build skills we have to start at the beginning. As Bob Mager states, "Before we prepare instruction, before we select procedures or subject matter or material, it is important to be able to state clearly just what we intend the results of that instruction to be."[1] Mager points out that the instructional objective should state the following:

[1] R. F. Mager, *Preparing Instructional Objectives*. Belmont, CA: Fearon Publishers, Inc., 1975, Preface.

1. What we want the learner to be able to do
2. Under what conditions we want the learner to be able to do it
3. How well it must be done

If we do that at the beginning, all design and delivery decisions are made under those criteria. In the end it is relatively easy to test for acquired skills. In addition, it is usually possible to go into the organization to find out whether the skills were used and what impact they had. We'll show how to do this later in this chapter.

Three Basic Measures

When management takes an active interest in training, it usually looks at cost first. Managers want to know how much was spent on training. The second and third questions are, How many people got training? and What did we teach them? Implied in the second question is the assumption that they learned something useful. The fourth and least considered issue is, Did anything happen in the organization as a result of the training? If we design training programs along the lines Mager suggests, we will be able to answer those questions.

The three general measures of training are cost, change, and impact:

- *Cost*: expense per unit of training delivered
- *Change*: gain in skill or knowledge or positive change in attitude by the trainee
- *Impact*: results or outcomes from the trainee's use of new skills, knowledge, or attitudes that are measurable in monetary terms in the organization's productivity, quality, or service results

We will examine each of these measures by using different analytic models to illustrate the many ways in which training and development can be evaluated quantitatively. As always, the issue is not whether it can be done but finding a better way to do it.

Cost

Cost is the easiest variable to measure. As long as accurate accounting is maintained, cost measurement is simple. The easiest calculation is a matter of adding up all expenses and dividing the total by the number of people trained. Expenditure variables vary with the number of direct and indirect costs that are included. Some of the most obvious out-of-pocket direct costs are:

- Consultant fees and outside services
- Training room rental (if off-site) or facilities expense
- Equipment expense or rental
- Supplies and program materials
- Refreshments
- Travel and lodging (trainees and training staff)

Examples of indirect costs would include mostly overhead types of factors such as the following:

- Trainer's salaries and benefits
- Trainee's salaries and benefits
- General overhead costs

Hence, the calculation for cost per trainee (training cost factor) is as follows.

TRAINING COST FACTOR

$$\text{TCF} = \frac{\text{CC} + \text{TR} + \text{S} + \text{RC} + \text{TL} + \text{TS} + \text{PS} + \text{OH}}{\text{PT}}$$

where TCF = cost per trainee
      CC = consultant costs (e.g., $7,000)
      TR = training facility rental (e.g., $500)
       S = supplies, workbooks, paper, and pencils (e.g., $2,500)
      RC = refreshments (e.g., $780)
      TL = travel and lodging for trainees and trainers (e.g., $3,500)
      TS = trainers' salaries and benefits (e.g., $1,500)

PS = participants' salaries and benefits (e.g., $6,800)
OH = training department overhead (e.g., $960)
PT = number of people trained (e.g., 25)

EXAMPLE

TCF

$$= \frac{7,000 + 500 + 2,500 + 780 + 3,500 + 1,500 + 6,800 + 960}{25}$$

$$= \frac{23,540}{25}$$

$$= \$941.60$$

A Training Cost Spreadsheet

If we have an automated training registration and scheduling system, we can capture training costs easily. If we do not, a simple database multilevel program can be structured to capture the related costs. As costs are accumulated, they can be entered into the appropriate cell by line item. Thus, when we are finished with a course, we can look at its costs compared to those of other courses. We can also match the cost against the budget for a planned versus actual review.

A basic training program cost report would include variables such as the following:

- Total training costs
- Total hours of instruction
- Total number of trainees
- Trainee cost
- Training cost per hour

Training cost per hour is a finer and more valuable measure than cost per trainee. The use of hours normalizes or standardizes the denominator across programs with different lengths. The calculation for training cost per hour is shown in the following formula.

TRAINING COST PER HOUR

$$\text{TCH} = \frac{\text{TC}}{\text{TH}}$$

where TCH = trainee cost per hour
      TC = total cost of training (e.g., \$23,540)
      TH = total training hours [e.g., 400 (number trained $\times$ hours of training, e.g., $25 \times 16 = 400$)]

EXAMPLE

$$TCH = \frac{23,540}{400}$$
$$= \$58.85$$

In addition to looking at the raw cost of a program, we can do comparison costing. That can consist of a comparison of training expenditures among various groups. We could check to see the amount of money being spent on exempt versus nonexempt employees. We could look at it across departments, locations, equal employment opportunity categories, job groups, or any other demographic variable. The purpose would be to make sure we are training everyone to the necessary extent.

We can also compare program costs between internal and external sources. Which is the cheaper source will vary depending on several factors. The most common are the following:

1. The scale of the program. Is this a one-off experience, or will we be training hundreds?
2. Is this a common topic or a special topic? Common topics usually can be purchased off the shelf from a training company.
3. Will there be travel involved? Usually it is cheaper to bring a program in-house than it is to send people to it.

All of this is necessary if we want to show management the less costly approach. However, there is more to training than cost. We may not be able to provide the same level of quality if we do it in-house. The staff instructor or the department may not be as expert in the subject as the outside presenter is. That problem is solved if we hire the outside expert as a consultant to conduct the program. However, there are other benefits from outside programs that cannot be matched. The opportunity to associate with people from other companies is often very valuable. A trainee has a chance to pick up knowledge beyond what the trainer offers. Some people are sent away to programs as a reward or to give them a break from work. People even get sent to off-site programs to give their supervisors a break from them. Whatever the reason, off-site training may be the appropriate choice. Networking is an effective training experience in itself. However, if cost is the key consideration, it is always possible to show that it is less expensive to do a program in-house. The main reason is that the fee per student will be lower if we have a group. Also, we won't have to spend as much for nontraining purposes such as travel, lodging, food, and sundry expenses.

Make or Buy

The final cost issue that we will deal with before looking at one of the analytic models is the make or buy decision. The number one cost question underlying training is, Is it cheaper to train employees or to recruit them? We have seen how to calculate employment, turnover, and training expenses. We often find that it costs more to recruit people with certain skills than it does to train the existing staff, especially when there is a shortage of skilled labor. Nevertheless, some managers don't want to wait because they are under the gun. One advantage of training over recruiting is that the current employees are a known quantity. No matter how good the recruits look, they are a question mark. We do not know how new people will fit with the employee group, the organizational philosophy, or the operating style. Training the existing staff is also a deterrent to turnover. We saw earlier that one of the principal reasons people leave is their perception that there is no room for growth or advancement. If we know the relative financial and human costs of the make or buy choice, our information should add value to the decision process.

Input Analysis

An input analysis approach is a systemic method of identifying and comparing the many costs involved in two or more training programs. It does this by breaking down the total training process into its main phases, which are then matrixed with the basic inputs. The matrix is shown in Figure 12-1. Each cell is filled in with the appropriate cost figure, and all phases and inputs are totaled. One matrix is completed for each program under consideration. The final set of matrices is compared for cost differences. This shows which program is most cost-efficient, but it says nothing about which will be most effective.

Whether or not a comparison is desired, every training program should be subjected to an input analysis. Over time we should be able to establish ranges of acceptable costs for various types of programs. They can be measured per trainee hour to normalize costs over programs with different lengths. Programs are the trainer's tool. We should know how much that tool is going to cost and how the cost breakdown looks before we start a program.

Change

Although it is important to know how much is being spent to train, how the money is being used, and who is getting the training, it is more important to know what the result or outcome is. Change can be measured at the individual level in terms of knowledge, skill, or attitude improvement. Comparisons can be made across groups as well.

	Inputs, in Dollars				
	People	**Material**	**Equipment**	**Facilities**	**Total**
Diagnosis					
Design					
Development					
Delivery					
Evaluation					
Total					

Figure 12-1   Training Input Analysis

There are several levels of sophistication in training evaluation. As the degree of sophistication goes up, the value tends to go up with it. Examples of before and after measures, which quantify the results of a training program, are presented in the following four formulas.

KNOWLEDGE CHANGE

$$KC = \frac{KA}{KB}$$

where KC = knowledge change
KA = knowledge level after training
KB = knowledge level before training

This information can be obtained by doing pre- and posttesting. Scores can be obtained before and after each class or before and after the total program. Not only does this demonstrate that people are learning what we want them to learn (i.e., the objectives of the course), test results point out specifically what is not being learned. By reviewing the tests in class, the trainer can reinforce the learning. The next formula produces a similar calculation for skill changes. What it does not indicate is whether the training is affecting the organization.

Precourse tests are used by some organizations to help students learn how much they already know about the topic. This saves people from spending time in a course where very little material that is new to them is presented.

SKILL (BEHAVIOR) CHANGE

$$SC = \frac{SA}{SB}$$

where SC = observable change in skills as a result of training
SA = skill demonstrated after training by work output, critical incidents of interpersonal relations, or other observable phenomena
SB = skill level existing before the training, using the criteria above

Data for this ratio can be gathered through questionnaires, interviews, demonstrations, or observation with trainers, subordinates, peers, or supervisors. The key to obtaining something of value from any measure is being specific in describing the skills or behaviors to be evaluated. We can't put a value on vague explanations, but if we see someone doing something, we can measure and evaluate it.

ATTITUDE CHANGE

$$AC = \frac{AA}{AB}$$

where AC = attitude change
     AA = attitude after training
     AB = attitude before training

If the objective is to go beyond knowledge or skill change to attitude change, the same pre- and posttesting method can be used. In this case, either a standard or a specially designed and validated attitude instrument is used. Since attitudes are particularly vulnerable to influences from the environment, thought should be given to the timing of the posttest. Attitudes immediately after the training may be affected when the trainee reenters the work environment. The change may be either positive or negative, and in either case it will confound the change attributable to the training. A test 6 months after the conclusion of training could indicate how much change has been driven or stifled by the environment.

If we find that the environment does not support the new attitudes, it does not make sense to continue to train. Unless we do posttesting, we will never know what happened. The most poignant example I ever saw of that was an ethnic awareness program that a company ran. In an effort to help everyone deal with an equal opportunity initiative, a large company on the West Coast put all supervisory personnel through a 2-day program dealing with cultural aspects of the various minority groups. It cost the company a lot of money. Through pre- and postsurveying they found that the course had had a negative effect because of the way it was conducted. If they hadn't checked and had carried it further through the employee population, it would have been a terrible waste.

PERFORMANCE CHANGE

$$PC = \frac{PA}{PB}$$

where PC = change in work performance as measured by the organization's performance appraisal system

PA = latest review rating or score from a performance appraisal conducted at least 90 days after the training

PB = performance review score or rating from the performance appraisal conducted before the training

In this case, since performance appraisal scales are usually small (e.g., 1 through 3 to 1 through 5), the difference in a single point may appear dramatic in terms of percentage change. Caution should be exercised in discussing an individual's performance change to avoid overstatement. This measure takes on more meaning when a large number of appraisals are compared and positive results appear consistently.

There may be a halo effect. That is, the supervisor knows the employee went through the training and accordingly expects improved performance. If the supervisor is not careful, something that is not there may be inferred. This is simply a rationalization on the part of the supervisor to fulfill his or her expectations.

Impact

The relationship between change and impact measurement is valuable. Whereas change and cost are two distinctly different variables, change and impact are sequential measures along a continuum. The following two examples may help draw the distinction.

A machine operator, Debra, is taught to run a new lathe. At the end of the program her skill and knowledge can be tested with a performance test. Before the class she could cut 80 units per hour on the old lathe. After the class a test shows that she can cut 100 units per hour. Clearly, the level of skill and knowledge changed in a positive direction: Debra is more efficient as a result of the training. If she goes back to work and consistently averages 100 cuts per hour, the impact of the training is felt in the cost of goods manufactured. Assuming that the reject and scrap rate is the same as it was before, Debra is now 25 percent more productive. That is the amount of change. The component cost of labor as an input to the cutting cost is thus reduced by 25 percent. That is the impact. If we didn't measure on-the-job performance, we would never know if the training was useful. However, there is a confounding force: Debra is running a new machine. How much of the improvement is due to her new skill and how much is due to the new machine? A simple way to determine this is to look at the specs of the old machine versus those of the new machine. If the new machine is not rated at more than 25 percent faster, part of the gain is skill-driven.

A salesperson, Peter, is put through a sales training course. The purpose of the class is to teach salespeople how to close a sale. At the end of class, a test of knowledge of the principles can be given and a simulated sales call can be practiced. If Peter performs according to the model being taught, we can claim a gain in skill and knowledge compared to precourse tests. The record of his subsequent customer calls and sales can be kept. If the ratio of sales to calls goes up or down, that is a change measure. In the up case, a cost-benefit analysis will show that as a result of the training, which cost X dollars, the company is now getting Y dollars of production from Peter. Presumably, Y is higher than X and is also higher than it was before the training. That is the impact. When we convert the difference into money, as shown by the impact, that is value added.

Most measurements of training are relatively simple. Except in running an experimental/control group comparison, we can get along without complex statistics. The key factors are the discipline necessary to make sure all the details are attended to and the accuracy of the data. Cost-benefit analysis is common sense: Add in all the costs and measure them against the payoffs. The benefits may be both quantitative and qualitative. Productivity measurement is a matter of comparing the cost of specific inputs to specific outputs. It is an idea similar to cost-benefit analysis, but it usually is applied to issues that are very specific, narrow in scope, and quantitative in nature.

Some trainers still balk at measuring impact and value, not because they're mean-spirited but because they don't know how. When we try to assess the value of training beyond sales, production, or service outcomes, we find that it isn't easy, but it can be done.

Levels of Evaluation

There are several levels of sophistication in training evaluation. As the degree of sophistication rises, the value tends to increase with it.

The first, most used, and lowest-value method is the *trainee reaction survey*, also called the "smile sheet." The nickname comes from the notion that if the trainer smiles a lot and the trainees have a good time, the trainees will give the program a good evaluation. Self-report data are very weak, yet this continues to be the most commonly used method. The second and slightly more useful method is the knowledge test. This is usually a paper and pencil or sometimes a computer-based quiz that measures how much the trainee knows. It is given after the program, and there is no pretest against which to compare the scores. Therefore, there is no proof that the trainee's knowledge level increased because of the program. The third level measures performance after the program. This is better because we look at the trainee's ability to perform, but there still are no comparative data. The fourth level measures performance before and after the program and includes a follow-up check several months later. This is a strong measure and the first one in which one can infer causal relationships from the training. The fifth level is the same as the fourth except that the control group is compared to the trainee group. The control group is very similar to the trainee group except that it does not get trained. If the trainees' performance improves and the control group's does not, it is reasonable to claim that the training was the primary cause—provided that there were no other identifiable intervening events. This is a time-consuming exercise and is not often done in industry. The final and most important level is the impact on the business. Can we discern a line-of-sight connection between the training and the operational improvement? A method for making this connection is called value analysis (see below).

Intervening Variables

The classic question in training evaluation is, How do we know that training caused the change? A counterquestion might be, How do we know that a salesperson is effective? The answer to both is, We don't know unless we conduct a thorough analysis. In sales it is assumed that when a salesperson brings in an order, he or she must be effective. In fact, sales or purchases depend as much or more on extraneous factors as they do on sales ability. Timing, product quality and price, competitors' actions, the general economy, and a dozen other factors affect sales more than sales ability does. Nevertheless, salespeople are paid on the basis of sales brought in no matter what caused the sales. In that case why do we ask the causation question of trainers? I believe that trainers seldom have good relationships with their customers.

In the cases we've witnessed over the decades, trainers who had established a partnering relationship found that their internal customers had no issue of causation. The trainers had reached a point where they were trusted to deliver. Here is how they can earn that position of trust.

They talk to the supervisors of the prospective trainees and discover what business problem a supervisor is expecting training to fix. If training is the appropriate solution, the trainers involve the customer in the design and planning. Then the program is delivered. After the training is completed, the trainers go back to the source— the supervisor/customer/partner—and ask what happened. The customers know either that nothing other than the training occurred or that something else did. They know that the trainee's process was or wasn't changed. They know if a new incentive pay plan or automation was introduced. If the market or the environment is affecting outcomes, they know. If any major change occurred, they know it and can describe it. Then the trainer and the customer discuss what caused the change. They can estimate the relative effect of training and the other variables. Statistical proof isn't necessary—or possible. Solid face-value evidence almost always does the job.

When we build a partnering relationship, we no longer have to prove our worth. The projects on which we partner become a joint venture. We sink or swim together; we learn together. No reasonable person in business expects to bat a thousand. He or she just wants progress. If you don't know how to partner and develop face-valid evidence of training's effectiveness, read on.

THOUGHT 13   *Effective, credible trainers establish themselves first by building partnerships with their customers and second by delivering solutions to business problems.*

Two Training Evaluation Methods

Throughout the text we have pointed out that effective evaluation can be carried out by using logical models. Training is a good example of that premise. More than any other function, training has control over its own environment. Trainers can close their doors and design their courses to fit the needs of the customer. Once they have the trainees in the classroom, the trainers are the boss. They can set up any reasonable sequence of events and put the trainees through it. With that type of power, it follows that trainers can make very definitive statements about their work, and they can support their claims.

The first example is a straightforward model that the author used when he was running training in a computer company from 1977 to 1982. Although today's environment is fast-moving and changeable, so was the computer business at that time. The second example is the result of an experiment carried out by 26 companies under the Saratoga Institute's direction in 1992 and 1993. It was detailed in *Training* magazine in the summer of 1994.[2] Companies now use this methodology to diagnose business problems, respond as needed, measure and evaluate the effects, and share the data. It can become a part of a knowledge management system.

The first system provides the trainer with the data to carry out an evaluation on the fourth level described earlier in this chapter. When a control group is added to the process, an evaluation on the fifth level is possible.

[2] Jac Fitz-enz. "Yes . . . You Can Weigh Training's Value," *Training*, July 1994.

The initial step is always to determine what the business problem or opportunity is. Training must never take place in a vacuum. After that step, if training is part of the solution, the company can proceed as follows.

1. Set behavioral objectives for the trainees. For each session (module) specify the desired behaviors, the conditions, and the criteria of performance.
2. Design the program to meet the objectives.
3. Collect baseline data from the trainees' department(s). The variables measured must relate to the upcoming training. (To have a fifth-level evaluation, select a control group at this point and collect the same data.)
4. Conduct the training. Give pre- and posttests of skills and knowledge (or attitudes, if appropriate) at each session.
5. Approximately 60 to 90 days after the final session, depending on the type of training and the time needed to show effects, collect data comparable to those in step 3.
6. Compare the step 3 and the step 5 data. This is the before and after course impact evaluation. It indicates whether the class appeared to make a difference. Look for extraneous variables that may have affected the results. (Compare to the control group if there is one.)
7. Approximately 6 months after the last session have the trainees return for a refresher day. Give them a retention test before starting the review. This tests how much they remember 6 months after the event.

If you have carried out all the prescribed steps, you will be surprised at the results of steps 6 and 7. In the 6 years in which this type of training was done in the computer company, the class average for the 6-month retention test was never below 86 percent, and the standard deviations were extremely low. People will learn, they will use, and they will retain.

The most important issue is what difference the training made in the operation of the company. If we partnered with the supervisors of the trainees, we could have them look at before and after production data to uncover differences. This is the ultimate measure of training effectiveness. This is the true return on investment (ROI) of training.

The second method is the value analysis. This process was developed at the Saratoga Institute in a project that included 26 companies from a dozen different industries. The basis for the success of the method is twofold: It was conducted as a partnership with the management personnel who are interested in solving the problem, and it is skill-focused. The process consists of four steps.

Situation Analysis

1. Study the business problem or opportunity looking for its source and the factors and forces driving it.
   a. Is there a productivity, quality, or service shortfall?
   b. What is the current performance level?
   c. How is that performance affecting the company's competitive status in the market?
2. Decide whether training might contribute to the resolution of the problem or the exploitation of the opportunity.
   a. What is the source of the problem?
   b. What looks like the best solution?
   c. Decide on the best solution and act on it.

This step looks simple and familiar. Almost every trainer says that he or she does this. The evidence is overwhelming that they do not do this well or completely. It is this failure to effectively and thoroughly analyze the true problem or opportunity that dooms evaluation. When it is not known what is causing something, it is not possible to plan a solution, deliver it, and draw a connection between the supposed solution and the eventual outcome.

Intervention

3. If training is deemed to be part of the solution, design and deliver it in a skill (not theory) form that is visibly linked with the business problem.
4. Monitor performance on the job (usually through the supervisor of the trainee's unit) after the training. Identify any extraneous variables that may have affected the outcomes.

Impact

5. When the data on performance change are in, did perform-ance change?
   a. If the answer is yes, how much change took place and in which direction, positive or negative?
   b. What drove the change, the training or an extraneous event?
6. Effect or impact can be, and often is, attributed to factors other than training. The supervisor is the authority and can testify to these effects.

Value

7. Calculate the value of the impact in monetary and, if appli-cable, human terms.
   a. What are the internal effects on productivity, quality, or service levels?
   b. What are the external effects on competitive advantage in the marketplace?

It is not necessary to do a statistical analysis of the proportional value of the training intervention versus the extraneous variables. Management is not interested and tends to view such attempts as wasteful and self-serving. If the matter was entered into as a part-nership, that type of analysis is irrelevant because the customer will gladly testify that the training had a substantial positive effect. In some cases training will be the principal and perhaps only visible factor. But whether it is or whether it has to share credit with other actions is not important. If training has a positive effect, everyone involved will be able to see it.

Measures of Management

In about 1977 a nationally recognized training "expert" stood before the audience at a training conference and declared that supervisory and management development programs could not be measured in regard to their effects. He was correct within the context of training as he saw it, but what he was talking about was education, not train-ing. He was referring to theoretical classes on communication, motivation, and leadership. As long as he viewed training as the presentation of principles and concepts, he was 100 percent correct.

But now we know different. We know we have to get off the abstract level and teach managers how to do a number of tasks better. If we do that, we will be able to measure their performance as well as the impact of that performance. We know that management is a concept, an abstraction. No one has ever seen anyone manage, much less lead. Management is not a concrete, observable single act. Concepts cannot be measured because they exist only in the mind. Management per se cannot be measured because measurement requires something to be visible and capable of specificity.

The solution is relatively simple and is to be found in the problem itself. If concepts cannot be measured because they are nonspecific and nonobservable, the answer to the problem is to reduce them to their discrete, observable components. This is the methodology that physical and social scientists have always used. To understand the whole, one starts by learning as much as possible about the parts.

The same approach can be used to understand more precisely what management is. Once we break down the process of management into a manager's many observable acts, the mystique disappears. Therefore, the real question is not, What is management? It is, What do managers do (effectively)? The answer tells us what we can teach and what we can measure.

We can show that managers perform their tasks better after a training program. They interview more efficiently and handle performance reviews and administer salaries with fewer problems. They coach, counsel, and discipline better. However, we must define the term *better*. They can be seen to budget more accurately, write more effectively, and schedule more efficiently. In short, they do the multitude of trainable tasks better.

Helpful and enlightening as that may be, it is only part of the picture. Ultimately, a manager is measured by the results of the department. Results are a reflection of the manager's ability to direct human, financial, and technological resources to achieve the department's objectives. If we can find connections between the tasks a manager performs and the output of the department, we can show that improved task performance relates to departmental results. The connections are these: The tasks are the contexts within which one communicates, motivates, and leads. It is by improving task perform-ance—that is, gaining competency in relevant areas—that we can help managers become better communicators, motivators, and lead-ers. Then we assume that communicating, encouraging, and reward-ing positive behavior and performance define effective managers. This leads to the final step: Effective managers are people who get results through other people. We can infer that the training programs make effective managers if we can show that we have helped them perform their tasks better, and we can demonstrate that if we follow a training system similar to the ones outlined in this chapter.

One broad way to assess the impact of all training and education efforts is through a bench strength measure. This is a percentage of key positions that have at least one person fully skilled and prepared to step into a vacated position above them.

Developing and Measuring Leadership

Leadership is clearly the most popular management topic. In times of transformation leadership is probably the most crucial prerequisite for success. We label it the extreme management game of the mil-lennium.

Yet in today's commercial world there is a dearth of leadership, according to surveys of employees. After thousands of books and articles we are still debating this mystical skill. What makes a leader, and how do we measure that?

We are not focusing here on the nature of leadership in all its models. Fitz-enz treated this topic in his book *The E-Aligned Enter-prise*[3] from the standpoints of inner strengths and interactions with followers. If we are going to talk measurement, we have to put a stake in the ground regarding our beliefs about leadership. I like Peter Koestenbaum's simple model in which leadership is divided into two aspects: authenticity and competence. Koestenbaum defines authenticity as identity, character, and attitude. He defines compe-tence as skills, knowledge, and know-how. The good news is that we

---

[3] Jac Fitz-enz, *The E-Aligned Enterprise*. New York: AMACOM, 2001.

can help people develop on both sides of this dichotomy, and we can measure changes.

Authenticity

Authenticity is not something that can be taught in a classroom. Attitudes can be altered through programs, but deep growth in identity and character requires personal counseling. Executive coaches usually work on competence and surreptitiously nudge the client toward greater authenticity. Because authenticity is so deeply personal, we would not want to attempt any type of formal measurement. The prudent thing to do, if we wanted to test progress at all, would be to reach an agreement with the appropriate top executive on the types of changes we hoped to see in personality. We would assume that if the subject began to shown higher levels of self-esteem (identity); made decisions based on higher-level, more ethical goals (character); and seemed more at peace with the self (attitude), we were making progress.

Competence

Competence is much easier to deal with. It is more visible through the execution of a person's responsibilities. We can see a person exercise a given skill, such as planning and strategizing. We can see knowledge exhibited in the oral and written words of a person. Know-how can be defined in terms of how the person is able to get along with and persuade a variety of people in a variety of conditions. While authenticity is the inner game of leadership, competence is more visible through interaction with others. This visibility is the path we will follow for measurement

Leadership Metrics

As we pointed out in the section on management, to make a concept measurable we have to make it visible. This is done by defining it as a function of a number of visible activities and results. The question is, What do people do that we interpret as examples of leadership?

The answer to this is open. You can make a list of visible behaviors that you say institute leadership. However, it isn't only what someone does that makes her or him a leader; it is the subsequent behavior of the *followers*. Leaders depend on followers; without followers there is no leader. If we are going to measure leadership, we have to look in both directions. When you see someone do something that you accept as an example of leadership behavior, what is it? Would you include some of the following in your list?

- Provides an exciting vision for others to follow
- Outlines a strategy and makes a commitment to it
- Describes a preferred corporate culture
- Acts in accordance with the culture
- Is consistent in word and behavior
- Treats all people with respect
- Gains commitment from the followers
- Acts ethically
- Is decisive
- Is approachable and trustworthy
- Sets challenging expectations
- Is a builder versus a maintainer
- Develops talent

These examples are a reflection of the value system and communicative skills of the leader. Behind each of them is the character of the individual. For measurement purposes we can make a list of 5 to 10 factors like these. Then we can set up a rating scale and score the subject on how she or he measures up to the list. This is highly subjective, but that is necessary since there is no single generally accepted model of leadership. In this case we need to assemble the people who are interested in measuring leadership development and have them generate an acceptable list.

The other side of the leadership issue is the results dimension. When a person exhibits the skills and attitudes on the list, how do people respond? The simplest and most valid way to measure this is through the performance measurement system of the organization. Does the leader move people to achieve the objectives of the business unit she manages or the goals of the enterprise he leads? These measures typically include financial targets, market share, customer relations, and company reputation. Ultimately, if the person is creating an organization that exhibits admirable characteristics and at the same time achieves operational goals, we probably would say that person is a good leader.

In summary, there are two types of measures of leadership. One includes the characteristics and behavior of the individual. These characteristics and behavior are measurable on attitude and value scales. In addition, those factors elicit behavior from the followers, and that too is measurable. The obvious follow-on is the other types of measures, which are the results within the organization the person purports to lead.

Business-Driven Action Learning

One of the most practical learning methods is hands-on experience. For that experience to be useful it should be directly related to the mission and objectives of the organization. Business-driven action learning (BDAL) is described by Yuri Boshyk as "a process and philosophy that can help change a company's strategy, and the behaviour of its people. In its most accomplished form it can provide break-through business results as well as highly rewarding personal and organizational development."[4]

There is ample evidence that two-thirds to three-quarters of an individual's development comes from on-the-job experience. Probably less than 10 percent comes from formal training programs.

BDAL interventions are highly measurable. However, the results are so obvious that the top executives see no need to spend time proving them. The process stems from work originally done in the United Kingdom by Reg Revens over 60 years ago. The most effective applications of BDAL involve five key elements:

1. The active involvement and support of senior executives
2. Work on real business issues and exploration of new strategic opportunities
3. Action research focused on internal and external business experiences

---

[4] Yuri Boshyk, *Business-Driven Action Learning*. New York: St. Martin's Press, 2000, p. xi.

4. Leadership development through teamwork and coaching on real issues
5. Implementation of recommendations and follow-up on the issues and learning that occurred, thus extending the results and ensuring that learning is greater than the standard rate of change

BDAL works because it is a process that incorporates many learning methods, all of which are focused on business problems. These methods include individual learning, consulting methods, benchmarking and best practices, team-based learning, and information technology. The key to success is clarity at the executive level in regard to expectations of business enhancement, plus individual and organizational learning. Thus, implementation of BDAL is both a science and an art.

Measurement of BDAL

By its nature the measurement of BDAL initiatives focuses on both business results and learning. Thus, BDAL answers the age-old question of how one can prove the value of training. While BDAL is not training in the traditional sense, it still answers the question. Although initiatives launched using this process seek to improve standard business processes, they often are aimed at answering questions of a more strategic nature.

First, strategy. Many BDAL programs have leadership development as a central part of the objective. To measure leadership development return to the discussion on leadership above. Beyond personal development, executives may want to know about new market opportunities, competitors' actions, evolving technology, or new process management methods. The goal in these cases is to help them make strategic decisions regarding the future investment of resources. They do not expect to reduce costs or improve service currently as a direct and immediate result of the research. In the course of the research there is an expectation that a good deal of individual learning and some organizational learning are attained. Therefore, measurement is less of an issue because it will be obvious to everyone if the objective of the project or program was achieved.

The only point that is critical is clarity on the front end. Did the sponsor clearly articulate the goal as well as any related process issues and boundaries of the research? Closely related to those types of strategic issues is leadership development.

Second, results. In this case we are more directly focused on improving a business process in the near term. The objective of the project can be to learn ways to improve productivity, quality, or service. Innovation is a subset of those three factors. New methods may help speed new products to market, and this is measurable in terms of revenue from those products. Of course, productivity is measurable in terms of the unit costs of products or services, quality in terms of error or defect rates, and service in terms of customer satisfaction, retention, and share of wallet. All these elements have been addressed directly or indirectly in earlier chapters.

Summary

If we want to measure the effects and value of training at any level, we can. In most cases we can even put a dollar value on the impact. The models described in this chapter prove that no matter what type of training has been applied, from entry-level skills to leadership development, it can be measured and evaluated. The only proviso is that we follow the principles and the steps described here.

Trainers and managers get into trouble when they try to shortcut the systems. We can't jump from a situation analysis to value with any degree of certainty. In short, we're just guessing. To find value we have to follow every step, linking one to the others, until we reach the end of the value trail.

If it were easy to measure training effects, everyone would have been doing it for decades. As a result, training departments and trainers would not be the early victims of every cutback. At the time of this writing, the economy is slumping, layoffs are accelerating, and training is being curtailed or eliminated. It is obvious that most executives still view training as a discretionary activity rather than a task as vital to success as production and sales. When we start to show management exactly how much value a program has contributed, we will never again be viewed as administering a "nice to do" activity.

Career Management: Tracking the Value

Whither Careers?

The central question at the beginning of the twenty-first century is, what does a career mean? Until about 1990 careers were well-defined progressions up the ladder of technology and/or management until one retired. However, starting with the massive layoffs of the last decade of the twentieth century, the psychological contract between worker and company has been shattered. Today there is no such thing as job security. This is the case not because the captains of industry don't like people but because the pace of competition, technology, and market change is so rapid and unpredictable that no one can afford to offer lifetime employment.

This raises the basic question of what the deal will be between companies and employees in the future. There are a number of hypotheses about this. One of the more radical is espoused by Stan David and Chris Meyer in *Future Wealth*[1]. Their idea is that a person is like a portfolio of marketable securities. The individual can trade those securities, (skills and knowledge) for money, position, or what-

---

[1] Stan David and Chrisy Meyer, *Future Wealth*, Harvard Business School Press, Cambridge, MA, 2000.

ever. If that is the case, the individual begins to see herself or himself as something to be actively traded, to be lent to the company where the best return on personal investment can be found. That is a new kind of career model.

Bill Bridges claims that organizations are being "dejobbed."[2] He means that instead of a fixed job model organizations are moving to a "field of work to be done." This has given rise to the contingent worker, who now represents between 12 and 20 percent of the American workforce, depending on whose numbers are used. What is the career track of a contingent worker? If there is one, it is as a member of a temporary staffing company.

Edward M. Marshall pointed out in *Transforming the Way We Work* that downsizing, reengineering, and outsourcing have altered the way companies are structured.[3] Now a more fluid process demands that employees move around the organization to meet the continually changing needs of the business. This changes relationships between supervisor and employee and clearly breaks down the traditional career model.

If these people are correct in their analyses, what does career development mean?

The New Look of Employee Development

Traditionally, employee development was approached as a duality: from the viewpoint of the job or organization and from the viewpoint of the employee. We tried to fit people to the job or the job to people, or we tried to do both simultaneously. Each rationale had its purpose and value. First, we wanted to ensure that the organization's needs were being fulfilled. Second, we hoped to provide an incentive for people to stay by giving them opportunities to learn, grow, and advance.

However, in the last decade career development has been presented with a new challenge. As organizations reduced the number of levels and concurrently moved toward cross-functional and self-directed work teams, the question became, What do we prepare peo-

---

[2] William Bridges, "The End of the Job," *Fortune*, September 1994.
[3] Edward M. Marshall, *Transforming the Way We Work*, New York, AMACOM, 1995.

ple for? The predictable, fixed, multilayered job hierarchy has all but disappeared. It is not likely to return in light of the intensity of global competition and the need to control expenses. Therefore, it is logical to assume that we need new methods or at least new thinking regarding what a career is and how to develop people.

There are three issues for people to consider if they are interested in a long-term career. The first is the need to understand the business processes of the organization. Whether one works for a bank, an airline, a petrochemical company, or a software developer, there are processes by which inputs come into the organization, are employed in the transformation or value-adding stage, and leave the organization bound for the customer. Employees obviously need to learn how to apply themselves in this endeavor. The second developmental requirement is interpersonal skills. As organizations require flexibility and move toward team processes, the ability to interact with peers and others becomes critical. More people fail for interpersonal deficiencies than for lack of technical skills. The third issue focuses on analytic capability. It is a paradox that as information is becoming more readily available, people are not developing analytic skills simultaneously. We are literally drowning in data, yet most of the data are wasted because we have not been trained to understand them. It is true, as Peter Drucker has said, that today's managers don't know what information they need, how to get it, or what to do with it when they have it. We have experienced this with human resources (HR) staffs. They are either not interested, intimidated, or ignorant about the availability or use of data. Effective use of hard and soft data is a competitive advantage that cannot be ignored.

General versus Specific Development

The old attitude that if we knew how to manage one situation we could manage any situation is passé. The world has become too complex. Specific knowledge is becoming more highly prized. Talented people may be able to do several jobs well, but not every job. Practically speaking, all people are somewhat limited by their aptitudes. This leads to the conclusion that the most effective development approach probably combines elements of both the work and the individual.

Experience with organizational training and development over more than 25 years leads me to state that it is more training than development. Professional and managerial training often takes place in a partial vacuum. Much of it is program-driven rather than objective-driven. Many training programs are designed and conducted without a specific long-term goal in view. In short, many programs are isolated educational or skill development efforts that do not have a visible purpose. There is a place for general education and training, but from a priority standpoint there are many more immediate specific needs. The following section will describe a methodology that is logical, specific, measurable in terms of results, and much more efficient than the current standard approach. It is called the targeted method.

The Development Trend

There is a very definite shift toward self-directed and self-paced development. Organizations are moving the responsibility for career development away from the organization and toward the individual. Development professionals are advising employees that they must take an active role in their own career growth. Until about 1985, development was scripted by the organization, and the individual went through the procedure step by step. This used to be refered to as "getting one's ticket punched," meaning that a person had fulfilled the requirements for promotion. This is no longer the case because of the rate of change. Since events are so uncertain and change is so rampant, organizations don't know what to prepare people for. Because of that, there are other paths that should be followed to give people the practical skills and knowledge that most likely will be needed in the future.

The place to start with career development is the creation of a development team. Collaboration is essential in today's complex, fast-changing world. Because employee development is a complex art, several disciplines must play a role. First, a representative of line management must be included from the area we plan on servicing. After all, the development of employees is a manager's job, and the training department is there only to support that effort. Next, we will need representation from HR planning, staffing, and career development. The planners in the organization should have a unique perspective because they are closer to the corporate business plan than is anyone within HR development. Their job is to see that the business plan is translated into an HR department plan. Staffing is involved because normally these are the individuals who have to find the people who will later be developed. Career development people do career counseling and assessment and should handle the job-posting program. Job posting is more effective when it is run as a career development system rather than as an adjunct to employment. Job posting should be used to develop people by moving them into jobs that they are interested in doing and that suit their aptitudes. The last group to be involved in the development team consists of the trainers who will design and deliver, or broker, the training intervention part of the development system. Each function represented on this team brings with it a unique viewpoint and a special set of skills and knowledge. Cumulatively, they should be able to select and design the most effective program in the most efficient manner.

When the team is ready, a target development area is selected. This can be done in many ways, but usually it is done from a functional point of view. For example, suppose it has been decided that the area that most needs development is customer service. To match and develop people for jobs in customer service, it is necessary to do two things. First, the duties, responsibilities, and required skills and knowledge have to be defined. Competencies, not jobs, are the foundation of career development. Jobs change, but competencies are transportable.

Then, a model of effective customer service needs to be developed. There are many methods for doing this, examples of which can be found in career development textbooks. Fundamentally, the model describes the behavior and the results obtained by an effective customer service representative or manager. The data are drawn from records and interviews within the customer service department and from contacts with people who interface with the department, including customers. The result of this two-pronged approach is a clear picture of what we are trying to find and develop in customer service staffs. There are selection methods, such as assessment programs and testing, that will reveal the people who have the best aptitude and potential for being successful in customer service work. These people should be the first to be developed. We are in the business of helping people grow and succeed, and this method offers them an excellent chance to do that. How well they do can be tracked and compared to the results of the traditional hit-and-miss method. The results should show that the resources put to this program generated a favorable return on investment.

Another procedure targets current and foreseeable business problems and opportunities, looking at career development from the outside in. When a training experience that upgrades specific critical skills is developed quickly, quality, productivity, and service issues can be addressed and solved cost-effectively. This puts the company on the front end of the competency curve. If we view the organization from the standpoint of the customer and the competition, we will find many places to apply training-counseling or on-the-job experiences. Given the new or enhanced knowledge or skills, people will perform better. This means the organization gains competitive advantage.

Career Development Measures

One way to measure career development is to view the job-posting system as a career development activity. No matter who runs it, we can still measure the relationship of the job-posting system to the development of employees. As organizations flatten, lateral movement and building a broad range of experiences and skills are one of the best career moves a person can make.

Mechanically, the posting process works the way the staffing process does. We produce applicants, make placements, and spend resources doing that. The first thing we can show management is the volume of applicants and placements handled each month. This type of information lends itself to bar charting. Each month we can present a graphic report representing the number of applicants and the number of placements. A quick visual survey tells the reader something about the trend in workloads as well as the results.

The second issue is the cost per placement. Earlier in the book we showed how to calculate the cost of hire and the cost of replacement from internal sources. Using those two figures, we can demonstrate how much we save the organization on the average every time we fill a job through the internal system. This number could appear on one side of the monthly report. If it is shown as a cumulative cost savings report, management can see the numerical increase each month. These data can be summarized on a quarterly basis, and year-to-year comparisons can be made. If we use common financial-style reporting (i.e., quarterlies with year-to-year comparisons) the documentation will begin to look more like standard business reports. This lends credibility to it and stimulates readership.

The third and probably the most important issue is retention. Applying self-paced learning, job-posting, and other developmental experiences will improve the organization's ability to retain the talent it most needs and wants. Making self-paced training available is an excellent starting point for career growth. When a person is placed through the internal system, he or she should be talked to about how the organization sees this move as a good career step. Even if the person is only trying to escape an unpleasant situation, there is something to be learned from that. At the Saratoga Institute we have conducted exit interviews for dozens of companies for the last 6 years. One thing we have learned is that people leave organizations where there is abundant opportunity simply because no one has talked to them about their careers. Personal attention is one of the most effective methods for generating loyalty. Nothing is more desired than personal attention and a demonstration that the organization cares.

Organizational Shifts

Often employees use job transfers as a way to develop their careers. This is seen especially in departments going through extreme change, such as those involved in technology change. When employees are challenged on the job, they naturally seek to further their careers. A specific metric that shows what percentage of the organization is being promoted versus transferred is the career path ratio.

CAREER PATH RATIO

$$CPR = \frac{P}{P + T} \quad \text{or} \quad CTR = \frac{T}{P + T}$$

where CPR = career promotion ratio
   CTR = career transfer ratio
      P = number of employees receiving a promotion (e.g., 24)
      T = number of employees transferred (e.g., 59)

EXAMPLE

$$CPR = \frac{24}{24 + 59}$$
$$= \frac{24}{83}$$
$$= 29\%$$
$$CTR = \frac{59}{24 + 59}$$
$$= \frac{59}{83}$$
$$= 71\%$$

To further identify movement, this can be measured by functional group, department, and exempt versus nonexempt. Measurement is more than an exercise in collecting and reporting data. It can identify problems by type.

Summary

Career development is about retaining and enhancing skills. Population statistics have alerted us to the continuation of the labor shortage that started in the late 1990s. Despite all the change that has taken place in the last decade, the central issue still is how to develop and retain individual competencies in concert with the needs of the organization. Training is one part of career development and job posting is another, but personal counseling is probably the most important. The purpose is to retain good people and help them grow as far as they can in ways that help the organization achieve its goals.

Over the last decade there have been two significant changes in employee development thinking and systems. One is the move from a job focus to a competence focus. Jobs change rapidly today. Older, rigid systems of jobs and pay no longer work. We need to develop portable skills. However, there is a lot of work to be done in the understanding and development of competencies. The second change has been a shift of responsibility for employee development from the organization to the individual. This is unlikely to change in the foreseeable future.

Although development is a personal matter, risks are increasing and the consequences of errors are more painful, and so there is an increasing need to take a systematic approach. When people from both the line and staff sides are involved, all perspectives and values can be considered. Optimum efficiency and effectiveness can be achieved if all processes work in concert toward a common purpose. Those who argue that things are too uncertain today to plan for anything are showing their ignorance regarding how to cope. We've got to do the job and do it right or we won't be competitive. There is ample evidence that the best companies have a programmatic style. While acknowledging that they don't know what is coming, they attempt to improve the odds that they will have the right answer by working through a well-thought-out system rather than reacting after the fact.

CHAPTER

14

Organization Development: Measuring the Business Outcome

Organization Development: Past and Future

In the early 1980s I wondered if organization development (OD) would evolve from the touchy-feely, humanistic psychology, 1960s–1970s model to a more concrete, business-oriented modus operandi. In the beginning there was no clear definition of the boundaries of the practice. It was spawned by the socio-tech movement made popular by NTL in Bethel, Maine, and by the work at the Tavistock Institute in the United Kingdom. In time it included the whole range of practices from a classroom trainer saying a team exercise was OD to academics developing complex instruments in a vacuum.

With the massive restructurings of the 1990s, OD took on a more practical face. While line management usually leads restructurings, OD is increasingly playing an important supporting role. It is actively partnering, creating, or guiding change management processes. OD practitioners are helping organizations solidify the business strategy, determine the gaps between current conditions and the desired future state, and prioritizing systems, processes, and frameworks that will help close the gaps.

One of the reasons for the change in OD is that many executives are becoming more enlightened about the management of people. Management also is becoming more demanding about the return on its investments. With markets becoming more competitive, managers everywhere have no choice but to become more productive and efficient if they want to survive. OD not only can make a contribution in today's market, it can prove its contribution; that is, it can evaluate its outcomes in quantitative as well as qualitative terms. The issue that has blocked measurement efforts is not the mechanics of mathematics or experimentation but an unwillingness to attempt measurement. To survive in this intensely competitive world OD practitioners have to accept and internalize the fact that they are part of commerce, not an esoteric adjunct function. The good news is that most of them have made that transition.

Organization Development and the Organization

Edgar Schein, one of the fathers of OD, provides a workable definition of an organization:

The rational coordination of the activities of a number of people for the achievement of some common explicit purpose or goal, through division of labor and function, and through a hierarchy of authority and responsibility.[1]

The key words in that definition are *people, activities,* and *achievement.* These variables are all measurable at one level or another. To find out how, it is necessary to look at the organization as a system. The organization is an open system that is characterized by inputs, processes, and outputs. It exists within a larger environment, which is now dominated by the capabilities of the World Wide Web. The organization draws resources from the environment, processes them,

---

[1] Edgar Schein, *Organizational Culture and Leadership,* 2nd ed., Jossey-Bass, San Francisco, 1992.

and returns them in a changed and value-added form. Within itself the organization has smaller systems that act in the same manner. They draw resources from the external environment as well as from other internal subsystems, process them, and pass them on in an improved form. Hence, the idea of the organizational system has the characteristics of interaction and interdependence of elements, plus the goal of creating value-added outputs. To see how this relates to OD work, we must seek a definition of organization development.

There are many descriptions of what OD is, all of which say pretty much the same thing. The late Richard Beckhard offered one that is still comprehensive and appropriate for our time:

> **Organization development is an effort (1) planned, (2) organization-wide, and (3) managed from the top, to (4) increase organization effectiveness and health through (5) planned interventions in the organization's processes, using behavioral science knowledge.[2]**

Note that the goals are to increase organizational effectiveness and health. The issue of health is concerned with individuals' feelings and with interpersonal and group relationships. The assumption here is that with improved individual work-related health, the person will become more effective on the job. This should lead to greater organizational effectiveness and profitability.

In summary, an organization is a collection of people, activities, and objectives. It is characterized by inputs, processes, and outputs that add value. OD is a planned intervention aimed at improving individual and organizational health and effectiveness. There is nothing in those statements that prohibits quantitative as well as qualitative evaluation.

OD's Opportunity

The world has turned in the direction of organization development. Benchmarking, reengineering, and other forms of process improve-

---

[2] Richard Beckhard, *Organization Development: Strategies and Models*, Addison-Wesley, 1969.

ment can use OD skills. Since OD specialists understand the human element of work processes, they are a natural resource for restructuring projects. Reengineering stumbled badly when it failed to recognize that the hardest part of making a redesign effective is dealing with the human element. What is more threatening to an individual than to have someone appear on the scene and state that he or she is going to reengineer the workplace?

Many restructuring projects such as reengineering fail to deal with the impact the project is likely to have on the people involved. They are rationalized behind the cliché, "business need." The fact is that the solution is often suboptimized or lost because of failure to acknowledge the humanity involved. It's hard to make simple process improvements and persuade people to go along with them, and OD can help.

Organization development is grounded in interpersonal dynamics. Teamwork, communication, and conflict resolution are the meat of OD. With their knowledge and skill in human psychology, OD professionals can facilitate a smoother transition. They do not have to worry about measuring their work because the results will be obvious. Unit managers understand process variables because that is what they manage. Changes in production cost, process time, and the quantity and quality of products or services will be monitored to learn how the restructuring has affected performance. All that OD people have to do is stand up and be counted as part of the success or failure.

Why Organization Development Is Not Quantitatively Evaluated

Since measurement is clearly possible, why is it seldom attempted? There are several reasons, and they are very similar to the excuses managers in all functions make for not measuring. First, some feel that since evaluation has not been demanded in the past, why offer it now? The second reason is that many people simply do not know how to measure beyond basic production and financial variables. The third and most difficult obstacle is that many people, OD professionals included, do not want to measure. The idea of measurement, proof, or the very introduction of objective methods into the field went against the value system of the early OD practitioners. They believed that OD should be excused from the rigors of the scientific method. Their position was that this method somehow impedes the process, focuses the effort on irrelevant matters, and makes the whole thing less useful or usable. Some of the people who held this position were close to being fanatics about it. Some of the most well-known OD types were so zealous in their love for OD that they could not bear to speak of it in business terms. These people loved the process so much that they could not accept the constraints and expectations that science and business impose. The irony was that although they sometimes dealt with the most intimate issues in the lives of their clients, they did not want to stop to look at the effects of their work. The few of these types who remain probably will never be persuaded to measure their outcomes.

Most human resources (HR) professionals have reached the point where they no longer ask the business world to accept HR purely for its inherent "goodness." OD also is moving in that direction. The following discussion should provide both sides with enough measurement alternatives that a few suitable ones could be adopted.

Measures of Effectiveness for Organization Development

The objective of the remainder of this chapter is to demonstrate how the effectiveness of both individuals and the organization can be evaluated at points across process and outcome levels. We will show how we can start with several broadly stated factors and find measurement opportunities within subsystems and with specific independent variables.

Before any OD project gets under way the first question must be, Why are we doing this project? Another way of stating this is, What is the problem? A penetrating and truthful answer to this type of question will point out the issue, which may be measurable. If that is too simple or does not yield a satisfactory answer, the framework that follows should reveal it.

The six factors in Figure 14-1 have a time aspect. The time dimension enters the picture when an organization is conceptualized as an element of a larger system (the environment). Over time the organization acquires, processes, and returns resources to the envi-

	Time Period		
	Short Term	**Intermediate**	**Long Term**
Productivity	X		
Quality	X		
Service	X		
Responsiveness		X	
Development		X	
Survival			X

Figure 14-1   Time Elements in Organizational Development

ronment. Accordingly, a time line with three ranges can be constructed. These ranges describe broad periods in an organization's life cycle. They are the *short run*, the *intermediate run*, and the *long run*. Some criteria exist across all time periods; others are primarily period-oriented.

The X's in the figure indicate the time period of primary consideration. Clearly, issues such as productivity, quality, and service are always important. The focus in this case is usually on short-term measures that are continuously moving. Responsiveness and development are intermediate-term signs of organizational health. Even here there are goals and objectives that can be defined, described, and measured. One would hope that top management has at least one strategic imperative that deals with its employees.

Survival is a set of longer-term goals that literally determine the viability of the company. When we think of measurement in terms of processes and results, a warning sign should be posted. We can certainly talk about and sometimes measure process changes such as flexibility, responsiveness, and adaptability if we define them in visible terms. The question is, If the process is now more flexible, responsive, or customer-focused, what difference does this make? How will it affect the base business measures of productivity, quality, and service?

Enterprise Factors

Here is how the basic factors of an enterprise, profit or not for profit, can be viewed, worked on, measured, and evaluated.

Productivity

Productivity is the measurable ability of an organization to generate goods and services in the quantity and at a price the market demands. Examples of production criteria are tons of steel, barrels of beer, dollars of sales, invoices processed, and new accounts opened. These are the dependent variables (outcomes) that can be affected by an OD intervention such as team building, process redesign, or conflict resolution.

The typical question asked is, "How can I relate a small OD effort in one department to the number of tons of steel my mill rolled last month?" The answer is that it depends on the business problem that drew OD in and the value of solving that problem. If it's a production problem, look for tonnage out the door. If it's an administrative process problem, look for the desired result: hiring, paying, billing, training, report generation, accidents, building maintenance, and so on. The following are two simple examples.

If we go out to the rolling mill floor and work with the crew to improve cooperation, team problem solving, or a work process, other things being equal, we can see the effect. More important, our client, the process manager, will see the difference. Remember, this isn't a doctoral dissertation or medical research. We don't have to prove it at the .05 level of statistical significance. As long as the client can see and appreciate it, we are halfway home. Then we can work out a range of value based on increased tonnage or less scrap or faster delivery. The same thinking applies to any tangible outcome.

Moving off the plant floor to the office doesn't change anything except the output. Assume that we are working in accounts receivable, redesigning the workflow. That may not affect the number of tons of steel rolled, but it may affect the cash flow of the company. If helping the accounting staff reformat its receivables processing improves the throughput and error rate of invoices, that should speed up the payment of bills and accelerate the influx of cash.

If we connect our work to the appropriate variable, we will see the result. If we want to affect any output, we have to go to the place where that output takes place. There are many people-based activities in a rolling mill, a semiconductor plant, a warehouse pick-and-pack system, and a customer service department complaint function that OD may be able to improve.

Quality

Quality traditionally is referred to in terms of the number of errors or defects in the end product. Since the advent of the quality movement in the United States in the early 1980s, the term *quality* also is being applied to measuring the cycle time of the process.

A team-building project that shortens invoice processing time may not be as exciting to an OD devotee as one that changes a supervisor's leadership style, but it is a lot easier to track and verify. It probably also has a much better chance of happening and is viewed by line managers as more relevant to their goals. However, if we are able to work with a supervisor to adopt a more effective interpersonal style, it may help improve the efficiency or effectiveness of a work group. If it does, we should be able to establish that fact through interviews and quantify the benefit that ensued by using the workers' examples.

Service

Service is important to two groups: employees and customers. First, we are concerned with employees' feelings. They are important because people are intrinsically important. Feelings are also important because they affect individual productivity and customer service. Obviously, we want the customers to be satisfied with our products and services; without customers we have no business. The key point for OD practitioners is to see people in two ways: as human beings worthy of ethical and uplifting treatment and as instruments of production. OD can help people realize their potential and also must help people produce.

OD can measure the outcomes of its work in several ways. It should affect not only production and service variables but also human issues such as turnover, absence, tardiness, and grievances. It is clear that OD can do many things of value besides making people feel good. Positive attitudes, reduced stress, strong group cohesiveness, and supportive interpersonal relationships can all be related to organizational productivity, quality, and service variables. The key variables are customer retention and share of wallet. The first is like a happiness scale; the second is a financial ratio of customer spending with us compared to the competition.

Timeliness is clearly a service measure. It also applies to quality in terms of cycle time and to productivity in terms of on-time completion or shipment. However, there is a broader aspect of timeliness that is called responsiveness

Responsiveness

As we move from the short run to intermediate outcomes, it becomes more difficult, though not impossible, to find measures. In the case of responsiveness, the truest test is when the company is faced with a need or opportunity and rises to or fails to meet the challenge. OD can do something in this arena, but it is more difficult to show cause-and-effect relationships. The reason for the difficulty is the intervening time. We might conduct a series of very useful team-building sessions that result in improvements in responsiveness or time to market performance criteria. Later we might see that the company can shift strategies much faster than it used to. We may feel that our work had a lot to do with that improved capability, but we can only infer that. The broader the effect is and the longer it takes to occur, the more difficult it is to establish a correlation.

However, this is the same in all disciplines. Only in an extremely small number of cases can a cause-and-effect relationship be proved, and only in the simplest activities. We can say with confidence that we cannot prove anything in business because we are dealing with an open market where influencing factors are seldom known. Managers ignore this reality. They learned it so long ago that they accept it and live with the looseness between the cause and the effect.

Development

It has become fashionable to speak of establishing a "learning organization." Clearly, an organization must invest in itself to enhance its capability for survival. The measures here are not training programs or interventions run but competencies attained and used to achieve positive results. Much of business training is really education, as was pointed out in Chapter 13. It deals with concepts and increases the learner's breadth of knowledge. Knowledge is useful in helping people be more aware and logical, and it can give them more information with which to improve their decision-making abilities. However, skills also have to be developed. OD teaches people skills through simulations or on-the-job experiences such as business-driven action learning (see Chapter 13). These techniques help people learn how to increase their ability to interact, supervise, and be supervised, as well as to produce something.

The types of development activities that are easiest to evaluate are the ones carried out in formal settings. OD can do some of the same type of measurement if it carefully selects some baseline data before beginning its intervention. An OD consultant has some control over the intervention environment. Most interactive change efforts are less structured than a classroom training session. Nevertheless, they are, or should be, directed toward a goal. Either the goal or a subset of the goal will be visible behavior or concrete organizational results, which are usually quantifiable. If the goals are not quantifiable and connected to a business imperative, why would we be working toward them? The point is to make certain that the goal is a visible, quantifiable outcome.

Survival

Only in rare cases is an OD intervention close enough to a survival crisis for a cause-and-effect relationship to be drawn. In rare cases OD becomes involved in mergers and acquisitions after the fact. These are often survival issues since three out of four mergers and acquisitions have proved to be unsuccessful. I have been involved from the inside in four acquisitions, and only one worked out well. Two were total disasters, costing the acquirer a lot of money and wasting management time and energy. One could be considered neutral at best because it did not collapse, but it also did not meet expectations. As a result there was a lost opportunity.

In every case of missed expectations it had nothing to do with technology. In one case it was a culture mismatch. In the other two the acquirer did not understand what it had acquired and how to fit it into the new parent corporation. OD can help in these cases only if it can get the chief executive officer's attention and work on the fundamental issues of culture and fit.

Survival may seem like an extreme term to use, but there is a reason for using it. Because of its intense nature it keeps the issues assigned under it in everyone's consciousness.

Subsystems

Within each of the factors described above there are subsystems. A subsystem has three phases: input, process, and output (I-P-0). As we shift from the broad criteria through the subsystems and to the individual variables, there are an increasing number of opportunities to measure. The intervention and the measure have to be related to each other. This relationship must be established at the beginning for maximum credibility.

Productivity

The inputs to the production process are people, machines, material, energy, and capital, all working together on intermediate or final processes to create outputs.

Traditionally, OD is concerned with the human dynamics during the process stage. Examples of processes and their outputs are as follows:

- Programming: an output that is a software package
- Brewing: an output that is beer
- Filling in a billing form: an output that is an invoice
- Assembling: an output that is a circuit board
- Installing: an output that is telephones, computers, or washing machines
- Cashing checks: an output that is money and customer satisfaction
- Screening applicants: an output that is candidates

Some of these outputs are the end product of a company; some are both the end product of a department and an intermediate product of the company. In the case of service processes there are two basic outputs: the mechanical aspect of the process and the response of the customer in terms of satisfaction. There is a longer-term outcome from all of these outputs: the effect on the ultimate customer, which leads to customer retention or loss.

Quality

Quality is the time it takes to complete a process and the errors or defects in the final product or service. This measurement shows how well the I-P-O subsystem is operating. The variables in the situation have values attached to them and ratios calculated for them. The formulas are self-evident. The cycle time of the process is measurable in terms of anything from milli-seconds to years. Error rates in manufacturing are typically percentages of usable outputs from the process. This sometimes is called the yield rate.

An OD intervention might deal with the behavior of the input variable, people, as they interact in the process and be able to demonstrate that the group's time and error goals were met or exceeded. Surveys and interviews also might uncover data on other inputs that, if acted on, could improve ratios. OD has many faces and many tools. Measurement is possible in many different combinations. Fortunately, a plethora of data is sitting unused in organizations that demonstrates the result and implies the value of any type of work. We know from employee commitment research that the relationship of an employee with coworkers affects not only the quality and quantity of work but also the likelihood of that person staying with the organization.

Service

This subsystem deals principally with the feelings of customers and employees. The inputs are not only people but also the things in the workplace that impinge on the people and to which they must react. The I-P-O model is shown in Figure 14-2.

Clearly, the outputs are measurable. The employee satisfaction arena is a favorite one of the OD staff members, who are committed to making the workplace a more humanistic environment. If they can connect the human issues to improved feelings and attitudes and relate that to improvements in customer service variables, they can easily show the value of their work in business terms.

Responsiveness and development utilize the same I-P-O model, but over a longer time frame. The task for the OD practitioner is to be able to connect the work being done today on the criterion variables of productivity, quality, and satisfaction with the intermediate criteria of responsiveness and development. This is not possible to prove at the .05 level of statistical significance. However, management does not require such proof. A valid, easy to accept inference often can be established.

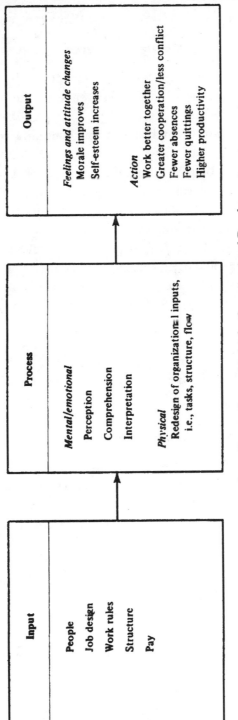

Input

People
Job design
Work rules
Structure
Pay

Process

Mental/emotional

Perception
Comprehension
Interpretation

Physical
Redesign of organizational inputs,
i.e., tasks, structure, flow

Output

Feelings and attitude changes
Morale improves
Self-esteem increases

Action
Work better together
Greater cooperation/less conflict
Fewer absences
Fewer quittings
Higher productivity

Figure 14-2 Input–Process–Output Model for Organizational Development

Change Measures

Each phase in the I-P-0 model has a number of variables that interact to contribute to the health and effectiveness of the individual and the organization. Many of these variables are quantifiable.

Assume that an OD intervention was done in a computer programming department. It could be that there had been conflict, unclear expectations, or other interpersonal issues that were affecting the output of the department. Figure 14-3 shows a number of variables that could be quantified on a before and after basis to measure the change that resulted from the intervention. Two types of changes are measurable. One relates to departmental health issues, and the other relates to productivity, quality, and service.

The list of variables is obviously not all-inclusive. One can think of many more items that could be evaluated. The key is the evaluator's ability to dissect an input, a process, or an output into the many elements that constitute it. If we take the time up front to understand the environment, just as we do when constructing the matrix, we will have no trouble finding variables to measure.

Scorecarding

A scorecard could be developed using the six factors described above plus any "Others" that you want. "Others" could be a set of objectives that stem from a merger or acquisition. For example, time and cost objectives for the integration of systems could be tracked and measured.

There are many ways to design scorecards. Some people use the dashboard approach that Jac Fitz-enz outlined in *The ROI of Human Capital*.[3] Another model is a game scorecard shown in Figure 14-4. It could be filled in with the appropriate tactical measures. It has the advantage of being able to show time dimensions with changes from one period to the next. As a result, the movement or change in performance is easy to see.

[3] Jac Fitz-enz, *The ROI of Human Capital*. New York: AMACOM Books, 2000.

Phase	Productivity/effectiveness	Health
Inputs		
Programmers	Baseline data gathered	
Salaries	before intervention on costs,	
Computers	timeliness, quantity and	
Job descriptions	quality of work, as well as	
	the attitudes and feelings	
	(and maybe interpersonal	
	skills) of the programmers.	
Processes		
Writing code and	Systematic observations and	
documenting	data collection, which lead	
program	the organizational	
Writing user manuals	development consultant to	
Communications	design the intervention that	
	seems most appropriate.	
Outputs		
Programs	Reliability, efficiency, cost,	Fatigue and stress levels
	on-time completion, amount	
	of redesign	
User reactions	Satisfaction with design and	
	capability acceptance without	
	revision	
Documentation	Readability, completeness	
Manuals	Trainees' and operators'	
	acceptance or complaints	
Feelings and		Degree of satisfaction,
interpersonal		stimulation, clarity about job,
behavior		cooperation, accomplishment

Figure 14-3   Variables Affected by Organizational Development Intervention

As an example, consider a basketball game that has a number of time periods similar to business quarters. In this case the number posted in each quarter could be a percentage of change or a percentage of target achieved. We could have any number of intermediate objective measures under each goal. In the right-hand column could be a cumulative annual percentage of achievement or an index number for each of the factors.

Goals Objectives	Quarter 1	Quarter 2	Quarter 3	Quarter 4	Year/Index
Productivity Unit cost On-time shipment					
Quality Rework rate Customer returns					
Service Service contact cost Customer satisfaction					
Responsiveness Time to market Time to fix*					
Development Competency† Bench strength					
Survival On-line and on- budget completion of the acquistion					
Other					

*Time to fix is a measure of how fast we not only respond to the customer but, more important, how fast we solve or "fix" the problem to the customer's satisfaction.

†Competency can be a ratio or percentage of an employee target population that has achieved a defined core competency. A number of these would be going on continuously, as competency development can never stop.

Figure 14-4   Organizational Development Scorecard

Value Chain

The four components of the value chain were introduced previously. The basic notion is that there is a linkage between work processes and monetary value. No one disputes this in sales and production, but when it is brought up in other functions, people are sometimes skeptical. Figure 14-5 shows how the linkage works in a variety of functions.

First, if we make a change in a process, we usually get a different outcome. That is simple cause-and-effect logic. That outcome, when compared to another outcome prior to the process change, is called the impact. The impact is the difference. It answers the question, So what? It is hoped that the change is positive. Usually it can be described as an improvement in quality, productivity, or service resulting in expense control or revenue increase. Once that is apparent, it is a simple matter to put a dollar value on it.

This linkage is the logic core of most business management measures. When we understand the value chain, we can find value in practically any change. All it requires is knowledge of the process and the ultimate values of different types of outcomes. As staff people we may not know that, but if we work closely with our customer-partners, we provide the logic questions, and they provide the answers and values.

Summary

It is clear to the authors, based on 30 years of contact with organizational development, that the issue of measurability once was overwhelmingly one of conflicting personal values. Fortunately, most OD professionals are now in the world of practicality and are more willing to accept responsibility for business results. This does not mean that they have given up trying to make organizations more humanistic. Today, more than at any time in the last 50 years, people are extremely stressed in the workplace. They are desperately seeking meaning in their work and balance in their lives. With the change in attitude within the profession the OD staff is beginning to see how it can serve both the worker and the organization by focusing on desirable business outcomes. Additionally, measuring those outcomes is proving to be a positive experience.

OD is a methodology with great promise. The measures described in this chapter are basically the same ones that all functions seek to improve. Everyone works on some form of productivity, quality, service, or organizational renewal. The renewal issues are also

Process/Practice > > >	> > > Outcome > > >	> > > Impact > > >	> > > Value-Added
Centralize hiring	Lower agency rates	Lower hiring cost	Reduced operating expense
Simplify hiring process	Shortened time to hire	Jobs filled sooner	Less overtime or temps
Improve claims response	EE claims paid faster	Fewer EE follow-up calls	Higher productivity
High quality salary actions	Fewer paycheck errors	Less rework time	Reduced process cost
	Fewer unhappy employees	Greater productivity	Lower product cost
		Better customer service	Fewer lost customers
Upgrade training methods	Increased ROI from training	Better Q-P-S	Lower product/service cost
Survey information interests	Improved EE communication	Higher morale/less turnover	Retention savings
Install succession planning	Fewer emergency hires	Less recruitment expense	Lower operating expense

Figure 14-5   HR Value Chain

aimed at improving P-Q-S. These are the bedrock metrics of organizations. When we improve them, we satisfy customers, increase profits, and increase shareholder value. No matter how fancy we get in describing our processes and goals, we are all working to improve P-Q-S. OD practitioners need only do the following things to demonstrate their value added as it relates to P-Q-S:

1. Establish partnerships with the clients
2. Identify the business issue behind the symptom of human behavior or organizational structure/process
3. Set and communicate clear business goals for solving the problem
4. Use the Value Chain as a logic guide to trace change and find value

PART
V

How to Measure Employee Relations and Retention Programs

ER: Field Leaders

In the last 5 years the value of the employee relations (ER) function has become much more visible. ER has always been the depository for any task that didn't fit neatly somewhere else. If one didn't know what to do with a certain task, often something no one wanted to deal with, it was dumped on employee relations. The attitude was that ER didn't hire, pay, or train people; they also didn't process benefits or negotiate labor contracts and grievances. They were the ultimate "people" people. Over the years surveys showed that about 60 percent of human resources services were provided by the employee relations people. The range of activities covered such dissimilar tasks as new hire orientation, unemployment compensation administration, recreation and social programs, counseling, surveying, employee communications, suggestion systems, and food service management. Overall ER engaged in a lot of invisible activities that make up the human resource infrastructure of the organization. This history has obscured the skills and value added by ER. The diversity of jobs demands a range of skills unequaled by any other function in the organization. It is simultaneously the softest and hardest of all functions. ER is there to counsel and comfort. Conversely, it usually is called on when there is widespread associate unrest, terminations, or other unsavory issues.

ER professionals should take great pride in their work. They can and do make a significant impact on employee satisfaction and productivity, supervisory performance, and talent retention. This group not only supports the corporate culture, it is often the last line of defense that saves the company from embarrassment and worse. Because of ER's scope, it is difficult to know where to start and what to include. It is impractical to attempt the measurement of more than half a dozen different tasks. Clearly, we must be selective. We must pick those activities we believe are the most important and focus on them. We have chosen to look at key activities such as new hire orientation, counseling, absence turnover or retention management, employee surveying, and unemployment compensation administration. Labor relations is usually a separate function. However, rather than create a section devoted solely to labor relations, we have included it with employee relations in this section.

Orientation and Counseling: Measuring Connections and Cost

Getting Started

New hire orientation is an activity that is seldom subjected to measurement. One reason for this is that the objectives of orientation are often not clear. Generally speaking, it is assumed that new employees are oriented to speed their integration into the organization. That is a difficult result to isolate and evaluate. Most managers now realize that the time spent in orientation is worthwhile because it shortens the acclimatization period of the new employee. Today most companies require a new hire to attend some type of formal orientation program shortly after reporting for work. In the hurry-up decades of the 1970s and 1980s that was not universally true.

At Spherion, the Saratoga Institute's parent company, orientation includes a process called Journey to Greatness in which each new employee is given a "passport" for his or her journey. The new employees are required to visit the department heads listed in the passport and have the passport stamped. What makes the process unique and effective is that the passport takes precedence over *everything*. When the new person arrives at the department head's office, that person stops whatever he or she is doing and spends a couple of minutes welcoming the new hire and describing what the department does for the corporation. This goes all the way up to the chief executive officer, whom I have seen stop a transatlantic phone call to talk to a new arrival. What is most interesting is the reaction of the people in Europe who are waiting and hearing part of the passport conversation. Rather than being put off, they express surprise and pleasure at this practice. One can imagine the impression it makes on the new employee.

In most companies new hire orientation is now an act of faith, and thus it is almost impossible to assess its effectiveness. If measurement is desired, cost and impact goals must be specified beforehand. Given a set of desired outcomes, a quiz can be designed to evaluate whether the knowledge goals were achieved.

Most new employees arrive at work the first day in a positive frame of mind, highly motivated to work, and somewhat confused by the new setting. During the first few hours on the job the strange new environment intimidates some. A new hire orientation program is an excellent way to deal with this problem. When employees are put at ease and helped to be mentally alert yet relaxed, they learn faster, make fewer mistakes, and develop on-the-job confidence.

One major electronics company has become known for its secondary orientation that takes place on the job. It goes beyond the general program, which is designed to communicate the information needed by all employees. This departmental orientation covers issues indigenous to the department. Five subjects are discussed:

1. *Jargon.* New hires are taught the company's and the department's language. Every industry and every organization has a language of its own. New employees are often confused and embarrassed and make mistakes because they do not understand the language.
2. *People.* The orientation discusses the kinds of people with whom the new employee must deal. Idiosyncrasies, styles, and personalities are covered so that that person knows what to

expect and can figure out how to work effectively with new coworkers.

3. *Resources.* The new employee is shown where to find the tools and supplies needed to do the job. Information is provided on the administrative procedures that need to be followed to obtain these items.

4. *Problems.* Every organization has problems. This company tells people what kinds of problems they can expect to encounter. It also teaches them acceptable ways to handle the resulting frustrations.

5. *Priorities.* Last, and probably most important, the goals of the work group and the company are explained. The purpose is to let the new employee know where to focus his or her energies in both the short run and the long run.

All this is part of acculturation. Many companies have adopted corporate visions, which they share with the new hire at the time of orientation. This helps the person learn quickly what is expected and accepted, what is celebrated, and what is not allowed.

Orientation Cost

Since orientation is a discrete, identifiable event, it is relatively easy to measure. Cost can be measured at three levels: cost per employee, cost per department, and cost of staff time to orient. The first measure is cost per employee, as shown in the following formula.

ORIENTATION COST FACTOR

$$OCF = \frac{[T \times (R/h \times E)] + DC}{E}$$

where OCF = average cost of orientation

T = time to orient (e.g., 6 hours)

R/h = average hourly rate of pay for attending employees (e.g., $25.75)

E = total number of employees oriented [e.g., 16 (one session)]

DC = human resources department cost (e.g., \$375)

EXAMPLE

$$OCF = \frac{[6 \times (25.75 \times 16)] + 375}{16}$$

$$= \frac{[6 \times 412] + 375}{16}$$

$$= \frac{\$2{,}472 + \$375}{16}$$

$$= \frac{\$2{,}847}{16}$$

$$= \$177.94$$

This basic ratio can be computed either by using the actual hourly rates of each new hire or, more easily, by using an average hourly rate for each job group represented in the orientation. If this task were done on the job by the local supervisor, it would cost more and be less effective. Supervisors and managers do not know corporate policies as well as the employee relations staff does and therefore cannot produce the same quality of information in the same time frame. Orientation cost is part of the cost of turnover. It goes into the indirect cost line on the turnover cost estimator (to be discussed later in this section).

The second cost measure, cost per department, deals with the lost productivity a department suffers when a new hire is in orientation. Since this is a total cost and not a ratio, the calculation, as shown in the following formula, is a straight multiplication problem.

ORIENTATION COST FACTOR BY DEPARTMENT

$$OCF/D = TO \times R/h \times N$$

where OCF/D = orientation cost per department

TO = time spent in orientation (e.g., 6 hours)

R/h = average hourly rate (e.g., \$25.75)

N = number of new hires in orientation from a given department (e.g., 6)

EXAMPLE

$$OCF/D = 6 \times \$25.75 \times 6$$
$$= \$154.50 \times 6$$
$$= \$927.00$$

This formula can be extended to the total organization. If the orientation were taking place within the department, the cost of lost supervisor time would have to be added in. Although at first glance it may seem that a significant amount of wage and salary time is being lost by production to orientation, when the cost of many supervisors' time is added in, it is clear that handling the process in the human resources (HR) department is more efficient. The third cost measure, the cost of the HR staff, as shown in the following formula, makes this clear.

HR DEPARTMENT ORIENTATION COST FACTOR

$$HR/OCF = \frac{T \times R/h}{N}$$

where HR/OCF = HR orientation cost per new hire
$\quad\quad\quad$ T = ER staff time spent preparing and conducting orientation (e.g., 18 hours)
$\quad\quad\quad$ R/h = average hourly rate of employee relations staff, including benefits (e.g., \$32.20)
$\quad\quad\quad$ N = number of new hires oriented (e.g., 16)

EXAMPLE

$$HR/OCF = \frac{18 \times 32.20}{16}$$
$$= \frac{579.60}{16}$$
$$= 36.23$$

Clearly, a manager cannot orient a new hire for anything close to \$36. That is less than one hour's pay for the average manager. The issue of the quality of the orientation does not even have to be discussed when the cost disparity is as great as it is here.

Evaluating the Impact

As in most measurement cases, the result is more important than the cost of an activity. When I was an HR director, I always wanted to know the new hires' reactions to the orientation program. An easy way to learn that is through a simple quiz or on-line survey. A sample of that type of survey is shown in Figure 15-1. These are some of the basic questions to which a recent hire can respond accurately and without fear. By making the name optional, we probably will get the most truthful results. As long as we have a job title or department number, we can trace back any problems that show up.

The most valuable question is one directed to the accuracy of the orientation. There are supervisors and managers in every company who believe that they are the sole authority on everything in their department. If they are administering policy and procedures in a manner contrary to company intent, we want to know about it. There are supervisors who take a new employee under their wing on the first day and say something like, "I know what they told you in orientation, but let me show you how things really work here." If that is going on, we may find out about it through a survey.

Mentoring

Before we discuss counseling, a word about mentoring is appropriate. Mentoring used to be an automatic process. One of the old hands would take the new kid under his wing and help her learn how to operate in that culture. Most people like to be mentors. It makes them feel good to do something to help the new hire.

When the downsizings of the late 1980s and early 1990s became the principal employee relations program, many would-be mentors, such as experienced supervisors and middle managers, were let go. The people who were left no longer had the time, and in some cases the motivation, to help new employees. As time went on and the volatility increased, employee tenure dropped. A recent statistic (2001) revealed that the average 32-year-old has had nine jobs. With this much churning, managers may feel that it is pointless to spend time with a person who won't be around more than a couple of years. The practice of long-term commitment has significantly diminished,

To assist us in evaluating our New Employee Orientation Program, please complete the questions below and return to Personnel. You need not sign your name, but please indicate your job title, department, and the requested dates.

Instructions: Circle the number that best describes your feelings about each statement below. For instance, if you strongly agree with the statement, circle number 6; if you mildly disagree with the statement, circle number 3; etc.

	Strongly disagree	Disagree	Mildly disagree	Mildly agree	Agree	Strongly agree
1. I felt very welcome and at home after my orientation.	1	2	3	4	5	6
2. The information I needed to know on the following subjects was clearly provided:						
(a) Insurance and benefits	1	2	3	4	5	6
(b) Familiarity with the facility	1	2	3	4	5	6
(c) Policies and rules	1	2	3	4	5	6
(d) Affirmative action plan	1	2	3	4	5	6
(e) Safety/security	1	2	3	4	5	6
(f) Forms and records	1	2	3	4	5	6
3. The orientation leader was well informed and answered my questions.	1	2	3	4	5	6
4. What I was told at orientation proved to be accurate in my daily work.	1	2	3	4	5	6
5. I learned in orientation where to find the additional information I might need.	1	2	3	4	5	6

Comments or suggestions: _____

_____

_____

_____   _____
Name (optional)   Job title   Dept. #

_____   _____
Date of orientation   Date questionnaire returned

Figure 15-1   Orientation Survey

and with it the human bonds that were part of the workplace. It is no wonder that employees feel more alienated today.

Organizational stability and effectiveness are built on relationships. No one works alone in a company of any size. Everyone is dependent on the knowledge, skills, and cooperation of others. Collaboration is the hallmark of a competitive information age organization, and mentoring is a key element in a collaborative environment. The effects of mentoring can also be obtained through an employee survey. We can ask people if they have a mentor, how they feel about that relationship, and what they might want to share about their experience. The results are almost always positive. They can be used to encourage management to make mentoring an essential part of the corporate culture.

Counseling: The Early Warning System

Counseling is what happens when people don't have a mentor or another source of support. Counseling of employees can be a continuous process that takes place anywhere at any time. The counseling staff cannot go a day without someone stopping them somewhere for information or advice. No place is sacred, no place secure from the person who needs counseling or wants to lodge a complaint (nor should it be). The counselor has to deal with employees in the office, the hallway, the shop floor, the cafeteria, the parking lot, and sometimes the rest room. We don't realize what a valuable, indispensable role employee relations (ER) people play until we walk down the hall with them and see how often they are stopped or sent an e-mail by an employee with a question or a problem. If the issue, no matter how minor, is not dealt with, the employee is not totally focused on the job. We know from other research that human beings do not use their full capabilities most of the time. Imagine how much productivity is lost if we add personal concerns to standard dysfunctionality.

In effect, the ER staff is like a safety value, always on hand to release some of the pressure that naturally builds up from friction within an organization or problems that employees bring in from outside the workplace. When I was an HR director, I thought of my staff as the lubricant of the company. They helped the parts work together with less friction and heat.

Ad hoc situations such as counseling impede most attempts at measurement. They make data collection a complex problem. The nature of a great deal of counseling rules out the usual forms of effectiveness evaluation. The only practical way to deal with this dynamic, amorphous phenomenon is to start at the beginning.

Since counseling takes place everywhere at any time, data collection is difficult. If counselors counseled only in their offices, it would be relatively easy to keep track of the number, type, and duration of counseling sessions. Since much counseling is unplanned and takes place away from the office, it is believed that precise records cannot be kept. That is true in part. The standard method of record keeping on counseling is to create a simple electronic spreadsheet that has fields for name, department, type of counseling (the topic), time spent, action taken, and whatever else might be desired.

As counselors move about the organization, they may talk with several people on different subjects for different periods of time before returning to their offices. When they return, they may get involved in other duties and forget to log the talks. Therefore, there will always be a margin of error. However, precision is not the issue, and record keeping of counseling sessions is not as difficult as one might think. There is a simple way counselors can log all pertinent data as they go: keep a small pad in their pockets, purses, or briefcases. If they carry a personal digital assistant (PDA), they can set up a log that can be updated as they go. Later they can download the PDA files to a desktop computer. The problem with data collection is not the inconvenience but the fact that the counselors don't like to do it. They like to hug people, not keep records.

When I was an HR director, I used to talk to my ER staff periodically about their chance encounters. I estimated that they were about 95 percent accurate in their recall of sessions. They almost always remembered who they talked to, what departments the employees were from, and what the subject was. They were about 90 percent accurate in recalling the amount of time spent per session. Those people were professionals. Their dedication to the job and interest in maintaining the system were such that they were able to keep very accurate information on counseling. When they knew they needed to remember, they did.

Before we are misled into believing that this is not a problem, let me mention that it took some time for the counselors in my department to reach acceptable levels of precision, although that wasn't because they didn't know how to keep records. In the beginning they openly opposed the idea, and the excuses they used were numerous and highly imaginative. Once I gave them the "or else" option, they fell into line. The turning point came when they began to believe in the value of keeping the data. Shortly after the counselors started turning in their monthly consolidated reports, they saw the benefit to themselves and to the department. They could see how much they had accomplished the previous month. They began to see trends, which we used to head off problems before they became unmanageable. The longer this went on, the more value they found in the reports. As they came to realize the benefit, they sharpened their memories. Within a few months they gave up the belief that the data would be inaccurate. From then on we never worried about the validity and reliability of counseling reports. The key here, as in all other attempts to persuade people to do something, is to lead them to see the benefit in doing it. Reasonable people will respond when they are shown the payoff.

The best way to run a measurement system is to have all those involved collect as much of their own data as possible. At the end of a reporting period the data can be consolidated into a single file, and a collective report can be produced at the click of a computer key. One of the most comprehensive report forms in the system is the employee relations counseling summary shown in Figure 15-2. Basically it is a spreadsheet adapted to this use. The counseling summary contains four categories of information. First, across the top it lists the types of counseling subjects covered. This list is based on experience. If we keep track of counseling by subject matter for a month or two, we will be able to consolidate the data into a manageable number of categories. Down the left side we put in the departments, job groups, levels, or other classifications of employees who used the service. The most common way to do this is to list departments. In a computer-based system we can sort the list by as many categories as we have identified previously. The greater the

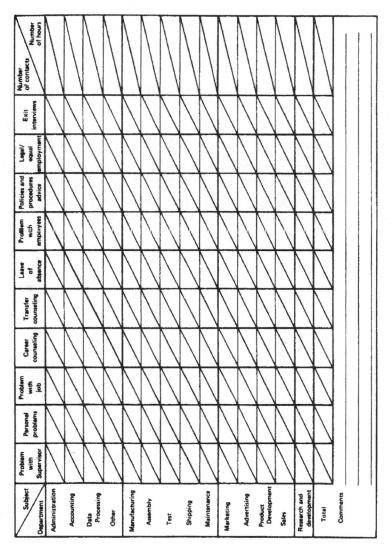

Figure 15-2 *Employee Relations Counseling Summary*

number of sorts, the greater the value of the information. Looking inside the cells, we see that they are divided. The subdivisions are for the number of contacts made per subject and the number of hours spent discussing the subject. The column on the far right is a total contacts and hours summary by classification.

When this report is completed for all counseling conducted during the month, we may find that there are a few blank cells. That is fine. In fact, it is exactly what we are looking for. Because problems tend to run in cycles, from time to time a particular issue is not a question or a problem for some departments. Therefore, we can see problems emerging and disappearing. Overall, the filled-in form has an overwhelming amount of data. Careful analysis will disclose a richness of information that will point the manager directly toward the most pressing issues of the day. Ultimately, the purpose of this data collection is to provide ER with an early-warning system that keeps the company out of trouble. By seeing trends early we can react before there is a major problem.

Analysis Calculations

We can do an eyeball analysis of the data on the summary form and pick up most of the pertinent information. However, if we have the data in an electronic file, we can run a few other computations that will add to our understanding of the employees' mind-set. Experience has shown me that an in-depth analysis of counseling data is a much more accurate display of the state of mind of the employees than is an attitude survey. Attitude surveys suffer from a number of inherent weaknesses. Here are a few:

1. Unless we have norms against which to measure the results, they are of little value. Numbers are relative, which means that we need comparative numbers from repeated surveying. If we survey only every 2 years, the population may have changed by 25 percent or more. The remaining employees may have changed their idea of what is acceptable, and part of the survey population is new.

2. A corollary is that surveys are a snapshot of one day in the life of an employee. Many extraneous issues may influence the responses on the survey day. Something as unrelated as a fight with a spouse that morning can turn an otherwise satisfied employee into a grump.

3. Surveys supplied by outside companies may offer regional or national norms against which to compare our responses. These norms can be useful if we keep in mind that no other company has the same mix of people, products, objectives, philosophy, and style that ours has.

4. Unless the responses have an importance scale built in, it is hard to tell whether it is necessary to respond to a low score. Maybe employees do not like something, and maybe they don't care.

5. All survey methods suffer from weaknesses of validity and reliability because they survey human beings. People change. Some are too frightened or angry to give honest responses.

6. After decades of research that has resulted in a great deal of ambiguity about attitudes, Fishbein and Ajzen tell it like it is:

Unfortunately, despite the vast amount of research and publication on the topic, there is little agreement about what an attitude is, how it is formed or changed, and what role, if any, it plays in influencing or determining behavior.[1]

Survey technology continues to evolve and become more accurate. Nevertheless, until companies are committed enough to hire professionals and support valid research projects, we are better off dealing with what employees do than with what they think. The following formulas provide examples of the several perspectives used to analyze counseling. The first, counselor percent by department, takes each department population into consideration. In effect, it weights the volume of counseling by department size so that each department can be viewed relative to the other departments.

---

[1] M. Fishbein and I. Ajzen, *Belief, Attitude, Intention and Behavior: An Introduction to Theory and Research.* Reading, MA: Addison-Wesley, 1975, Preface, p. v.

COUNSELING PERCENT BY DEPARTMENT

$$CP/D = \frac{SD}{DP}$$

where CP/D = departmental counseling percent
SD = sessions per department (e.g., 50)
DP = department population (e.g., 230)

EXAMPLE

$$CP/D = \frac{50}{230}$$
$$= 22\%$$

This measure allows two types of analysis: How much counseling is taking place relative to other departments? and Is the trend increasing or decreasing overall? It is a volume analysis that acts like a thermometer. It gives a reading of the general level of employee attitudes. It does not segregate sessions by type, as does the next resource, counseling reason percent.

COUNSELING REASON PERCENT BY DEPARTMENT

$$CRP/D = \frac{R}{SD}$$

where CRP = percentage of each topic discussed
R = number of sessions on that reason (e.g., 14)
SD = total sessions for the department (e.g., 60)

EXAMPLE

$$CRP/D = \frac{14}{60}$$
$$= 23\%$$

This measure will reveal the topic or reason for counseling that comes up the most. When tracked from month to month, it will show trends in counseling topics. It can be compared across departments to see whether a topic is a concern for the whole organization or only for isolated departments.

Another issue besides number of contacts is the amount of time being spent by reason and in total. Time is probably the more important issue, since it usually indicates the severity of the concern. We found that the relationship of contacts to time also was interesting to watch. If we look at the average time per reason over several reporting periods, we may find it increasing or decreasing at a significant rate. These early-warning signs are most valuable for an employee relations manager who is trying to be proactive.

COUNSELING TIME BY REASON

$$CT/R = \frac{RT}{N}$$

where CT/R = average time per topic

RT = total session time per topic (e.g., 12 hours)

N = number of sessions per topic (e.g., 14 sessions)

EXAMPLE

$$CT/R = \frac{12}{14}$$
$$= 0.85 \text{ hour (51 minutes)}$$

This formula can be used in the aggregate to measure the average session time for all sessions. This provides an overall feeling of the level of intensity. However, the most useful application is the one just shown.

These measures can be used for classifications other than departments. Electronic technology provides the capability to do multiple sortings of the data. We can apply these measures to levels (exempt and nonexempt), job groups (programmers, technicians, accountants), or equal employment opportunity–1 categories. The more sortings we can compute, the more data we have to manage the problems.

COUNSELING COST FACTOR BY REASON

$$CCF/R = (TT \times ERC) + (TT \times ECC)$$

where CCF/R = counseling cost by reason

TT = total time by reason (e.g., 12 hours)

ERC = average hourly pay rate for ER counselors (e.g., $32.20)

ECC = average hourly pay rate for employees (e.g., $25.75)

EXAMPLE

$$CCF/R = (12 \times \$32.20) + (12 \times \$25.75)$$
$$= \$386.46 + \$309.00$$
$$= \$695.40$$

COUNSELING RATE BY REASON

$$CR/R = \frac{CR}{TCS}$$

where CR/R = counseling rate by reason

CR = number of counseling sessions for reason A (e.g., 24)

TCS = total number of counseling sessions (e.g., 126)

EXAMPLE

$$CR/R = \frac{24}{126}$$
$$= 19\%$$

At the beginning of this section there was a summary table of counseling data that presented a great deal of information. Its only weakness is that it shows only one month's activity. Some other formats also provide a full breakdown and also show more than one month at a time. Bar graphs can provide a multiple-month perspective. Each month you would drop off the oldest month and add in the newest one. Segmented bar graphs offer the advantage of being able to show trends across several topics simultaneously. This type of graph points out increases or decreases in counseling reasons.

The issue of rising counseling rates would lead us to the employee relations staff to ask what is happening. They can check their individual records and usually pinpoint the sources. They may say that the problems are spread across the organization or are confined to a given department or group of people. Once they isolate the source, we can usually do something to fix the problem or find the right person to fix it.

When we solve a problem, we see the results in decreasing rates. For instance, if we hire a large number of new employees and supervisors over a short period of time, we may find them besieging the staff with policy questions. Then it is a simple matter to run a training program for supervisors and watch the volume go down. By calculating the time, and thus the dollars, wasted in one month versus the next, we can show a quick cost-benefit analysis of our training class. Remember, it takes two to talk. The 37.4 hours in October only covers the person with the problem. While employees were off the job talking with the staff, our people were precluded from doing something else productive. Hence, the production time lost was really at least doubled because more than one person may come in on a contact. Time is money, and by multiplying the time by the salary rates of our people and the complainants, we generate the cost of the counseling. Then, when we multiply the decreased rate by the salaries involved, we have the difference that the training made. It is a simple method that will not stun the audience with its impact, but it will show that we are making a contribution and are bottom-line-oriented.

There is one note of caution with any calculation of counseling time. Although we may see counseling employees as serving a useful purpose, some managers view this as wasted time. They see it as an excuse for an employee to take some time off the job and shoot the breeze with our staff. We must assure them that this is worthwhile time and that our staff does not conduct coffee sessions to keep the employees amused. The question is, What is the value of counseling?

We can point out that if our staff were not dealing with issues that the supervisors obviously cannot deal with, the problems would remain unresolved. They might seem to disappear, but actually they go underground if they are not addressed properly. Instead of one employee being off the job talking about a concern and getting professional help, there would be two or more employees off-line, probably making a molehill into a mountain.

It is a great temptation, once the system is up and running, to go to the boss's office and declare how well the system is operating.

Remember that the boss has a different perspective. What we might think of as a vindication of our program, the boss might see as a job that does not necessarily need to get done. The point is to be prepared with evidence that there was some tangible value. Value is a subjective thing. What is valuable in the boss's mind? That is what we want to link our work to.

THOUGHT 14   *Success is defined by value-adding results, not expensive activity.*

The Value Question: Was the Problem Solved?

It is possible to calculate the percentage of counseling effectiveness by dividing the number of satisfactory resolutions by the total number of counseling sessions, but that probably isn't the most useful or relevant statistic. Besides, there may be a problem in reaching agreement on what a satisfactory resolution is. Follow-up cannot be done on many issues because of their sensitive personal nature.

However, some cases are a little more obvious. Very often there is simply a question to be answered. Sometimes we can see that we prevented an unwanted termination. If a conflict has been resolved, that can be shown. When unproductive employees have their concerns taken care of and their productivity goes up, that is a measurable payoff. A rehabilitated alcoholic is an obvious result of professional help. The policy training program mentioned above is a very visible example. There are some instances where we can show unequivocally that counseling paid off. Reductions in turnover and absenteeism and increases in productivity are measurable results.

If we can show that we have had a number of successes, we do not have to quantitatively evaluate everything we did in employee relations. It all comes down to the difference our work makes. What was the problem or purpose behind the counseling? Was it merely general advice? Was it a specific, visible event such as employee or supervisor behavior? Was there unsatisfactory work or a personal issue on which someone wanted counseling? This might be a quality, productivity, service, or interpersonal relations problem. To measure the result of any action, whether improving employee productivity or counseling a confused or troubled person, we have to decide what the purpose is behind the action. If we know that and can put it into visible rather than feeling terms, we can measure it.

In the case of counseling, we may be trying initially to reduce the emotional or psychological stress an individual is feeling. That's fine, but if we want to find some tangible value, we must ask what difference it makes when the person is not stressed. Does that person produce more? Does he or she make fewer errors? Does he or she treat the customers better? These are the productivity, quality, and service improvements that can come from counseling or advising an employee.

THOUGHT 15 *When you are trying to locate value, ask what difference your action or the outcome will make; keep asking until a visible result appears.*

A Quarterly View

Financial reporting is typified by reports of earnings for the most recent quarter versus the same quarter a year earlier. The reason this method is widely used in businesses is that it shows trend. That is what management wants to see: Are we getting better or worse? Management gets paid to manage trend.

This approach can be applied in HR reporting as well. It works just as well with counseling as it does with financial reporting. Figure 15-3 shows a quarter-by-quarter comparison of counseling by topic, giving both the number of contacts and the total time. The example shown would be a year-end review. We want to learn two things from reports: Are things moving in the right direction? and What is the value of the movement? It's nice to see negative issues go away, but what difference does it make in the business?

In quarterly reports we can look for seasonal trends that predict probable occurrences. In the sample, the third quarter appears to be a time when there are fewer problems than there are in other periods. This may mean a slackening of the workload and a time when other types of activities might be planned.

The point of this kind of reporting is that it helps the employee relations manager plan and organize the staff for maximum performance. Good managers plan ahead, but that is hard to do when they have only a hazy notion of what to expect. A detailed knowledge of

	Q1 1992 #/hr	Q1 1993 #/hr	Q2 1992 #/hr	Q2 1993 #/hr	Q3 1992 #/hr	Q3 1993 #/hr	Q4 1992 #/hr	Q4 1993 #/hr
Policies and procedures	186/34	114/46.5	158/48.9	129/39.6	145/36.9	66/17.1	186/37.3	89/31.3
Employee performance problems	179/62	105/53.1	138/48.2	144/61.5	120/40	113/41.1	143/58	135/62.8
Personal problems	68/39.2	186/78.8	192/56.2	84/58.8	81/52.3	72/28.2	114/49	114/61.6
Job performance problems	68/31.2	99/51.6	149/64	63/42	116/43	84/28.4	111/46.1	92/48.5
Salary administration	44/24	0	37/15.1	0	33/14.8	1/0.3	38/17.9	4/2.5
EEO matters	4/1	21/24.9	5/2.6	3/1.5	22/12.9	6/2	10/5.5	4/2.3
Exit interviews	114/44.6	81/32.4	134/56	91/32.1	118/58.6	186/41	122/53	64/29.3
Career opportunities program	17/5.9	284/71.1	33/10.8	258/94.8	15/5.1	217/53.1	21/7.3	136/69.6
Career pathing	26/15.9	42/22.5	18/3.3	15/12	6/2	35/16	14/7	118/55
Management training	0	27/21	0	291/219	0	57/39.4	0	0
Employee training	0	12/12	0	45/72	0	6/3.8	0	13/26.8
Termination procedure	68/11.1	0	58/20.6	0	61/19.2	0	62/16.9	0
Total	758/268	813/406	906/318	1116/633	717/285	764/270	741/290	761/390

Figure 15-3 Counseling Quarterly Report (Headquarters)

what has gone before, along with the direction and strength of the trends, is invaluable in planning for the future.

Summary

Whenever I bring up the topic of measuring the effectiveness of counseling, I am confronted with the question of how one can measure the results of people talking to each other on such a wide variety of topics in so many different settings. The answer is to define what we are trying to measure. What are the people talking about? That is the topic category. How often do they talk about it? How much time is spent on it? Most important, why are they talking to us about it? What is the result they want to achieve? Any or all of these issues can be monitored and measured to one degree or another.

The monitoring system described in this chapter is a great early-warning device. It can tell us about simmering problems that we can jump on before they boil over. The most important issue is, Is there a connection between the topic and an organizational phenomenon such as absence, turnover, productivity decline, quality problems, or something else we can identify? Did our counseling affect that? Chapter 17 will show an example of how counseling affected absenteeism and saved a small company well over $60,000 in a year. In a large organization ER-driven savings often run into the high seven figures. We've seen many cases where the availability of an employee relations professional has obviously affected absence rates, turnover, formal complaints to regulatory agencies, and so on. The before and after records of these types of occurrences are so strikingly different that no one has to prove that an employee relations person made a difference.

The point is to systematically and regularly gather data on the work of the ER staff and then trace connections between ER activities and specific or general outcomes. When we pull all that together and apply our experience and intuition, we will be surprised at how much we will learn and how we will be able to show value added from employee relations work.

Absenteeism and Turnover: Understanding Costs and Reasons

How Absence Correlates with Turnover

Employee absence is a nuisance that if left unattended can become a significant expense. Today it is more difficult to monitor absenteeism because many companies abandoned absence monitoring of professionals and managers some time ago. They also instituted an overall pay-for-time-not-worked system in which they lumped all forms of absence. This includes a set number of holidays, vacation days, and absent or "personal" days.

There are many reasons for an employee to be absent from work, some of which are legitimate. Sickness, family emergencies, and personal business that can be dealt with only during working hours are things for which an employee reasonably takes time off. However, there are other, more capricious sources of absence, many of which can be prevented. Research has shown a correlation between absence and dissatisfaction with pay. It is an employee's way of "getting even." The rationale used is, "He won't pay me what I am worth, so I'll just take a day off and let him give me sick pay instead." Excessive absenteeism is a sign of turnover to come. Other sources of irritation and stress also can cause an absence. Poor supervisory practices most often correlate with turnover, but they also may foster absence. Excessive workloads for a long period of time can cause psychological or physical overload, resulting in an employee taking a couple of days off. In the worst cases high levels of stress can cause permanent problems. However the absence comes about, there are several ways to measure its rate of occurrence and its cost to the organization.

The basic absence rate calculation used in most national surveys follows.

ABSENCE RATE

$$AR = \frac{WDL}{HC \times WD}$$

where AR = absence rate (monthly)
  WDL = worker days lost through absence (e.g., 640)
    HC = average employee headcount (e.g., 1,100)
   WD = number of workdays available per employee per month (e.g., 22)

EXAMPLE

$$AR = \frac{640}{1,100 \times 22}$$
$$= \frac{640}{24,200}$$
$$= 2.6\%$$

As with most ratios, this one can be computed by department to find locations where absence levels are relatively high. It also can be applied to job groups to identify the types of employees who are often absent. For an absence control program to work there are two prerequisites: accurate employee time records and a standard acceptable absence rate.

Knowing the amount of time lost through absence is the starting point. The other issue is the hidden cost of absence. Kuzmits[1] pro-

---

[1] F. E. Kuzmits, "How Much Is Absenteeism Costing Your Organization?" *Personnel Administrator*, June 1979.

vided the basis for a formula that is still usable to measure the costs of absenteeism.

ABSENCE COST FACTOR

$$ACF = \frac{(WH \times EHC) + (MH \times MHC) + Misc}{E}$$

where ACF = absence cost per employee

WH = total work hours lost for all reasons except holidays and vacations (e.g., 39,165)

EHC = total monthly compensation for all staff × 0.35 for cost of employee benefits (e.g., $34.78) ÷ 173.33 (work hours performed)

MH = management hours lost because of employee absence based on sampling to estimate average hours per day spent dealing with problems resulting from absences: production rescheduling, instructing replacements, counseling and disciplining absentees (e.g., half hour per day × 1,200 employees × 6.4 occurrences = 3,840)

MHC = total monthly compensation for all managers × 0.35 for cost of manager benefits (e.g. $43.47) ÷ 173.33 (work hours performed)

Misc = other costs, temporary help, overtime, production losses, downtime, quality problems (e.g., $42,500)

E = total employees (e.g., 1,200)

EXAMPLE

$$ACF = \frac{(39,165 \times \$34.78) + (3,840 \times \$43.47) + \$42,500}{1,200}$$

$$= \frac{\$1,362,158 + \$166,924 + \$42,500}{1,200}$$

$$= \frac{1,571,582}{1,200}$$

$$= \$1,309.65$$

Measuring this quantity brings home to supervisors and managers the fact that absence has a high hidden cost. The peripheral costs of supervisory time, temporary help, poor-quality work, and so on, add significantly to the loss. Manufacturing companies that often experience high absenteeism rates can easily save hundreds of thousands of dollars annually in pay for time not worked.

Still another way of viewing absence is from the standpoint of its effect on workforce utilization. This can be seen in the two-step process that follows.

EFFECT OF ABSENTEEISM ON WORKFORCE UTILIZATION

$$WU = \frac{Nh}{N}$$

where WU = workforce utilization percentage
Nh = nonproductive hours: absence, breaks, downtime, prep time, rework (e.g., 380 hours)
N = work hours available (e.g., 10 employees $\times$ 40 hours $\times$ 4 weeks = 1,600 hours)

EXAMPLE

$$WU = \frac{380}{1,600}$$
$$= 24\% \text{ (utilization} = 76\%)$$

To show the effect of absenteeism, subtract absent hours (e.g., 80) from Nh and recompute.

EXAMPLE

$$WU = \frac{380 - 80}{1,600}$$
$$= \frac{300}{1,600}$$
$$= 19\% \text{ (utilization} = 81\%)$$

Utilization would have been 5 percent higher if no employees had been absent. In today's highly competitive marketplace workforce utilization must be maintained at high levels or jobs will be shipped offshore, where costs are significantly lower.

The effects of absence are insidious because they are often invisible. It is not so much a matter of something going wrong as it is a case of something that should occur not occurring. The missing occurrence is the arrival of a scheduled employee at work. When that does not happen, it sets in motion a chain of other events that negatively affect hard measures such as quality and productivity, softer measures such as customer dissatisfaction, and human stress imposed on other employees by the absence.

Value of Absence Control

Absenteeism also may affect things such as morale for the employees who come to work every day. It can create other types of dissatisfaction among employees in a work group, who may have to take time to indoctrinate temporary employees filling in for those who are frequently absent. By maintaining current data on absence and showing its negative effects, we can cause management to address an issue it would rather ignore. If the managers do that, we will have helped them save the company money and improve morale.

Most surveys have shown that Pareto's law applies to absences; that is, approximately 20 percent of the employees account for 80 percent of the absences. If we divided all absence into three types, we could label them capricious, personal business, and problem. The first category was mentioned before. It covers the days people take off because they are angry with the company or are not motivated to work that day. The first sunny day in spring, the opening of hunting season, and the morning-after blues are examples of no-work motivation. Personal business includes picking up one's grandmother at the airport, taking a child to the doctor, and handling a family legal or financial issue. The last category covers the gut-wrenching business of addiction, mental health, and family relations problems. Special employee assistance programs (EAPs) help employees with these traumatic issues. Absences by reason are very difficult to capture because of the abundance of general paid time off (PTO) policies. Employees no longer are required to indicate why they take days off. However, it is possible to track EAP use and see the connections to absence. These programs can be offered on-site; however, most are managed by external providers.

By computing lost time costs we can find the effects of absenteeism on the company's profit and loss statement. As the problems are solved, we can see the gains attributable to improved attendance, better job performance, and secondary effects on supervisors and fellow employees. We might find that an EAP pays for itself through these types of gains. Equally important, the rehabilitation of a sick employee or the rescue of a troubled family has incalculable value. To maintain employee confidentiality, most external EAP vendors provide summary reports (excluding employee name) that show EAP topics, number of employees seen, and time (which equates to time lost). To show a cost analysis, one simply costs it out by using a standard employee labor rate times the lost time.

Example of Counseling's Impact on Absenteeism

In my experience, counseling has had profound effects on absenteeism. Employees who use counseling services usually have high rates of absence. The counseling topics are largely personal issues: problems with families, substance abuse, financial difficulties, and so on. When absenteeism is tracked, the results usually are seen after professional counseling was applied. Not only does counseling pay off on a two-for-one basis in dollars through reduced absence, it positively affects the lives of the families involved.

In conclusion, absence affects both the hard data issues of productivity and human issues such as morale. Excessively absent workers affect the morale of the employees who come to work every day and can create other types of dissatisfaction among their coworkers.

Clarifying the Concept of Turnover

Movement of employees into and out of organizations, commonly called *turnover*, is one of the more heavily studied organizational phenomena. The U.S. Bureau of Labor Statistics uses the terms *accessions* and *separations* to describe movements across organizational boundaries. Transfers and promotions are not considered part of turnover because they do not involve movement across the membership boundary of an organization. Accessions are generally *new hires*. Separations are subdivided into *quits*, *layoffs*, and *discharges*. Turnover is further typed as *voluntary* and *involuntary*. Quits (resignations) are the normal label for voluntary departures. Examples of involuntary turnover are dismissals (firings), layoffs, retirements, and death. Under normal business conditions voluntary turnover is greater than involuntary. Voluntary turnover is more often studied by management, which wants to reduce it or maintain it at an acceptable level.

The extensive and repeated downsizings that began in the late 1980s and that have continued intermittently in the new century utilize a variety of methods of terminating people. Some are straightforward layoffs. Many also include so-called early retirement programs that have confused the distinctions between voluntary and involuntary. The underlying question is, When is early retirement voluntary and when is it the only real choice? There is no standard answer. The people on site must examine each case, and their determination must rule.

Zero turnover is not desirable for several reasons. First, long-tenured employees generally have higher salaries. This is one of the unspoken aspects of "retirement" programs. Companies trade off years of experience and skill for lower salaries. If all employees stay and the organization grows at a normal rate, most employees eventually will be at or near the top of their pay ranges and total salary expense will be very high. Second, new employees bring new ideas. A number of stagnant organizations have become inbred and are no longer in touch with their constituency. The automobile industry lost touch with its public in the 1960s and allowed foreign car manufacturers to take as much as 50 percent of some U.S. car markets. Labor unions have in some cases failed to develop new leadership from the rank and file. In the 1970s they found that the membership had developed new needs and new values, many of which union leadership was not aware of. Any organization must continually renew itself with fresh ideas from new members. Therefore, a small amount of turnover is healthy.

Rather than focus on the causes of turnover, we will concentrate on methods of analysis. The question, What is the turnover percentage in the organization? is too simplistic. A single number tells little. Even if the number compares favorably with a previous period, it is not very helpful. One number does not indicate who is leaving or for what reasons. As with most variables we have discussed, the data have to be cut into smaller, more discrete clusters to yield an understanding of the phenomena at work.

The two basic calculations from which all subdivisions are made are the accession rate and the separation rate.

ACCESSION RATE

$$AR = \frac{TH}{HC}$$

where AR = accession rate
TH = total hires during the period (e.g., 575)
HC = average headcount employees (e.g., 2,836)

EXAMPLE

$$AR = \frac{575}{2,836}$$
$$= 20\%$$

SEPARATION RATE

$$SR = \frac{TT}{HC}$$

where SR = separation rate
TT = total termination during the period (e.g., 684)
HC = average headcount employees (e.g., 2,836)

EXAMPLE

$$SR = \frac{684}{2,836}$$
$$= 24\%$$

For many years there was little agreement on the employee population figure that should be used. Some practitioners used the beginning of period population and others used the average or end of period population as the divisor. Average headcount has won out and become the standard figure. This factors out most of the effects of heavy hiring or terminating.

Subdividing for Understanding

There is practically no end to the ways in which turnover data can be cut. Basically, turnover can be viewed as follows:

Total Separation Rate

- Separations by equal employment opportunity job groups (managers, professionals, sales, office and clerical, operatives) and by job categories, level, and business unit/location
- Voluntary separations: total or by the categories above
- Involuntary separations: total or by the categories above

Voluntary Separations by Length of Service

- 0 to 1 year
- 1+ to 3 years
- 3+ to 5 years
- 5+ to 10 years
- 10+ years

In addition, separations can be studied by demographic group (age, race, sex, education, salary level, performance level, job classification, and reason for leaving). Subdividing separations by reason for termination provides an indication of organizational problems.

The formulas we use are quite similar. Except for length of service, it is a matter of dividing the number of employees in the group by the average population. One example, length of service or tenure, is computed in the following formulas.

AVERAGE TENURE—CURRENT EMPLOYEES

$$AT/C = \frac{TY/C}{HC}$$

where AT/C = average tenure, current employees

TY/C = total years of employment (e.g., all current employees, 9,764)

HC = average headcount (e.g., 1,200)

EXAMPLE

$$AT/C = \frac{9,764}{1,200}$$

= 8.14 average years of service—current employees

AVERAGE TENURE—SEPARATED EMPLOYEES

$$AT/S = \frac{TY/S}{TS}$$

where AT/S = separation tenure

TY/S = total years of employment (e.g., all separate employees, 374)

TS = total employees separated (e.g., 202)

EXAMPLE

$$AT/S = \frac{374}{202}$$

= 1.85 average years of service—separated employees

A comparison of the two results indicates that most employees who terminate have a short tenure with the organization. Experience indicates that the longer employees stay with the company, the more likely they are to continue to stay. Another way to view this is that most voluntary separations occur during the first 1 or 2 years of employment.

Proactive Retention Management

Very few companies work on retention until the eleventh hour of an employee's tenure. As the example above shows, most employees who leave have a relatively short tenure with the organization. We have observed that there are three points during one's tenure when a person is most likely to leave voluntarily. The first comes between about 18 and 30 months. By that time the person has learned a lot and received some training and a couple of salary increases and promotions. The employee begins to see himself or herself as a prized commodity in the job market. This is also a time when headhunters look for people who may be ready for a move. The second point comes at about 4 to 5 years. Here a person has a pretty good idea of what the organization offers. The employee might have gone to school and gotten a graduate degree or otherwise improved herself or himself. If the employee is young, he or she may have a growing family and a need to make more money. The third and last point comes at about 8 to 9 years. This is now or never time for many people. They can see where they stand in the organization and what their chances are to fulfill their aspirations. When a manager knows these three tenure points, she or he can make it a point to talk to those people. The Saratoga Institute's research on departed employees shows that people leave organizations that have a lot of room for advancement because no one has talked to them about their chances. A manager should work with all employees who aspire to career growth and help them map paths for advancement.

Many years ago I was with a West Coast bank in the training department. In the course of checking turnover patterns by length of service we discovered an abnormally high rate for people with 2 to 3 years of service. By digging into the records of all those who left we discovered that the management trainees from a certain college were leaving shortly after completing their training. Apparently, word had gotten around this school that we had an excellent training program. After finishing their training and getting 6 months or so of branch experience, they went back home, where they wanted to live all along.

Length of service calculations indicate whether the turnover rate for a given population, such as employees with over 5 years of service, is changing. They answer questions such as, Are our older employees leaving at the same rate as we would expect them to? We can calculate the rate for those leaving early in their career or after several years of service, as shown in the following formula.

VOLUNTARY SEPARATION RATE—0 TO 1 YEARS OF SERVICE

$$VS/0\text{--}1 = \frac{S/01}{TS}$$

where VS/0–1 = voluntary separation with 0 to 1 years of service
S/01 = total separation with 0 to 1 years of employment (e.g., 25)
TS = total separations during the period (e.g., 102)

EXAMPLE

$$VS/0\text{--}1 = \frac{25}{102}$$
$$= 24.5\%$$

VOLUNTARY SEPARATION RATE—10+ YEARS OF SERVICE

$$VS/10 + \frac{S/10 +}{TS}$$

where VS/10+ = voluntary separation with 10 or more years of service

   S/10+ = total separation with 10 or more years of employment (e.g., 12)

   TS = total separation during the period (e.g., 102)

EXAMPLE

$$VS/10+ = \frac{12}{102}$$
$$= 11.8\%$$

In this case, 24.5 percent of employees with over 0 to 1 years of service left compared to 11.8 percent for those with 10 or more years. That can be compared with previous experience, and a value judgment can be made.

The measures of voluntary separation by length of service also can be used as part of the recruiter effectiveness composite. Are employees with less than 1 year of employment leaving because of a "bad fit" with the department or job? Did the recruiter do an effective job of hiring a qualified employee? However, since a new hire's survival is out of the hands of the recruiter, this indicator should be used with caution. Quality hires are sometimes lost through subsequent bad management. In fact, other than exceptional outside opportunities or changes in one's personal life, why would an individual voluntarily leave an organization? Supervisor relations, coworker problems, noncompetitive pay or benefits, lack of opportunity, and boring jobs account for most turnover.

Multidimensional Analysis

It is often enlightening as well as practical to look at turnover from several perspectives simultaneously. For example, we could correlate voluntary turnover data by age and level of performance. First we could compute the percentage of turnover for age groups (e.g., 20 to 24, 26 to 29, 30 to 34). Then we could do the same for levels of performance. There are two ways to look at performance, as shown in the following formula.

TURNOVER/PERFORMANCE RELATIONSHIPS

$$PT = \frac{R}{L} \qquad PT = \frac{R}{TR}$$

where PT = percent terminating at each performance level
     R = number rated at each level
     L = total number terminating
    TR = total rated at a given level

EXAMPLES

$$PT = \frac{27}{225} = 12.0\% \text{ or } \frac{27}{79} = 34.2\% \text{ performance level 6}$$

$$\frac{79}{225} = 35.1\% \text{ or } \frac{79}{365} = 21.6\% \text{ performance level 5}$$

$$\frac{63}{225} = 28.0\% \text{ or } \frac{63}{593} = 10.6\% \text{ performance level 4}$$

$$\frac{42}{225} = 18.7\% \text{ or } \frac{42}{53} = 79.2\% \text{ performance level 3}$$

$$\frac{8}{225*} = 3.6\% \text{ or } \frac{8}{10} = 80\% \text{ performance level 2}$$

*Column adds to 219 + 6 who did not get rated.

    In the sample 225 employees terminated voluntarily. Twenty-seven were rated 6, the highest level in their performance. In the total organization 79 were rated 6. Thus, while 12 percent of the terminations came from level 6, 34.2 percent of the organization's highest performers left. An additional measure that can be obtained is the performance level of the average terminee. This can be obtained through a weighted average calculation of the left column. The answer in this sample is 4.27. To correlate age, performance, and turnover we need to have both the age and the performance rating of each terminee.

    When we have the three types of data, we can enter them in an electronic spreadsheet and plot them all on a line chart. In the sample shown in Figure 16-1 we are interested only in high performers who left voluntarily. They are defined here as employees with perform-ance ratings of 5 or 6 on a 6-point scale. Employees with ratings of 1 to 4 are not included.

This example shows an organization with some problems. We can see that turnover is highest from about age 27 to age 38, which is also the age group that has a large percentage of high performers. In addition, as age increases, the percentage who are high per-formers decreases. The age profile shows a very large group in the range of 45 to 54 years. If we put some of these findings together, we can see that there is reason for concern across all three dimen-sions. This is an example of the way in which multidimensional anal-ysis can take us inside the numbers to find correlations that point to otherwise invisible organizational phenomena.

THOUGHT 16   *Understanding relationships among data opens the door to improvement.*

Before we leave this area, more should be said about looking at the reason for leaving. Most organizations collect data at termination

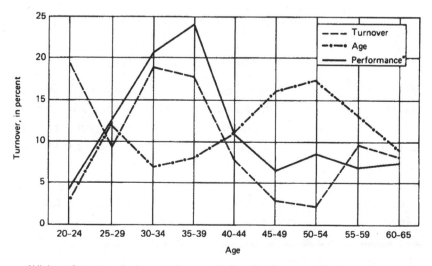

*High performers only: i.e., employees with 5 or 6 ratings on a 6-point scale.

Figure 16-1   Age-Performance-Turnover Relationship

time regarding the reason for the termination. If the data can be considered reliable, the information can be displayed very effectively in a multilevel bar chart. It also can be displayed in a bar chart with an individual bar for each reason. All the other formulas we have looked at indicate who is leaving; this tells us why. Unless we know the why, we cannot do much about the who. After we know why, we can figure out what to do and where to do it. That kind of analysis and action is bound to produce positive results. The critical point is that the data must be reliable. This is why we suggest that a third party conduct exit interviews. That costs more than a do-it-ourselves method, but what value is there in obtaining data that are not reliable? Everyone knows that departing employees seldom tell the employer the true reason for their decision to go.

The Full Hidden Cost of Turnover

Everyone knows that turnover is costly. Just how much it costs depends on what we include. Expenses fall into four basic categories: termination costs; replacement costs, which can include orientation and basic training costs; vacancy costs when no one is there to do the work; and lost productivity or opportunity costs that result from the learning curve of the new employee. Vacancy cost often is ignored because people say that they are saving money while the job is vacant, and besides, other people can pick up the work for a while until a replacement is found. This is partly true. Others can and do pick up the work, and if the job can be divided and parceled out to others with no loss of productivity on their part, there is no reason to refill the job—one should just eliminate it. However, if problems arise from others trying to fill in, the position needs to be filled as quickly as possible. Each case is unique, but as a general rule, when someone leaves, there is a loss of output and that is a loss of value.

It is impossible to calculate exactly what turnover cost amounts to, but it is substantial and it is possible to come up with a very good estimate. If we want to be very accurate we can use a form such as the one shown in Figure 16-2, which lays out all the typical types of costs. To keep the job simple, we can develop standard costs for different categories of jobs. The most formidable issue seems to be calculating lost productivity. We suggest pulling together a group of

Direct Hiring Costs

New Hires

1. Advertising $_____
2. Agency and search fees   _____
3. Internal referral bonuses   _____
4. Applicant expenses   _____
5. Relocation expenses   _____
6. Salary and benefits of staff   _____
7. Staffing office overhead   _____
8. Recruiter's expenses   _____
9. Total direct hiring costs   _____
10. Divide line 9 by number hired. Cost per hire   _____

Indirect Hiring Costs

11. Management time per hire   _____
12. Supervisor/lead time per hire   _____
13. Orientation and training per hire   _____
14. Vacancy cost   _____
15. Learning curve productivity loss or opportunity loss per hire   _____

16. Total indirect hiring costs per hire   _____
17. Total hiring costs per hire   _____
18. Multiply line 17 by number hired. Total hiring costs   _____

Direct Internal Replacement Costs

Replacements

19. Applicant expenses $_____
20. Relocation expenses   _____
21. Salaries and benefits of staff   _____
22. Employment office overhead   _____
23. Total direct replacement costs   _____
24. Divide line 23 by number placed. Direct costs per placement   _____

Indirect Internal Replacement Costs

25. Management/time per hire   _____
26. Supervisor/lead interview time per hire   _____
27. Training time per hire   _____
28. Learning curve productivity loss or opportunity loss per hire   _____
29. Total indirect replacement costs per placement $_____
30. Add lines 24 and 29. Total cost per placement   _____
31. Multiply line 30 by number placed. Total internal replacement costs _____
32. Total turnover costs   _____
33. Target percentage reduction   _____
34. Potential savings $_____

Figure 16-2   Turnover Cost Model

managers from each function for an hour or two. In that time we can reach a consensus on a standard cost by level or type of job. From then on we simply plug those values into an equation and multiply the answer by the number of terminations in that group. This gives us a workable, if not precise, figure for trend analysis and problem identification. Once we have the formula we can drop the costs into the four categories shown in the previous paragraph and use that as a timesaving method for the future.

Unemployment Claims Control

An important but seldom undertaken activity is a review of the un-employment insurance claim process. This is another hidden cost that often is neglected. Since cost control or cost reduction is a major issue in the new millennium, periodically we should take a look at the cost of unemployment claims. In many states, when an applicant's claim for unemployment benefits is denied, this is reflected favorably in the employer's experience rating. Accordingly, it behooves the company to contest all claims from former employees that it believes are unfounded. Often this task is the responsibility of the employee relations group. A simple but effective way to report the results of that cost containment effort is shown in Figure 16-3.

Note that the savings from the two previous years is shown in the upper right corner. This serves two purposes: One is public relations, and the other is motivational. First, assuming that this is a report that is updated monthly or quarterly and distributed outside the department, the report continually reminds the executive reader that we are cognizant of the value of cost containment. Using this reporting philosophy, it does not take long to convince line management that rather than being a cost center we are an integral part of the profit team. Second, keeping past performance visible for the employee relations staff stimulates them to do better. I remember how a determined employee relations manager reacted when I told her that I thought we could save an additional 25 percent in the coming year. I thought it was a formidable goal, one that I would have trouble selling to her. She looked at the report and saw how well she had done for the last 2 years. Then she looked down the savings column for the current year, month by month. For a long

1991 Year-end total							68,835.00
1992 Year-end total							128,227.60

1993	New claims contested	Determinations		Appeals			Potential savings, in dollars
		Won	Lost	Won	Lost	Pending	
Jan	15	3	0	0	0	12	4,873.00
Feb	16	2	5	1	0	21	4,680.00
Mar	15	2	5	0	0	29	4,810.00
Apr	10	1	1	0	0	37	2,912.00
May	20	2	0	0	0	55	4,602.00
Jun	18	12	7	0	1	54	32,162.00
Jul	9	5	1	1	0	57	13,754.00
Aug	16	6	2	1	1	65	17,030.00
Sep	15	6	3	1	0	71	20,020.00
Oct	19	7	6	2	0	77	20,098.00
Nov	10	4	6	0	0	77	9,906.00
Dec	8	10	5	2	0	70	26,314.00
1993 Totals	171	60	41	8	2	70	163,161.00

Figure 16-3   Unemployment Insurance Record

time she sat there, and I could see the wheels turning in her head. Finally, she looked up and said, "We can do it!" She knew from looking at her past performance, exceptional as it was, that she could try new or better techniques and meet the objective. I am convinced that without the past record of success to convince her, she would have been reluctant to commit herself.

One of the great unseen benefits of measurement is motivation. When people see that they can do something and do it well, they are motivated to surpass themselves. There is a cycle to high performance that is based on a person's inherent self-esteem. For people to build and maintain high self-esteem, they must be successful. By starting with reasonable, attainable goals and achieving them, a person feels a sense of increased self-esteem. This motivates him or her to try for a higher goal. If the goal is challenging but possible, the chances are that it will be reached. Success once again increases self-confidence and self-esteem, and the upward spiral continues. Everyone wins: The person grows, the department succeeds, and the organization prospers.

Managing Workers' Compensation

The same principles that were applied to unemployment insurance can be employed in managing workers' compensation claims. In essence each claim is a case to be managed. Although the details are different, the dynamics are similar. We can contest a workers' comp claim. If we win, we chalk it up as an implied saving. For example, if we fight an alleged back injury and show that it wasn't caused by work, we save what the average back injury case costs. Even when there is a legitimate claim, we can manage it to keep the costs to a minimum. Our workers' compensation carrier should be working those cases as a matter of routine service. When we manage a case effectively, we will see the dollar difference it makes.

In all these cases of cost management we can look into the viability of outsourcing them. We might not have the staff to chase down all these items. But if we outsource the work and find we are saving money for the company (after the cost of the outsourcer), it is wise to do it. We suggest running a pilot test for several months with a vendor of outsourcing services. If it is paying off, continue it. If not, find another vendor or bring it inside. When we show managers that we are saving money, we have fewer problems persuading them to give us the resources we need to add even more value. But without data we are left in a begging state.

Summary

Absenteeism, turnover, unemployment, and workers' compensation claims offer the human resources professional an excellent arena in which to exercise analytic and creative skills to obtain visible, quantifiable results. Everyone can appreciate the value of reduced absence and turnover and controlled claim costs. Best of all, from our standpoint, the results are quantifiable: We can show management exactly how we are contributing to the bottom line. In addition, line supervisors universally are annoyed by these lost time and turnover cases. By working closely with them we can show them that we are truly a problem-solving business partner.

The costs of these events are very significant in an era when operating expense is under great pressure. Savings in excess of $1 million a year for large companies are commonplace. Absence and turnover also increase stress for coworkers and supervisors. Somehow the absentee's work must get done, and usually coworkers absorb some of it. Even if they don't, an absence may impede their work.

Ongoing massive layoff programs can skew separation rates by destroying old patterns. Nevertheless, unwanted turnover creates problems and demands attention. Turnover needs to be subdivided into categories for better understanding. Then its cost should be calculated and presented to management. There are many remedies for excessive turnover, but first we need to isolate where and why it is happening. Then we can show the cost to get management's attention and support for attacking the problem.

Unemployment and workers' compensation cases are annoying as well as costly. There is a good payoff for our efforts in managing these issues. Even medium-size companies can save hundreds of thousands of dollars by vigorously managing these phenomena.

Labor Relations

In the 50-plus years since the end of World War II the American labor movement has experienced huge losses of membership in private industry. If it were not for government employees, unions would represent less than 10 percent of American workers. The reason for this is that management finally got smart or less greedy, depending on whose view one subscribes to. Historically, unions came into being to serve a real and important purpose. The early leaders of the industrial revolution generally treated the working man, woman, and child very badly. When it became clear that only a show of unity would transfer some power to the workers, they organized themselves. Eventually, as a result of cruel reactionary tactics on the part of some owners, the federal government stepped in and provided additional protection. In the period between the two world wars union membership grew until approximately 40 percent of the direct labor force in American industry was represented by a union.

After the World War II management began to provide better working conditions, greater safety, and improved health and welfare benefit programs. Whether the motivation was altruism or expediency is debatable. In either case, management began to take some of the force out of the unions' traditional demands. Gradually, the main bargaining tools of unions were co-opted. In addition, social factors such as a better-educated workforce and improved technology made workplaces somewhat safer and cleaner. All this has resulted in a 75 percent reduction in union membership since 1950. The net effect is that unions and management are finding more common ground. In many cases the century-old adversarial relationship is softening. Despite this general trend, unions are still a factor in some industries, and so labor relations staffs are not about to be out of work.

Measuring Effectiveness

The effort of the labor relations staff doesn't lend itself readily to ratios and formulas. That work can be viewed in two ways: a confirmation of "system" maintenance such as the benefits of keeping in touch with employees and union officials and "project" or situational responses such as grievance handling and contract negotiations.

The first case involves what might be described as preventive maintenance. Keeping the system clean and well-oiled (with friction at a minimum) means there will be few breakdowns. When employees feel they are being treated fairly and are being listened and responded to, there is no need to file a grievance. Thus, it makes sense for labor relations specialists to work with first-line supervisors, foremen, and leads to avoid problems. In the second case any analysis of legitimate grievances often shows they could have been prevented through astute handling when they first appeared as irritations. It takes a lot less time, money, and effort to keep problems from occurring than it does to deal with arbitration or a strike. Therefore, evaluation of labor relations work follows a combination path of prevention, resolution, and negotiation, not necessarily in that order.

Level I: Prevention

The first level to look at is the incidence of problems or grievances. What is the rate of questions, problems, and grievances occurring during this period versus the last? One must differentiate between a question, a problem, and a grievance. What is the topic in each case? How often does each topic come up? In which business unit is it occurring? Tracking frequency by topic and unit indicates how successful the preventive maintenance program is. If the system is running comparatively smoothly, the rate of occurrence will be low. If the rate rises in one unit or on one topic, that is a sign that more maintenance is called for.

The next question is, How do we put a value on low occurrence or incident rates? This is the same question asked of any preventive program. Safety, security, and employee relations are faced with the same question. The answer is simple. What is the cost of a typical incident? On average, how many resources does an incident take? Resources are time, money, and possibly equipment and materials. In the case of safety there is lost time and sometimes material and equipment losses, not to mention possibly serious injuries. In security breaches there is time and possibly facility damage and material losses. In labor relations what happens when a question, problem, or grievance occurs? At the least, time is spent on it, and there may be direct costs as well. One must play through several scenarios and see what truly happens. Then we can attach an average cost to each type of issue. Thus, the answer is twofold. First, we trace the number of incidents in this period versus the average period. If we are starting from scratch, we have to wait a few months until we have at least a couple of quarters behind us. Second, what is the typical or average cost per incident? This is like the standard cost in any other type of evaluation. The value of work can then be calculated as the saving in cost or time or any other resource between the standard and current level of performance. Figure 17-1 is a simple matrix that can help us calculate the cost of each type of issue.

We can put the matrix on a spreadsheet and see how the resources are expended for each type of issue. Probably more important than the immediate cost is the lesson we can learn from each occurrence.

Issue / Cost	Question	Problem	Grievance	Arbitration	Total
Money					
Time					
Material					
Equipment					
Other					
Total					

Figure 17-1   Labor Relations Cost Matrix

Learning Points

With companies becoming learning organizations, what can we learn from these labor spats? What clues do we get about what is wrong when we look at these experiences? What patterns, if any, are apparent? If we dig into the testimony of all sides, what do we think is going on? Are they all really random? What are the sources of the issues? Is it pay, working conditions, supervisory behavior, or something larger over which we have no control? If the company is in trouble, some people get nervous and look for problems. Whenever there is a lot of publicity about an environmental issue, some people swear that company is suffering from it no matter what evidence is presented.

Look for repeating data. Look by department; by level; by job type; by supervisor; by age, race, or sex; and by any other categories you can think of. You can make a big matrix and check every time there is an issue of a given type or in a certain place. There is usually a pattern, particularly if there are a large or a growing number of complaints. If you see a pattern emerging, you can often get to the source of the issue before it becomes a full-blown problem. Some of the most effective union avoidance programs use this type of tracking mechanism. An early warning is the best warning. In either case, you are able to identify and thus measure a change.

Level 2: Resolution

Grievances are the first formal level of labor action. Sooner or later, no matter how effective a preventive maintenance program is, a formal grievance will be filed. It may be legitimate, or a malcontent may be stirring up some muck of his or her own making. In any case, we will respond. Measuring the effectiveness of grievance resolution is not as simple as an outsider might think.

Obviously, we can add up the time spent by all the parties involved and determine what that costs directly and indirectly in terms of wages and lost productivity. If we are going to do that, we should develop some standard costs per hour for different types of people so that we don't have to calculate it anew every time. Then we can add in the cost of any settlement. Eventually, we will have a total cost, which we can compare to the average grievance cost. However, this is where the complexity comes in.

We can settle a grievance quickly by giving the complainant what he or she wants. In some cases that is the wise thing to do. Again, to the casual observer it might look like a low cost in terms of time. But what is the cost of giving in? In both the short term and the long term what will it cost the company? If we project the effect that the settlement might have not only on the plaintiff but on all the employees affected by the settlement, the cost could be very great over a long time period. We also may be setting a precedent that will adversely affect the company's bargaining position in the future. It goes like this: Does allowing X imply that Y and Z are also acceptable? Does allowing X under these conditions imply that it is also acceptable under other conditions? This is a tricky business, as labor relations people know.

Therefore, grievance resolution must be considered very carefully. We need to educate supervisors. Most companies do have training for first-line supervisors regarding the terms of a contract and its implications. However, labor relations training often is looked at only from a negative standpoint. The real question has always been, Is there some way to play a positive, proactive hand in this game? Clearly, when we look at anything purely from a negative point of view, we can only expect to experience negative occurrences. Perhaps if we examined labor relations from an objective perspective we might obtain some new insights.

Level 3: Negotiation

This level completes the circle and ties back to maintenance. Through better agreements or contract negotiations we set new levels of performance for the system. That may imply new, more, or different performance measurement activities. One of the first lessons of contract negotiations is, not to set up something one can't live with. This is what happened from 1950 to 1980. Management continuously gave away the right to manage the human asset in exchange for labor peace. Eventually, this went so far in some industries that management didn't have any flexibility. That almost destroyed several major industries in the United States. Today the vulnerability still exists in contracts where only a union member from Local X can turn a knob on a machine. People have to sit and wait for someone who isn't there to be found to come and perform a task that a 2-year-old could do. It is embarrassing for the waiting employees, and the message it sends is that management is a bunch of dummies for letting this happen. It is stupidity beyond imagination. Ultimately, it does no one any good.

How can we describe the value or effectiveness of a negotiation? The simplest way is to ask how close the agreement came to the original goal. There is no absolute value. What were we willing to give, and what did we want in return? What were the relative values of each of those elements? Clearly, we can cost out a contract. That is the absolute cost, but it is a relative value. The value is relative to the objective. What did we get in return for what we gave? What is the economic value of that? Did we give job security in return for flexibility? If so, what is the net trade-off today, next year, and 5 years from now?

Performance measurement is all about tracking relative values as they move through time. What is getting better, as we see it? What is getting worse, from our perspective? That is what management is about as well: monitoring progress toward specific goals. If we know what we want from labor relations, we can measure how successful we are at any point in time.

Measuring the Upside

Typically, we think of performance measures in relation to problems. Let's turn that around and look at positive performance measures. The upside deals with improvements in the three basics of management: quality, productivity, and service. When these things are attended to, the result is almost always reflected in increased profits. There have been a number of studies confirming this. Schuster,[1]

---

[1] Frederick Schuster, *The Schuster Report: The Proven Connection Between People and Profits.* New York: Wiley, 1986.

Kravetz,[2] and Huselid[3] have all conducted research and found evidence that supports correlations between so-called enlightened management practices and improved profitability.

Mark Huselid's work is the most recent. It takes an understanding for statistics to grasp the full implications of his research. Nevertheless, common sense and a little intuition show what he is trying to say.

Essentially, Huselid tested the link between human resources (HR) management practices and objective measures of turnover, productivity, and financial performance. For the causal variable he used an index of HR management practice sophistication (HRSOPH) that had been developed in a U.S. Department of Labor study. That index measures the amount and quality of attention paid to personnel selection, performance appraisal, compensation, grievance procedures, information sharing, attitude assessment, and labor-management participation. HRSOPH has a range of zero to 100, with higher numbers indicating sophistication. Huselid contacted 3,400 firms that had over 100 employees and $5 million in sales. He obtained data from 968 firms in 35 industries.

His first finding was that high HRSOPH was positively related to company size (number of employees), industry type, capital intensity, business planning sophistication, formal HR planning, and the number of years HR has been involved in the company's strategic business planning process. HRSOPH is negatively related to the extent of union coverage and the use of cost leadership as a competitive strategy.

His general findings were that larger firms and firms that spend more money on capital equipment also invest more in sophisticated HR practices. Firms with more sophisticated business planning see the value of HR planning. Finally, large differences were found across industries.

It was acknowledged that employee behavior cannot always affect financial performance (competitors, the general economy, and so on,

[2] Dennis Kravetz, *The Human Resources Revolution*. San Francisco: Jossey-Bass, 1988.
[3] Mark Huselid, *The Effects of Strategic Human Resource Management and Human Resource Planning on Firm Performance*. New Brunswick, NJ: Institute of Management and Labor Relations, Rutgers University, 1993.

have an effect). Therefore, the first payoff associated with the use of HRSOPH was sought in intermediate outcomes, such as turnover and productivity. In the first test Huselid found that high HRSOPH was associated with low turnover. His second test showed high HRSOPH positively affecting sales per employee (productivity).

Huselid went on to calculate the impact of increasing HRSOPH. He found that an increase of one standard deviation (16 points on the index scale) from an average of 56 to 72 would raise net sales an average of $8,337 per employee per year. Over a 5-year period, using an 8 percent discount rate, this translated into $33,287 per employee.

To link all this to a firm's financial performance (profitability), Huselid used both accounting profit calculations and economic profit calculations. He found that increasing HRSOPH one standard deviation produced a 5-year market value increase in profits of $7,868 per employee.

These remarkable results were confirmed across a wide range of industries and firm sizes. This general study supports the belief that when we invest in employee management, we increase profitability.

Summary

Labor relations work can be viewed from three perspectives: prevention, resolution, and negotiation. The objective in each case should be to find a position that creates the best win-win situation for both parties. The stance that labor and management are intrinsically enemies is an anachronism. It is too inefficient. Companies cannot compete, increase their market share, and provide jobs if there is continual fighting between bosses and employees.

Try to think about labor relations activities from a positive viewpoint. Train supervisors to see that there is another way to look at their relationships with employees. The Japanese supervisor is much closer to his or her employees than is the typical Western supervisor. That personal touch had a lot to do with the self-sacrificing attitude of Japanese workers over the last 40 years. I'm not suggesting that Western management try to emulate Eastern methods, but inside those methods there is a kernel of human relations wisdom that we would all be wise to note.

PART
VI

E-HR: Moving HR to the Web

Trends

This part is different from those preceding it in that they were about the *processes* of hiring, paying, developing, and retaining talent, and so on. This part focuses on the tools—hardware and software—used to speed, expand, enhance, or facilitate those processes. In the last 5 years technology has had a profound effect on most human resources (HR) departments. The first human resources information system (HRIS) product came on the market about 1970. It was purely a record-keeping software program. In its time it was a clear advance over the existing manual systems. Gradually automation came to HR. The next big leap was Peoplesoft's product, which was much faster and more user-friendly. Other Enterprise Resource Planning programs (ERPs) followed. The German firm SAP, which was dominant in Europe, invaded the North American market and became a competitor of Peoplesoft. What is now Best Software's Abra system gained a very strong market position in the small company arena. Its original name was Abra-Cadabra.

After a slow start HR has made the case for investments in computer and phone technology to improve processes and increase service without adding staff. For the most part this has worked well.

HR departments today are much more efficient and better service providers than they were at any time in the past.

Expert Opinions

We asked a group of professional colleagues from software companies, HR departments, and consultancies to give us the benefit of their experience and opinions in regard to the changes that have taken place in the last 5 years. These experts included a head of HR for a logistics management company, a knowledge champion in a financial institution, and an HR consultant, the former head of HR for a hospitality company.

The key issues they cited can be summarized as follows:

1. According to one person, e-learnng is probably the most important development while another person views it as "crap." Regardless of which side one takes on the effectiveness of e-learning, there seem to be some major forces that will push it along, such as the following:
   a. It is less costly than traditional central training facilities and can be accessed on a just in-time, as-needed basis.
   b. It suits a distributed workforce.
   c. There can be a close correlation between e-learning and communities. For example, one company has the names of everyone who has taken classes and is actively looking for ways to extend that learning experience among the attendees through communities of interest.
2. Several respondents pointed out that HR professionals have hidden behind the barriers of process and paperwork for so long that they have been unable to address the higher-value levels of work open to them. New technology available today enables line managers to complete information transactions and access databases directly, freeing HR staff for the more important roles of counseling and training. Open software architecture and querying tools make complex analyses more readily available to the practitioner and make advice based on these metrics more timely and valuable to the organization. Every HR professional needs to become conversant in this

new technological language to maximize his or her effectiveness in the organization.

3. Others noted that in regard to technology the most attention over the last decade has been focused on large-scale integrated personnel and payroll systems development (PeopleSoft, Oracle, SAP, etc.). Bringing these systems down to HR department desktops was a necessary and overdue tactical assault on the paperwork quagmire that personnel administration has become over that period. However, perhaps the more powerful, useful, and strategic efforts will be found in the current extension of data capture formats and the advent of data-mining tools for HR applications. Still, this will not be complete until HRIS becomes fully integrated within one unified, enterprisewide, performance-reporting and management system (EPM). These challenges are just beginning to be addressed.

4. Some of the people queried complained that there is almost too much personnel and business information that is or could be available, and it is constantly changing. Getting useful information out of the database is often a time-consuming challenge. Most report writers are somewhat unfriendly and unwieldy. Data-mining tools within HR applications are still limited at best. Current data transfer between HRIS and EPM databases is one way, at best. Today, HRIS feeds into payroll and general ledger, and payroll and general ledger feed into EPM, but financial and accounting systems do not feed back to HRIS. Until this loop is electronically closed, access to needed business data and effective measurement of human capital will continue to be a manual reporting process.

5. It was clear to others that an electronic personnel input form is the most critical technology need at present. To drastically reduce paper documents, the "employee status change form" must become totally Web-based on the company's intranet. We need an electronic "personnel jacket" for each employee because it is pointless to run this process just to have a clerk print copies to file in a cabinet.

6. The need for better statistical tools and report writers is being addressed, but this is an area that still needs much attention. One example of note is PRISM, recently introduced by Wm.

Mercer & Co. This on-line compensation tool simplifies survey completion input and allows data-mining output at the same time. Another example is SAS Institute's HR Vision. It expands the user's ability to draw data from several sources and load it onto a form of the user's design. As more such tools electronically extract from a company's EPM as well as HRIS, HR technology will reach the next needed step of development. Much of the information needed for operational analysis is not captured in any form: cost of hiring, training, employee relations programs, and so forth.

7. Finally, portals and self-service applications are making data available to both managers and employees at levels previously limited or restricted. The key need now is to develop the ability of people to use the data effectively. Analytic skills are lacking at all levels. Until this human issue is remedied, technology cannot deliver on its promise.

These comments are examples of the promise and problems of converting HR into e-HR. We are seeing only the beginning of the transformation that eventually will reconfigure the delivery of human resource services to the human capital, the talent of the organization. The next decade should see the launch of some very exciting capabilities for the benefit of HR and its customers.

Looking beyond Technology

Along with the proliferation of technology has come a growing concern about misdirection. A number of technology experts have pointed out that technology is a tool, not a destination. Their concern is that HR management might focus too much on internal technology applications. Greater opportunities lie in expanding the effects of HR's technology-enhanced services toward the business of the enterprise. Staff managers are susceptible to putting their heads down and working on their processes. They need to improve their ability to think beyond the day's work and the steps in their processes. The point of this and of all work is to serve the goals of the enterprise. This result, not the process, must be the focal point if HR is to transform itself from an expense center to a business partner.

HR needs to articulate a congruent information delivery strategy that its customers understand and can integrate into their daily work as well as their strategic objectives. Another way of saying this is that customers don't care how providers support them; they just want what they need when they need it. HR's technology strategy should describe how it intends to leverage the inherent talent of the organization's workforce with external and internal knowledge and technology to serve the enterprise's goals. When this is done well, it is much easier to monitor activities and processes to find measurable examples of value added.

Several vendors are developing products that move HR from back-office administration toward problem analysis and resolution and forecasting. Included in these systems are both quantitative benchmarks and employee survey data. By following decision trees using both hard and soft data, HR departments will be able to find quick solutions to present problems and begin to forecast the likelihood of various human capital occurrences.

Workforce Analytics: Supporting Business Decisions

The Information Age in Human Resources

Information is valuable only if it is used to pursue an organizational goal. The goal can be financial, production, or human-based. Over the last decade technological and telephonic inventions have made the acquisition and utilization of data much easier. With the advent of the World Wide Web everyone on the globe can join the universal conversation. Along with advancements in computing and communication has come a mountain of hyperbole that obscures and sometimes misleads. To understand how the human resources (HR) function can use the new tools we have to start not with the technology but with the strategic goals of the enterprise.

Enterprise Goals and Human Resources Services

Everything starts with the goals of the enterprise. Every function, whether line or staff, has the responsibility to make its unique contribution to the achievement of those goals. The HR function serves the enterprise's goals by supporting the work of the operating units, which in turn are supposed to be connecting their efforts to the enterprise's goals. The fact that in a significant percentage of cases the connection is weak makes tracking causal or even inferential relationships between actions and results difficult, if not impossible.

Figure 18-1 shows the structural connection between human capital talent management (HR services), the operating objectives of the business units, and the enterprise goals. The basic question is, How will HR do its part in managing human capital to facilitate achievement of the operating objectives and the enterprise goals?

Clearly, one of the most visible things that HR has done is to introduce new electronic technologies—both hardware and software—to cope with the emerging issues of the last 5 years. A number of surveys have shown that more than three of four HR departments have introduced new systems and programs in the last 2 years. These systems and programs have ranged from new versions of the Enterprise Resource Planning system to individual applications such as:

- Applicant tracking
- Portals to corporate and vendor sites
- Employee self-service call centers

Figure 18-1   Connection of human resources services to enterprise goals

- Training administration
- Distance learning
- Skill tracking
- Succession planning
- Performance review/appraisal
- Compensation administration
- Budgeting
- Reporting

The operational purposes of these investments have centered primarily on improving internal HR administrative productivity.

Next in importance are better service delivery and attempts to graduate to more strategic services. It is this that offers the best pathway for HR out of the traditional expense center syndrome to value added business partnering. It implies HR taking a more active role in

- Workforce modeling
- Performance management (beyond providing forms and record keeping)
- Employee communications
- Resource planning
- Leadership development

Measuring the Effects of Technology

As was pointed out in the introduction of this part, technology is a tool, not a result. Also, it is not the process. We are interested in the results of HR processes. From a measurement standpoint the result does not know the tool that drove it. Thus, the question is not how to measure the tool but how to measure the effects of this tool versus other tools that might have been used previously. That is, how will service quality and effectiveness be measured?

The underlying premise in measurement is always the same regardless of the application: Measure what matters. Focus measurement resources on those activities which make a difference to the organization. Should we commit to measuring hiring costs, training investments, compensation trends, turnover rates, or something else?

The answer is found within the goals of the enterprise. What human capital factors and forces have the greatest effect on the operating objectives of the business units and therefore on the goals of the enterprise?

Many years ago, when automation made its initial tentative steps into organizations, we learned a valuable lesson: Improve the process first and then automate it. If we do it the other way around, all we have achieved is an inefficient process that is now cast in stone. In part, this lesson led to the reengineering movement of the early 1990s. There a second lesson was learned: We can't ignore the human element when we redesign processes. These two painful mistakes must be kept in front of us as we change processes and introduce new technologies. If we fail to learn from the past, the subsequent measurement system will tell a confusing and disconcerting story.

In redesigning processes we have to start with the enterprise goals, as was pointed out above. Changing a process or even making it more efficient is not necessarily going to have a positive effect on the goals. Not only might it positively affect the work of our customers (the employees and managers of the company), it might have the opposite effect. Wouldn't it be logical to check with the people who will be affected by the changes before we make them? The more that technology advances, the greater will be the required investment to install and maintain it.

Back to Basics

From the preceding chapters you have learned how to measure and evaluate the effectiveness of HR services. Technology doesn't change the basic measurement paradigm. Let us repeat that the result doesn't know or care about the process. Process becomes an issue only if the result is unsatisfactory.

When we talk about measuring technology, we are really talking about measuring the result of introducing technology to a manual operation or employing technology in a new way or at a deeper level than before. We can do this at two levels.

Level 1

We can look at the situation at hand, for example, responding to an employee request for information. This can be viewed in terms of how quickly we can answer the question as well as how happy the employee is with the promptness, accuracy, and courtesy of the response. Then we compare these reactions and measures with previous instances where we did not have the same technology. For example, we might have used the telephone in each case, but in the current instance we had access to an electronic database instead of having to look up the answer in a manual.

Level 2

We can go beyond a simple case to look at what effect the outcome of the given case had on the productivity, quality, or service levels of the units for which we delivered the service. For example, if we introduced a computer-based training program on diskette and on the intranet, did we find any difference in a number of possible measures? The first measure would be the experience and reaction of the individuals using the two methods (just like the level 1 case). The second would be the effects on the business unit's performance on the acquisition and utilization of the skills gained in the training. Here one might ask, How can we sort out the extraneous effects of the environment on the result from the effects of the use of one type of technology versus the other? That is a legitimate question and leads into the heart of this chapter.

Our central purpose here is to discuss how to assess the efficacy of technology in regard to business performance. Any time we measure something in which there is a period of time between the intervention, such as training, and the point of measurement, there will always be the possibility of what are called intervening events. For example, we could teach people how to use a software program. After the training a new, improved version could come out that was faster than the old version on which those people were taught. If they didn't need extra training for the new version because the improvements were buried in the programming, we might have a problem stating that their faster performance was due to the training versus the program improvements. In more complex situations such as supervisory training there are many variables that can affect outcomes. They include not only the interpersonal, scheduling, policy, process, or other topics but also the behavior of the supervisees, changes in the business unit or company structure, and a myriad of other forces.

The basic question to ask is, Is this the only case where extraneous forces affect outcomes? The answer is obviously no. In all organizational situations there are many unaccounted-for forces at work. However, in practice, unless the forces are obvious or visible, we either acknowledge or discount them and attribute the change to whatever intervention took place. Take a simple example such as sales. When a salesperson makes a sale, usually we attribute that to that person's selling skills, yet a sale can be the result of many other factors. The same can be said of customer service. If an irate customer calls and as a result of the serviceperson's response the customer does not close his or her account, we say that the serviceperson did a good job. Yet we know nothing about the customer's level of anger, tolerance, alternative options, and the like. In a monopolistic situation or one in which the customer is totally committed to one technology, there is no way for the customer to defect. We have been measuring sales and service for so long that we accept those unknowns as givens and believe that over time they will even out. We should apply the same criteria to HR interventions that we apply to production, sales, and service activities.

If we want to measure the effects of technology on HR activities and results and the effects within the organization, we should start at a strategic level. If we start at the process point, we might achieve our measurable objectives while suboptimizing the value contribution of HR. This can occur when we improve a minor process but fail to operate with strategic goals in mind and therefore have little effect on the organization.

How to Develop a Measurable e-HR Agenda

Chris Ashton's study of e-HR programs lays a solid foundation for developing an e-HR agenda.[1] Figure 18-2 shows three agendas Ashton has consolidated from discussions with different firms. Let us look at the differences and the similarities. When we scan them from left to right, we see three different thrusts or foci. Case 1 has a strategic overtone. Case 2 is engaged in reviewing the business case

---

[1] Chris Ashton, *e-Hr: Transforming the HR Function.* London: Business Intelligence, 2001.

Case 1	Case 2	Case 3
1. Is there a clearly defined HR strategy?	1. Setting a business case is good professional and business practice.	1. Has the effectiveness of current HR service delivery methods been reviewed?
2. What are the links to corporate strategy and current or future perceived business issues?	2. Rigorously thinking through why an e-HR innovation is being considered.	2. Were different end-user populations consulted as part of the review process?
3. What main people issues does the strategy attempt to address?	3. If financials are to be used, deciding on the most appropriate metrics.	3. What limitations or different expectations has the review revealed?
4. Which elements of these issues can be realistically tackled through e-HR innovations?	4. Estimating the costs of e-HR developments and their risks/potential downside.	4. Has it highlighted a need for completely new HR services?
5. Which strategic elements cannot be, or are unlikely to be, addressed using technology and web tools?	5. Deciding when the payback periods are for any investments, along with interim results.	5. What new service delivery channels and methods are required to improve current provisions?
6. Does each innovation or several grouped together have a plan for resourcing, time, and deliverables?	6. Considering the value directly created from deploying technologies across HR services.	6. What is the HR case for shifting from status quo ambitions, goals, resources, capabilities, etc.?
7. Who are the principal end-users and stakeholders?	7. Estimating the value that will result from process improvements and service efficiencies.	7. Is there a financial justification to be made? Using which metrics?
8. In what ways have they been consulted regarding e-HR plans?	8. Deciding on implementation timescales, along with progress milestones.	8. What is the function's comfort level with regard to the speed of implementation and change?
9. What different benefits are anticipated for each discrete user population?	9. Considering nonfinancial outcomes from e-HR developments in relation to people policies.	9. Has a review of the softer issues been made—access to web tools, willingness to use them, etc.?
10. To what extent are general business conditions and specific e-business developments affecting the continued viability or effectiveness of e-HR plans?	10. Ensuring that an e-HR innovation has not been introduced for its own sake or just to make life easier in HR.	10. Have underpinning plans been shaped with regard to more open communications, service failure recoveries, end-user feedback, and their satisfaction with new service provisions?

Figure 18-2 Sample issues for e-HR agenda building

for e-HR. Case 3 looks at service delivery and the human element. Collectively, they cover every important issue or recommendation that we need to build our own agenda. The lesson is that an e-HR transformation is not a simple matter. In the process of moving toward e-HR we need to set points in time to monitor progress along with methods for assessing and evaluating our progress.

 With this as the starting point we are trying to answer the basic question, What is HR's raison d'être? Why do we have an HR function? In a recent survey for a client we found that HR said it was there to counsel management on the recruiting and selection of talent. Management said HR's job was to handle the administrative details around the process and not get in between the candidate and the hiring manager. Which is it? Is HR in business to process paper or to guide management on the acquisition, development, and retention of talent? HR must be able to handle the administrative work or it will never be given the chance to provide strategic input. It has been HR's inability to demonstrate quantitatively as well as qualitatively its effect on the business that has driven management's view of HR as an administrative expense center. That is what this book hopes to change.

The primary purpose of this book is not to help explain this strategic positioning question, although insights from it can help. It is focused on how we measure the result of both strategic and tactical-level activities. Let us now move on to the measurement of activities and their effects. It is by being able to measure outcomes at levels 1 and 2 that we can move HR from administrative to strategic work.

Tools

Most HR software vendors have moved beyond record-keeping systems to some level of analysis. In most cases it is still relatively simple and almost primitive compared to the financial analysis tools that are available. Nevertheless, it is a start that recognizes the approach of a new era in human capital management.

The currently popular term for this trend is *workforce analytics*. Software companies such as PeopleSoft, SAS Institute, Lawson, SAP, and Oracle are working on analytic applications. The idea is to put up-to-date data in the hands of the HR staff or supervisors and managers so that they can make informed decisions. The name of this application suite is less important than the utility of the tool and the data it manipulates.

Applications

Our human resources measurement system is designed to answer five questions about any activity or result. You know from earlier chapters that the questions are as follows:

- What does it cost?
- How long does it take?
- How much did we do?
- How many errors did we make?
- How happy is someone?

It's no different when we talk about applying technology to an activity. As was shown above, the level 1 application simply answers the question, What is the difference in this activity and its immediate result compared to what it was before we introduced the technological solution? At level 2 we ask, What difference did it make to the operating objectives of the business unit or the enterprise goals? If we use a software application, we want to be able to measure the effects on the immediate operation (level 1). Can we do something better (fewer errors), faster (quicker response time), or cheaper (more output for a given input)?

Examples

Let's look at examples from three software vendors to see where workforce analytics are focused. Their's is typical of what we currently see being pitched. Over time their words will change, but this is a good example of what they are all claiming. We'll excerpt some copy from their Web sites to make the point.

Example 1

Human Resources Meets Profitability.
(Welcome to the New, New Economy.)

Let's face it. In the new, New Economy, the entire human resources dynamic has changed. Today, you have to:

- Attract, retain, and motivate the best people
- Align the individual goals of your employees with your corporate strategy
- Demonstrate that your HR strategies and solutions benefit the company's bottom line

And at the end of the day, you're going to be judged on how much your HR organization contributed to the overall goals and profitability of the company. Big challenges, aren't they? That's why you need a powerful HR solution—one that combines world-class human resources functions, a global scope, and the power of the Internet. mySAP™ Human Resources (mySAP HR) is that solution.

It's All About Talent

Keep your talent from leaving—that's a primary goal in today's world of specialized skills and tight labor markets. With role-based portals, mySAP HR makes sure that everyone gets the right information to collaborate and make shared decisions. The net result is that mySAP HR helps you create a good work environment—a place where people want to stay.

Also, mySAP HR puts human resource management in the hands of operational managers—where it can do the most good. It combines strategic HR features with workforce analytical data so you can clearly demonstrate your contribution to the bottom line. No matter what size your company, you can truly optimize your investment in all employees.

With mySAP HR you can:

- Streamline HR processes and reduce administrative costs
- Maximize workforce collaboration and knowledge management with <u>mySAP Workplace</u>™, a role-based enterprise portal

- Support employee retention and total reward programs
- Measure the HR organization's contribution to corporate strategy
- Enhance networking and data sharing between departments
- Manage your global workforce with standard language, currency, and regulatory requirements for more than 35 countries
- Create standard and legal reports
- Improve decision making through enhanced HR business analytics
- Empower employees to manage their own life events through expanded employee self service[2]

Example 2

The following screen shot (Figure 18-3) is a typical example of the type of content and display these three vendors are offering. While they differ in the form of expression, they are all talking about the same idea. The concept is to move HR information systems from

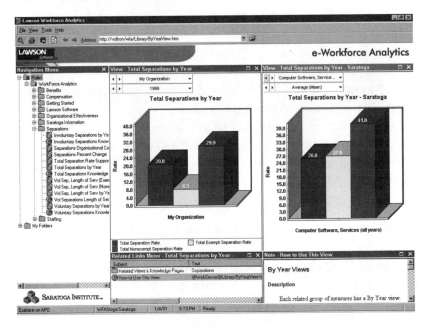

Figure 18-3   Lawson Software web page

[2] Reprinted from SAP's web site with permission.

record keeping and basic reporting to higher levels of performance analysis.[3]

Example 3

Optimizing Human Capital Performance, Achieving Maximum Employee Satisfaction, and Positively Impacting on Your Bottom Line

Your business is changing rapidly. If you don't make HR decisions quickly, you're wasting time and money. Now more than ever, HR professionals are being challenged to align their management goals and the individual goals of their employees with overall corporate strategy—to become more profit-oriented on every level.

You're being asked to:

- Attract, retain, and motivate the best employees.
- Challenge the view of HR as a cost center by becoming thought leaders and strategic advisors.
- Translate information—about your employees, your company, your industry, and your competitors—into knowledge you can use to make the right HR decisions.
- Monitor market conditions and adapt to new strategies as your organization grows and goals change.
- Put solutions in the hands of operational managers so everyone in your organization can explore, analyze, and present HR-specific information for decision making anytime, anywhere—without depending on IT.

Above all, you have to demonstrate how HR links people, strategy, and performance to add true value to the bottom line. How do you do it? With the only solution that combines award-winning data warehousing technology with Web-based HR-specific decision support—all designed by HR professionals—not statisticians. You get:

---

[3] Provided courtesy of Lawson Software.

- An HR-specific decision support system that combines strategic information with workforce analytics so you can clearly demonstrate HR's contribution to the bottom line.
- A solution that surfaces HR strategy and measures that strategy against key performance indicators. So you can spend more time developing organization and leadership strategies.
- Accurate information at your fingertips so you can make informed decisions based upon facts—not intuition—and adapt to changing market conditions.
- A solution for evaluating skills and resources and analyzing, forecasting, and modeling changes *before* they occur. Easy access to historical information so you can make predictions about employee recruitment and retention.
- Technology that manages and treats your people as your most precious asset. You can simplify processes, move information to user desktops, and align all human capital processes around common goals.
- Benchmarks that enable you to compare your company with best practices of others inside your industry and out.
- One solution from one vendor. SAS gives you the flexibility to add, change, and update information easily as your business needs change.

The net result? A world-class working environment that motivates people to stay. And because they're more productive and provide better customer service, that translates into increased profitability and stakeholder value. Linking people, strategy, and performance. That's SAS for Human Capital Management.

Take HR Decision Support to a Higher Level

HR Vision from SAS is a comprehensive HR decision-support solution. It enables proactive strategies for determining corporate goals while enhancing the task-driven routines that have traditionally formed the core of HR activities.

HR Vision sits on top of an ERP system and provides the analytic capability that extends the utility of the ERP. ERPs capture data but as of the beginning of the new decade are not easy to work with when it comes to analytic projects.

Increasingly, HR practitioners are required to provide human resources functions and information enterprise-wide . . . from the mailroom to the boardroom.

On an individual level, each employee requires a distinct service to track personal information about compensation, benefits, and retirement issues. Front-line managers require the HR department to provide services for recruitment, remuneration, and termination. These managers also need information relating to departmental dynamics such as personnel demographics, headcount, turnover, and position management.

HR Vision serves the needs of these internal clients by helping to:

- Gain a true understanding of the entire work force.
- Quantify the bottom-line impact of compensation policies, hiring decisions, and employee turnover.
- Quickly pinpoint and troubleshoot problem areas and reveal opportunities for improvement.
- Deliver information from data relating to all HR processes.
- Develop strategic policies critical to the organization's future development and success.

Make decisions with confidence based on timely, accurate, enterprise-wide knowledge.[4]

Proving the Value Added

The words and forms used by these vendors will change over time, but the thrust is clear. They want us to believe that the use of their products will measurably improve the attraction, retention, and productivity of our talented workforce. From HR's perspective it should help the staff demonstrate its contribution to the business's bottom line. A parallel business goal is to put human capital operating data

---

[4] Reprinted from SAS Institute's HR Vision materials, with permission.

in the hands of business unit managers. The premise is that it will help them optimize their return on human capital investment.

The question we want to ask these vendors is, How can you prove it? They should be able to show us direct and indirect connections between the use of their analytic tools and results that are better, faster, and cheaper than those in the past. We want them to demonstrate how their tools can make administrative work less costly and more valuable to the enterprise.

Let's take their statements point for point and ask for concrete examples of how the ability to call up and format operating data will help us drive reductions in *cost*, improvements in process *cycle time*, more *output* for a given input, fewer *errors*, and *happier* employees and managers. From previous chapters we already have over 100 metrics from which to choose. We can select a few of the ones that are most meaningful and ask the vendors to show how their tools can help make those improvements.

More important than process efficiency and even current employee productivity is the ability to analyze problems and trace them through to the most likely remedial actions. What would be even better would be the ability to forecast the effects of current decisions on future results. When they provide that type of functionality, HR will have the capability to move directly from administrative efficiency to strategic partnering.

When we apply this method to any technology solution, we will be able to make a case to management for investment in the technology. When the investment is made, we will be able to track the results and show return on investment (ROI) and elevate management's perception of HR.

Cost-Benefit Analysis

When asking top management to fund technology investments, it is reasonable to show the projected ROI through a cost-benefit analysis. I remember one case in which a chief executive officer (CEO) described the HR director's ROI approach. When the CEO asked what the benefit would be from an investment in a new software system the HR director described how it would make work easier in the HR department. This would reduce stress and speed throughput of HR processes. The CEO sighed and said that that would be nice, but what difference would it make on his strategic goals in the near future? The HR director looked blank. He had never thought of it that way. He didn't get the new software.

Cost-benefit analysis is an old and accepted process for analyzing the future result of a current investment. It is a simple process that anyone can do. It does not require any mathematical skills beyond four-function arithmetic and a minimal knowledge of accounting terminology. There are an infinite number of variations on this common technique. The following is a basic one that has worked for us.

1. *What is the business problem that this investment is aimed at solving?* This must be stated as explicitly as possible so that it can be converted into quantitative and financial terms later. It can be a process problem that is causing intolerable results in one group or across the entire company. An example could be that the cycle time to fill critical positions is too long partly because of an antiquated manual applicant-processing system.

2. *How is this problem negatively affecting the company?* Is it impairing productivity, quality, or service (PQS)? These are the fundamentals of every organization, whether profit or not for profit. Given the example above, where do we see the delay in hiring affecting PQS?

3. *What is the cost of this problem to the company?* Is it negatively affecting new product development, customer service, and thereby retention, or is it delaying the opening of a new store or sales territory? What is the cost of that? There are both fixed (plant and equipment and overhead) and variable (material and capital) costs. The other side of the income statement is revenue. Is the cost found in lost sales through an inability to get to market?

4. *What is the source of the problem?* This is the critical step that often is not well analyzed. Proposals often do not have solid evidence about the underlying cause of the visible PQS symptom. This happens in organizations where there is little cross-functional collaboration. Thus, one point of view is presented and not challenged. Make sure you know the true cause, which sometimes is hidden and flows across functions.

5. *What are the production, human, and or financial benefits from this investment?* Here again truncated analysis often looks only for financial ROI. But what will it do to people in the area where it will be installed? Will it have an effect on other related business units that are either suppliers to the process or customers of the output of the process? We must show some financial value from the investment or we will be like the HR director who was concerned only with his own people and process.

6. *Are the benefits greater than the cost?* First, is this going to yield an acceptable rate of return on the funds invested? Every company has an expected recovery or hurdle rate for its investments. Second, what are the secondary benefits? Some investments are made because they are good for the employees even though they do not promise a good financial return.

When we apply cost-benefit methodology to any technology solution, we will be able to make a case to management for investment in the technology. After the investment is made we will be able to track the results and show ROI.

The Next Generations

Let's accept the idea that the latest analytic products can help improve current operations and investments in human capital. But we need to go beyond process efficiency and current employee productivity to focus on the ability to pinpoint the source of problems and to ascertain the appropriate corrective actions.

Of still greater value is the ability to forecast the effects of current decisions on future results. If software vendors eventually provide that type of functionality, HR will be able to progress beyond mere administrative efficiency into a state of true strategic partnering.

Summary

When we approach technological investments, several perspectives are germane. They vary by organization, based on the enterprise goals. The goals vary over time but are all focused on financial, market, customer, and operational desires.

The fundamentals of business are efficiency and service whether we are talking about people or production. Through advancements in e-HR technology we are beginning to see the fulfillment of the promise of automation for the management of human capital and HR operations. As the new generations of software become available, HR professionals will have the ability to perform the same level of analysis of human capital operating data that finance and production professionals perform. By taking advantage of this opportunity HR will finally erase the age-old questions, What is HR's role? How does HR demonstrate its contribution in bottom-line terms? and What does it take for HR to become a strategic partner? The future for HR is very bright. We have only to grasp the new tools and learn how to use them effectively.

Communication: Reporting Outcomes and Trends

Impact of Technology on Employee Communications

Computer technology, especially intranets, allows an organization to distribute information on a selective basis. Rather than issuing a corporatewide blast the company can segregate information by practically any demographic category: age, job classification, function, level, or even known interests. Knowing the needs of individual employees, such as elder care, child care, medical needs, educational desires, and recreational preferences, helps a company reach out and connect with its people on a personal level. This is a key step in becoming an employer of choice.

A review of the annual *Fortune* magazine list of the best companies to work for reveals that those firms are especially adept at communicating and thereby bonding with their people. Communications, more than any single other act, causes people to commit to the organization's vision and stay during difficult times or when the job market is particularly hot.

What Organizations Should Know about Employee Communications

Organizations spend thousands of hours of work and sometimes millions of dollars annually on employee communications. However, they seldom ask employees three simple questions:

1. What do you want to know?
2. Who do you want to hear it from?
3. Which medium is the best for communicating each topic?

Companies spend great amounts of money to study customers' wants and needs but spend little to study employees' desires, especially when it comes to information. Can you answer the three questions above based on research, or is this something you think you "just know"?

What Organizations Communicate

When we look at employee communications programs, it becomes clear that organizations typically try to communicate fewer than 10 basic topics to employees. They can be divided into the following categories:

Personal information: pay and benefits

Job performance: periodic performance reviews/appraisals

Career opportunity: availability of training, job posting, and career planning

Management vision: vision, mission, and values

Company strategy: corporate plans and goals

Information on daily operations: scheduling, priorities, and responsibilities

Company performance: quarterly and annual financial results

Changes in structure: reorganizations, downsizings, and mergers

General company and employee news: recreational information, anniversaries, and so on

Market news: new products, financial results, and market penetration by competitors

Of course there are exceptions to this list, but it covers over 90 percent of what most companies attempt to communicate to their employees.

What People Want to Know

Surveys have confirmed a commonsense rule: People are most interested in information about the issues that affect them the most directly. We know that the three topics at the top of their interest list are

Job performance. How am I doing?

Career opportunity. Where and how far can I go, and what do I have to do to get there?

Pay and benefits. How are you going to compensate me for my effort and loyalty?

This holds true for almost all employees. Exceptions are due to age; most people over age 60 are not as interested in career opportunities for obvious reasons or personal intentions as are short-term employees. Nearly all employees, no matter how short- or long-term their job outlook is, want to know how they are doing. Everyone wants information on pay and benefits.

The topics of greatest interest beyond personal information are management's vision and strategy. These elements drive the organization by telling the people what the company stands for and where it is going.

The next level is a group of topics that are more variable in importance. They include the following:

Operating information. People need to know what to do each day.

Organizational change. When we started this research more than 20 years ago, change was not as continuous or widespread as it is today. Because of the frequency of change people are more attuned to every subtle shift in the corporate wind.

Financial performance. This is another phenomenon of the late twentieth century. Many employees now have stock options or have invested in other ways in the company's stock. They also know that if the company's performance falls off, it can become a takeover target. This moves the topic very close to home.

Market news. It used to be that only people in customer contact functions seemed to be interested in the competition. Marketing, sales, advertising, public relations, research and development, and production were more affected or even driven by the actions of the marketplace. However, in recent years, because of the uncertainty and turmoil of the market and because of stock options and other pay incentives, more employees in more functions have become more interested in market news.

General company news. People are very busy and often don't take the time to read the company newspaper or many of the e-mails from corporate communications. News of anniversaries, bowling scores, parties and reassignments, promotions, and so on, usually is interesting only to those directly involved.

How People Want to Be Talked To

The first rule of good communication is be honest. Tell the truth and most things will work out. While most of an organization's communication budget goes into formal media, the most effective employee communicator is the supervisor, for better or worse. Repeatedly people have told us that their supervisor is the person from whom they want to hear important information. This does not mean they receive that communication, only that they want it.

Depending on the content of the message, employees like to hear it from upper-level management within their department or division. If it is a corporatewide matter, they want the chief executive officer (CEO) to deliver it. Failure of the CEO or senior executives to communicate the state of affairs causes people to doubt their wisdom or veracity. In effect, the managers lose credibility in the eyes of the workforce. As we mentioned earlier, at the turn of the century people told us they were leaving because they had lost faith in top management's ability to lead. This is a message that the top team needs to heed.

Other persons can be effective deliverers of information to employees as well. The human resources (HR) department obviously must be the primary transmitter of data on pay and benefit programs as well as other HR services. People expect HR to do this, but after they get the message, they often turn to their supervisor for interpretation or elaboration. People naturally ask, What does this mean to me? and expect the supervisor to interpret the message for them.

Effective Media

As the topic becomes less critical to the receiver, having a supervisor use face-to-face methods is not necessary. Less personal means become acceptable. This is where most organizations do an acceptable to good job. A combination of e-mails, video and audio transmissions, and various paper media messages at all levels of import can be used effectively. The question is, Which medium is most effective for which topic? There is no way for an organization to know the employees' preferences without asking them. There is no single answer for all companies and all situations.

A Communication Survey

Figure 19-1 shows a template that can be used to design a communications survey. It covers topics, transmitters, media, and levels of satisfaction.

Reports: Communicating Upward

Knowing what to report is easy. There are two rules about measurement reports.

1. Rule 1 is to report on what interests the audience, in this case upper levels of management. Rather than flood management with information, we will prepare short reports that focus on issues it cares about. When there is something they ought to be paying attention to but aren't, we need to educate them. We can do this by introducing one issue at a time with a number or two and a brief description of the importance or implications of the issue. As we gain their attention, we can expand the message if necessary.

Topic	Transmitter	Method	Satisfaction Level
Job performance	Immediate supervisor	Face to face	High
Career opportunity	Department or division head	E-mail	Medium
HR systems/programs	Senior executive	Video conference	Low
Pay	HR executive	Audio conference	
Benefits		Newsletter/newspaper	
Recreation programs		Employee meeting	
Lifestyle programs			
Management's vision, mission, and values			
Company strategy, plans, and goals			
Daily operations, schedule, and responsibilities			
Company changes, including reorganization, mergers, downsizings			
Company performance finances, new products			
Market news Customers and competitors			
General company news			

Figure 19-1 Communications Survey Template

2. Rule 2 is to report what makes a difference. Don't waste space and drag the audience through issues that have little effect on corporate goals. We will tighten our report and tell what is happening in human capital factors that is important. Then we will explain what difference it makes that the data are moving in one direction or another.

Scorecards

In my last two books I showed examples of several different types of scorecards, including a balanced scorecard for HR.[1] Balanced scorecarding became popular in the last few years of the 1990s. As with every other management tool that has come along in the last 50 years, some companies are using it to great effect while others are adopting a weak version to go along with the flow.

Basically, a scorecard is a concise form for communicating quantitative data. It leads any narrative discussion of what is happening. Typically it should show trend data, since a single point in time means almost nothing.

Summary

Communicating to employees and management is more an art than a science. Although there are rules for effective formats, they vary by audience and can be learned through trial and error. The most important issue in communications is integrity, closely followed by accuracy. Being honest, accurate, and focused on the audiences' interests usually results in effective communications.

The connectivity of the Internet has stripped all pretense and doubletalk out of organizations. No longer can management keep a problem quiet or isolated. Now anyone can and often does share information with friends outside the organization. Even strangers hear what is happening in the organization as employees express their frustrations in a chat room. The lesson is clear: Be honest and forthright in communicating.

---

[1] Jac Fitz-enz, *The ROI of Human Capital*. New York: AMACOM, 2000; *The E-Aligned Enterprise*. New York: AMACOM, 2001.

**PART
VII**

How to Measure
Alternative
Methods Value

Trends

Although outsourcing and contracting for human resources (HR)
services are not new, they took off in popularity in the early 1990s.
Like most ideas, sometimes this went too far or too rapidly without
sufficient consideration and planning for the change, and disappoint-
ment resulted. In many cases, the pendulum swung back too far and
many outsource contracts were canceled without a thorough analysis
of the reasons behind the failure to meet expectations. As we entered
the new decade, outsourcing came back again. Early results show that
we have learned from our mistakes and that it is a more effective
method this time around.

Almost any process can be outsourced. Smart companies are
looking at outsourcing much of their general and administrative
(G&A) functions. These functions include some parts of accounting
and finance, corporate services, human resources, information tech-

nology, and legal. This strategy, combined with the widespread use of contract technicians and professionals, can erode an organization's intellectual capital. When a nonemployee is working under contract, we are receiving the services desired but are not learning anything that can be used in the future unless we have a system for capturing all knowledge. Almost no one has that. With the cessation of the contract the intellectual capital—the knowledge of what works and what doesn't—walks out the door. Under such circumstances it is hard to imagine how a company can gain competitive advantage in G&A other than some cost savings. Contractors are free agents, and outsource providers can work for anyone. Thus, whatever is learned not only is lost to us but also might be used by the contractors when they work for a competitor.

Business versus HR

When we talk about measuring outsourcing, especially when we talk about call centers, we are not focusing on the HR process. Once we move an administrative process out to a vendor, we are really looking at a business contract that is established between, in this case, HR and the vendor. Although we might be measuring the same cost, time, volume, quality, and satisfaction outside that we would inside, we are measuring the work of the vendor, not the work of the HR staff. HR has shifted from being the provider to being the manager of the provider. This is a fundamental difference in terms of HR operations. At the same time the organization is looking to HR to be accountable as the provider, one step removed.

This means that HR exercises different skills and knowledge as a contract manager than it does as a hands-on provider. This is similar to an individual who moves from being an assembler to being the supervisor of assemblers. In both cases it is an example of the old maxim that management is getting work done through others. In the early wave of the outsourcing movement that accompanied the downsizing of the late 1980s and early 1990s some people thought that once they had signed the contract, they could relax and only periodically review results and pay for services. They were surprised to find that vendors have their own performance problems and have to be monitored closely. To avoid unpleasant surprises, the terms of the initial contract have to be explicit and measurable. Incentives and penalties have to be included to ensure that the vendor will do the best job possible. Just as it is perfectly reasonable to change vendors when a vendor does not perform satisfactorily, it is common to share savings with vendors that find ways to be more efficient or effective.

Benefits

Outsourcing can be a very effective way to deliver HR services. It offers the possibility of using state-of-the-art technology without having to make a capital investment. It should produce excellent service, probably better than could be provided by HR staffs that do not have access to the latest technology. Finally, outsourcing allows HR and senior management to focus on value-adding business issues rather than on typically no-win administrative services.

Outsourcing and Call Centers: Assessing the Value

Outsourcing

The earliest and most commonly outsourced function was payroll, followed shortly by benefits plan administration. Outsourcing of administrative and even some production tasks was and still is most common in smaller companies. In a production situation a small company may not have the capital to invest in equipment. In human resources (HR) services these companies don't have the staff or the expertise to keep up with the frequent changes in regulations and taxes. Furthermore, they have to manage costs even more rigorously than do larger firms and commit their limited staff resources to core functions.

In making outsourcing decisions some people have ignored the hidden costs of doing work with the internal staff. Among these hidden costs are absence and turnover as well as the variable cost of productivity and quality. If a company outsources a function, issues such as absence, turnover, supervision, productivity, and quality become the problem of the vendor. That is one of the main benefits of outsourcing. The vendor is committed to providing a negotiated level of service, and the company does not care what it has to do within its own company to maintain or exceed that level. Our only cost is the time we spend managing the vendor or dealing with problems inside our organization that result from unacceptable vendor service. If an employee complains about the outsourcer's service, we have to deal with it as the middle person between the vendor and the customer, our employee.

Outsourcing has had a mixed history. As was mentioned above, in its earliest days there was a learning curve that HR and other functional heads had to come up. That has largely been achieved through trial and error. Now outsourcing can be an effective method for cost reduction, service improvement, and/or avoidance of capital investment.

Critical Factors

The Outsourcing Institute conducted a survey in 1998 to find out what factors contribute to effective outsourcing.[1] The top five were

1. Understanding company goals and objectives
2. Having a strategic vision and plan
3. Choosing the right vendor
4. Continuous management of the relationships
5. A properly structured contract

None of these factors involve the direct performance of the service. They are all managerial responsibilities.

Outsource Measurement

The measurement of the performance criteria of an outsourced function is the same as it would be if the company maintained the function internally. The basic five measures always apply:

1. What is the cost to us for the service on a unit or total basis? We have to be certain that we account for all costs, including

---

[1] Outsourcing Institute, Survey of Current and Potential Outsourcing End-Users, Jericho, NY, 1998.

the internal cost of supervising the vendor and dealing with any problems. Is the cost turning out to be what we expected, and is it higher or lower than it was when we did it ourselves?

2. How quickly is the process(es) being completed? What is the cycle time to process a benefit claim, answer and solve an employee question or problem, and so on.

3. What is the volume being processed? How much is being done, and is the volume increasing or decreasing? Does the contract call for a set rate or a piece rate price?

4. What is the error or complaint rate? Are errors frequent or infrequent, important or trivial?

5. How satisfied are employees and management with the performance of the vendor? Are we hearing complaints regarding the service? How often is this happening? We can be certain that if the service is not excellent, the employees and/or their supervisors and managers will let us know. Is the satisfaction level at least as high as it was when we did the work internally? One of the hidden costs of employee dissatisfaction is lost productivity. Employees can't be tending to their jobs at the same time they are in the HR office or on the phone trying to resolve a service problem.

We have to monitor on a regular schedule more than one of the five factors to know how well we are doing. Costs could be low, but errors may be rising and satisfaction may be falling. Overall performance is always a combination of more than one of the five factors.

Call Centers: A Customer-Centered Approach

Call centers can be set up to handle almost any type of incoming contact. This can include calls from employees as well as calls from external customers. We inserted the adjective *external* to make a point. Employees are customers of HR and in a sense customers of the organization. Employees trade their intellectual capital, motivation, and goodwill for pay, benefits, and respect. Therefore, they are entitled to the same or better treatment as are external customers who exchange their money for the company's products and services. Without motivated and skilled employees there will be no customers.

Common Measures

There are a number of common measures that apply to call centers. Most of them focus on time and volume with some quality data included. The next most common measure is customer satisfaction. In the early days of call centers the most controversial activity was the automated monitoring of call center personnel, typically called agents. Most call center operators have a variety of visible and invisible means for knowing exactly what an agent is doing at any moment in a shift. When these so-called Big Brother techniques were first introduced, there was a great cry of foul. However, after many years in use they have been refined and have come to be accepted as part of the job.

The HR Response

As you read through the following metrics, keep one question in mind. Given the outcome expressed by this measure, what human capital factor is involved here? That is, what might we do in the way of HR services to help the business unit manager improve the number? Can improvement be made by doing a better job of hiring, paying, supporting, developing, or retaining the members of the workforce? This includes supervisors and managers. Where is there room for improvement in the behavior of any level of management?

In the examples below the business issue will be obvious. The cost can be too high, response time or wait time cycles can be too slow, the volume of work output may not be sufficient for the amount of staff and facility invested, or there can be quality or customer satisfaction problems. How can HR respond with an HR service or by partnering with management to improve agents' performance?

Agent Measures and Customer Reactions

A great number of measures are or can be used to measure agent's performance. The most common ones are the following.

Average Time per Call

Usually called average handle time (AHT), this is the most common agent measure. Automated systems track the number of minutes spent on a call individually and compute averages. Many center operators set optimum times. They do this for a couple of reasons, which are often in opposition to each other. For example, while they want friendly service, they don't like agents to become "Chatty Cathys or Charlies." They also want as many calls handled as quickly as possible to keep waiting to a minimum and maintain high levels of customer satisfaction.

Number of Calls Handled per Shift

This is a productivity measure. It is computed by adding up all the calls handled by all agents. It is a basic starting point for many other metrics, such as average time per call. It also helps management staff for peak load times between and within shifts.

Agent Active Time

Telephone surveillance systems record every time an agent signs on or off line. If agents take themselves out of the system for any reason, that is noted. Sometimes agents have to sign off to take care of a special business or personal situation. If an agent's inactive time is beyond tolerable levels, management can investigate. The system can monitor these times between calls as a way to determine how busy the agent is or perhaps how complex the calls that are being handled are. There may be additional training needed, or perhaps counseling or another form of support from the supervisor.

Agent Behavior

All of us have heard a recording saying that our call may be monitored for "training purposes and to ensure quality." This is a nice way of saying that if a problem arises, the center's management has a voice record of every call. The objective is not only to catch the agent doing something wrong; it can also protect the agent if a customer makes an unfounded complaint or files a suit for an alleged offense by the agent or the company. There is no metric involved in this case.

Quality

There are what are called remote agent monitoring applications that record both audio and video data on calls. This allows the quality assurance (QA) staff to check not only what is said but how the conversation and the agent's activity within the program are coordinated. For example, if the agent says that he or she is looking at the caller's account or some product information, is the agent actually doing it at that time? How long does it take the agent to come up with the right response? Did the agent ask the right questions of the caller to facilitate the service or a sale?

Holding Time

Incoming calls are clocked and reviewed to learn how long the customer has to wait before an agent comes on to handle the call. Customer satisfaction is a key reason for this metric. If you are the HR person who is monitoring the performance of the employee call center operator, you want to know how long the employees have to wait for service.

Abandonment Rate

When callers tire of waiting, they usually terminate the call. In some situations where we are servicing external customers there is a direct correlation between the abandonment rate and lost customers. Unhappy customers tell friends, who pass the story on, and in time hundreds of people have heard about the poor service provided by a company. In highly competitive, commodity-based businesses unhappy or impatient customers can hang up and turn directly to a competitor for the same product or service. Management will monitor abandonment rate by time of day to see when peak times occur. In the case of an employee call center, excessive wait time and abandonment can affect employees' attitudes and productivity.

Staff Loading Costs

Several of these measures help center managers set work schedules. They try to balance staffing schedules so that they have the optimum number of staff members on duty at all times. One of their incentives is the cost of the staff. If they can hold down the number of agents needed per shift while maintaining customer satisfaction, they may be able to cut their operating costs and earn an incentive payment. However, they also have to show that they are holding abandonment rates within tolerable levels. One way they do this is by shifting calls automatically from one busy call center to another less, busy center. The caller does not know or care where the agent is located as long as the call is handled promptly and the need is satisfied.

Queue Size

At all times the center knows how many callers are waiting in the queue for service. We have all called into a service center and heard a message that told us the average waiting time for service is a certain number minutes. Agents can check the queue size constantly. It is visible on a screen somewhere in the room. When a center is well managed and the agents feel they are treated properly and are a team, they often pick up a call rather than relax for a few seconds or go off line.

There are standards that are based on a number of factors. For example, a common expectation is that 80 percent of incoming calls will be answered within 20 seconds. In revenue situations such as a sales center experience tells management that the average call handled produces a certain number of dollars. The longer it takes to handle calls, the more money the company loses.

The Effect of Service

In the world of the Internet everyone is connected to everyone else in the world who is also on the Net. Dissatisfied customers often take out their frustration by telling their story on the World Wide Web. There are Web sites that invite such stories. If one person goes on-line and sends a message to 20 friends, who in turn send it to 20 more, and this is repeated only two more times, how many people will have gotten this story of poor service? The answer is 3.2 million! That can happen literally overnight. The moral of this mathematical exercise is that good service is a critical competitive advantage.

Management Measures and Employer Responses

Call center managers have their own measures that are part of the contract. The objective is to provide an incentive for the vendor to do the best job possible. The following are typical management measures.

Timely Reporting

Most contracts specify what types of management reports are due and when they are due. The employer needs these reports to monitor operator performance. The center management, as part of its incentive package, must file them on time.

Control or Containment

Agents who are found to be leaving the premises with unauthorized equipment or data violate the control measure. Even if there is no intention to steal, this act can draw severe penalties for both the agent and the center manager.

Customer Satisfaction

Measures of customer satisfaction are taken at regular intervals. They are used as a basis for evaluating the center operator. They also become a very important part of the vendor's incentive package.

Cost Reduction

When a center operator finds a way to save the employer money outside the normal center operations, the operator can be rewarded. In one center this happened when the center manager knew about some idle employer equipment that could be used by one of the employer's departments instead of having to buy extra items. When this opportunity was pointed out, part of the saving was awarded to the center operator.

Manager Performance

The basic measure of a center manager's performance is the aggregate of the measures described above. Achievement of standards is easy to monitor since so many data are being generated on a continuous basis. Bonuses and salary increases are driven by how well the manager is able to meet the standards.

Graphic Representation

Figure 20-1 is a graphic representation of the measures used in call center management. It provides a mental picture of the three basic

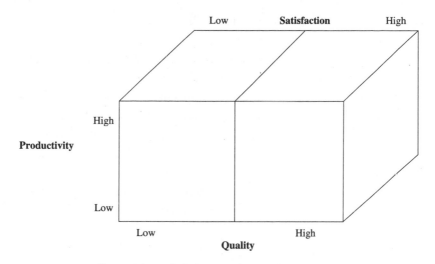

Figure 20-1   Call Center Measures by Importance

categories of measurement: productivity, quality, and satisfaction. As agent and management measures are deemed to be more or less important, they can be moved right or left, up or down. We can spot our agent and management measures on this template to suit our situation.

However, each contract and every situation are different, and so the display changes. When the model is completed, both the call center operator and the contracting employer can see and discuss how well the operator is meeting the specified goals of the operation. As the forces change, the mental model can be reviewed and modified. Going through the exercise of discussing and spotting measures helps us question our assumptions about the relative importance of each issue. Over time untested assumptions can fall behind changing market and customer variables or fail to recognize the emergence of important new variables. Finally, this type of mental picture helps us see patterns or connections between variables.

By plotting our measures on the template in accordance with our judgment we can have not only numbers but also a graphic representation. The numbers can be displayed in any tabular or graphic format, including trend data. When the numbers are viewed in toto, both the call center operator and the employer can see where to focus resources and attention. Later they will tell us how well the operator is meeting the specified goals of the operation in accordance with the necessary or desired levels of productivity, quality, and service.

There are many ways to present the data in great detail. Dashboards, balanced scorecards, tables, and charts all work well. Computers can print out or display the measure in colors, for example, green, yellow, or red to indicate where performance is satisfactory, marginal, or a problem. When choosing the method or presentation we would keep in mind the preferences of the management group that will be viewing the data. Effective communication always depends on recognition of the audience's viewpoint rather than our own perspective.

Employee Self-Service: Gauging Effectiveness

Trends

Since the downsizing binge of the late 1980s and early 1990s employee self-service has gained popularity. This attempt to make American businesses more competitive by driving out costs originally demanded not only a reduction in staff sizes but also more efficient ways to support employees.

Taking a page out of the service industry, companies began automating many formerly labor-intensive human resources (HR) services. Benefits enrollment is one of the more common applications. Employee record changes, training class enrollment, job posting and application, career assessment, and self-directed training are other examples. Every day we hear about HR departments that have put another program or service at the fingertips of the employee.

Effectiveness

When this trend started there was great concern on the part of HR staffs that the employees would not like it. They reasoned that employee's had come to rely on the type of personal attention that only an on-site, face-to-face situation can provide. They also claimed that without the hand-holding to which they had become accustomed there would be a high error rate, which would lead to dissatisfaction and loss of productivity as the problems were sorted out. None of this turned out to be true. It was a reflection of HR personnel who were locked into an obsolescent system that they enjoyed overseeing. It took a few dramatic cases for them to see not only that there was a better way but that it was imperative to find more cost-effective ways to support employees.

One of the early cases in which we were involved was at the Mellon Bank headquartered in Pittsburgh. It was reported in detail in *The 8 Practices of Exceptional Companies*.[1] In 1993, Mellon decided to introduce managed care into its employee health program system. This required 22,000 employees to reconsider their options and enroll. The HR staff at Mellon took a big chance by putting the enrollment process on a touch-tone telephone system. Employees were given instructions on how to review and make changes or add services to the package. When this high-risk experiment was launched, the results were remarkable.

1. Individual employee enrollment time was reduced by nearly 50 percent.
2. The error rate dropped from 12 percent in the old paper-based system to 2.5 percent.
3. Thirty thousand pieces of paper were saved, and the cost for temps to process it was eliminated.

This example and others shortly thereafter broke through HR's fears and were a driving force that began to bring HR out of its administrative myopia and let it see better, value-adding ways to run the function. Today no one would dispute the efficacy of employee self-service.

Typical applications include the following employee access capabilities:

[1] Jac Fitz-enz, *The 8 Practices of Exceptional Companies*. New York: AMACOM, 1997, pp. 94–95.

- Complete and submit their time sheets
- View their career and pay history
- Enroll and change benefits
- Update personal data in their files such as address changes
- Obtain employment and salary verification for lending requests
- Obtain reprints of certain personal data

The Prime Measure

In a service situation the prime measure is always customer satisfaction, although some people claim that cost is the prime measure of any business function. In this case especially, if the employees are not happy, their attitudes are reflected in their productivity and the quality of their service. Everything else is secondary.

When we studied the *Fortune* magazine list of the 100 best companies at which to work over the last 2 years, it was clear that the success of those companies was based largely on a culture that respected, cared for, and challenged the workforce. Employee self-service systems (ESSs) promote that in a real but subtle way. Basically the ESS says to the employee, We respect you as a mature individual who is capable of handling important issues without the intervention of a third party. By putting access to data in the hands of the employee, management makes the message clear and positive. People solve complex, sometimes highly emotional problems outside the work situation every day. Clearly, they should be capable of handling personal administrative services internally without having to go through a staff specialist all the time.

Formal and Informal Methods

That presumption of maturity and respect leads to monitoring and assessing employee satisfaction with the various ESS applications. We can use formal and informal means to do this. Effective HR departments maintain close relationships with many of the employees. In the course of those interactions there are many informal opportunities to ask for direct feedback on an ESS or the total system. Open-ended questions can be asked such as the following:

How do you feel about the employee self-service system?
Is the service working for you?
Which parts of it do you use the most (the least)?
Which parts do you like the most?
How do your associates feel about it?

It is important to use the word *feel* because satisfaction is more an emotional issue than an intellectual one. During the course of the reply and subsequent discussion we can steer the conversation toward specific functional aspects of the service to help pinpoint areas that may need improvement. There is no scoring system for this informal method. We simply take the testimony and add it to other informal impressions we've picked up.

Employee attitude surveys are the formal method most often used to obtain feedback from the workforce. You know how to structure these because you are already surveying. It doesn't matter what scoring system you use as long as it has two characteristics: simplicity and consistency.

People are stressed and want a task to be made as simple as possible. Don't ask compound questions that include "this and that." The respondents don't always know what we are looking for. Make each item a discrete question. This makes tallying the responses easier and eliminates bad data. In terms of consistency, try to use the same question time after time in situation after situation. We use a common set of questions to survey all groups, from those who reject job offers through the existing workforce to those who have left voluntarily. This produces a thread that can be traced to uncover endemic problems as opposed to specific problems. We might find that all the respondents complain about the consistent delays they experienced during the selection process, while they were employees, and even when they were quitting and being processed out. A delay in responding to someone is a sign of a lack of respect. We have found that this is a primary reason for rejecting job offers. The attitude is that if this is the way they treat applicants, how must they treat employees?

Focused Scoring for Better Service

One of the survey scoring methods that we have used for years is to pose a question in two parts:

1. How important is this to you?
2. How satisfied are you with it?

When we have collected the responses, we calculate a gap score, which is the difference between the average importance and the average satisfaction levels. The reason for including the importance question is that we don't want to spend resources fixing something that few people care about. We can set cutoff points at which we decide we need to respond. For example, using a 5-point scoring system, we might decide that a gap of more than 1.5 points means that we need to look into it. Importance often is scored higher than satisfaction, but we don't want to overreact if the gap is less than 1 point.

Importance often varies by group. Sorting the responses by demographic classifications helps uncover a group of people who are underserved, misunderstand a service, or need something we didn't foresee. An example of the latter could be the emergence of the need for elder care. We might have offered a referral service for people who need support with aging or ill relatives. Not everyone has this problem, but we want to know who has it and how many have it. By sorting by age, sex, location, or another demographic, we may notice that there are a number of women in a certain part of the city, state, or country for whom this is a troubling need. Knowing that it is isolated to that group, we can work on improving the service there without going into a universal campaign. This helps us use our benefit dollars more efficiently. It is also a great way to cut turnover for groups with special needs. We know from experience that a significant number of people stay with an employer who provides for a critical need.

Secondary Measures

Having said at the outset that cost is not the prime measure, we now want to acknowledge its importance. Of course, in business cost is always an issue. As managers, we want to provide the best possible service at the lowest cost. The cost of the self-service system can be compared to that of the direct contact, on-site, staff-based method. While it is almost always more cost-efficient to have people handle many of their own administrative service tasks, the human touch cannot be ignored.

No self-service system can handle all the subtleties that a direct conversation can. Second- and third-level questions ("But what if . . . ?") are not always answerable through touch-tone telephone methods. The volume often does not cost justify the maintenance of a 24/7 or even a 10/5 system. There are also expectations set and tested to determine if employee queries are handled promptly and accurately. Measures similar to those described above for call centers can be applied.

E-Mail

E-mail is more common than audio responses for most companies, although interactive voice response (IVR) is becoming more popular. Incoming e-mails are time- and data-stamped, and the response also is stamped. This allows for response times to be tracked. It also shows where the queries, or complaints are coming from. Management can see who sent a message and when it was received. It can also monitor the response in terms of what was offered and how.

The Future

It seems clear that more enlightened attitudes are emerging regarding the character and ability of employees. As management continues to gain confidence in the ability of employees to handle sensitive information, employee self-services will expand. To maintain or improve competitive costs it is necessary to put more data into the hands of responsible employees outside the HR function.

Epilogue: Where HR Goes From Here— Prospects, Problems, and Payoffs in the Twenty-First Century

The Human—Technology Interface

The impact of technology, especially communications, is having a profound effect on people that promises to increase in intensity in the future. This is both good and bad news. The good news is that it will become increasingly easier to communicate with a larger number of people, faster than ever before, anywhere in the world. It is also bad news because those people can communicate with us as well. Sometimes it seems that all of them are.

The essence of technology is that it replaces the direct contact a human being has with the natural world. As cave dwellers began to domesticate beasts of burden and invent tools and vehicles, they made life easier but gradually lost some of the feel of the earth between their toes and in their hands. Today many people in large metropolitan cities seldom, if ever, walk barefoot in the city or dig into its soil. That does not bother most people, but because people can communicate through the latest wireless tools, they don't see their friends and neighbors as often as they used to. Who takes the time to select nice paper and write a personal letter anymore? That can be good or bad, depending on one's viewpoint, but it is a loss of human contact at a more personal level.

The Search for Meaning and Connection

The fact that people can e-mail or phone someone thousands of miles away affects the intimacy that people need as part of human nature. When we expand this into the workplace, it can dehumanize jobs. The key dilemma of the new millennium is finding a way to use technology without losing meaning in work. More and more we are removed from the tools of production, particularly those of us in service professions. Although we in human resources can communicate more efficiently with our associates in the department and throughout the enterprise, we are concurrently losing the intimacy of earlier times.

Intimacy is a remedy for stress. The comfort of another human being's physical presence is increasingly uncommon. As more work is conducted remotely at faster rates of speed, and as constant change pounds down on us, it will become very difficult to *feel* the goodness of our interactions and accomplishments. Many of us won't know why we are so stressed beyond the fact of increasing volumes of work at increasing rates of speed. The reason is the lack of true connection along with the intimacy and comfort that come out of it. What does this mean for us?

Backing into the Future

Many people are content to live in the past. They hark back to the good ol' days, forgetting that at that time they said things like, "In the old days things were simpler and a lot better." In decision making they vacillate between precedent and gut feeling, uncomplaining that they don't have enough time, energy, or data to look into the future. While it is always easier to look backward than forward, we cannot live in the past. This is not as new a phenomenon, as some people think. Although the pace of change is rapid and radical today, in 1990 I pointed out that we already were dealing with evolutionary change at revolutionary speed.[1] If anything, that was an understatement.

Walking backward into the future is a sure way to stumble, fall, and be overrun by the competition. The history of companies and

---

[1] Jac Fitz-enz, *Human Value Management.* San Francisco: Jossey-Bass, 1990, p. 10.

whole industries that have fallen to competitors because they did not focus on the future is well documented. This is not a behavior exclusive to Americans. Europeans and Asians have lost markets to competitors by resting on past glory and depending on government to maintain trade barriers. Inevitably, the markets have to be opened to competition, and then the complacent will be wiped out or bought out. The question before us is, How can we reduce some of the uncertainty of the future?

Human Resources in 2010

The human resources (HR) function of the twenty-first century is riding on the horns of the technology-humanity dilemma. To be a value-adding function at the highest possible level HR will have to look ahead to balance efficiency with intimacy. Forecasting is essential. On the one hand, HR professionals will continue to introduce and refine the application of various technologies. On the other hand, and more importantly, we will find ways to promote humanity within vast global organizations. We need to do this not only out of altruism but also for survival. People can take only so much before they need support and comfort. Letting technology affect the mental and physical health of associates is bad business.

When the time comes to review and perhaps update this book again we expect that the HR profession will have fulfilled its promise of operating as an equal partner in the business. The issues of measurement and benchmarking will have risen from the administrative level to the strategic arena. Forecasting will be a common HR activity. The road to this is open. Executives are looking for all the help they can find in the management of human capital. As HR professionals step forward with their knowledge, skills, and tools to respond to this need, they will make life better for themselves and, more important, for the millions of people who toil in organizations. As this comes to fruition HR will be able to claim rightfully to have made a very positive difference.

INDEX

Page numbers followed by *f* indicate figures.

About the Authors

Dr. Jac Fitz-enz is acknowledged worldwide as the father of human capital metrics and benchmarking. He carried out the original research in the 1970s during the founding of the Saratoga Institute. Dr. Fitz-enz has published over 130 articles and reports as well as seven books, two of which won national book awards from SHRM. He has trained over 50,000 managers in 40 countries. Previous to founding Saratoga, he held human resource vice presidential positions in major finance and technology companies.

Barbara Davison is Principal Consultant with Saratoga Institute. She worked with Jac Fitz-enz on the original research and development of HR metrics. Ms. Davison has held several director-level HR positions at Motorola and ARA.